Literary Lives

Literary Lives

Biography and the Search for Understanding

David Ellis

Edinburgh University Press

For Frank Cioffi

© David Ellis, 2000
Edinburgh University Press Ltd
22 George Square, Edinburgh

Typeset in New Baskerville
by Florence Production Ltd, Stoodleigh, Devon, and
printed and Bound in Great Britain
by The University Press, Cambridge

A CIP Record for this book is available
from the British Library

ISBN 0 7486 1372 2 (hardback)

Contents

Preface

GENERAL TALK ABOUT LITERARY matters comes naturally to many people, but for those brought up with Blake's 'To generalise is to be an idiot' ringing in their ears, it goes against the grain. The provocation for going against it in this instance was my responsibility for volume 3 of the new Cambridge biography of D. H. Lawrence (*Dying Game*). In his 'Foreword' to *Fantasia of the Unconscious*, Lawrence claimed that his novels and poems 'came unwatched' out of his pen whereas his discursive writings were 'inferences made afterwards, from the experience': the result of 'the absolute need which one has for some sort of satisfactory mental attitude towards oneself and things in general'. One way in which biography is unlike poetry or fiction is that it is hard to imagine it ever emerging 'unwatched'; yet my own volume of Lawrence's life was no doubt written more easily than it might have been because its outward form had already been largely determined by its two predecessors. That questions of scale, or the role of the works (in their often uneasy contrast with the 'life'), had been more or less decided, was in many respects a great advantage; but it was one which somehow seemed to make it even more imperative afterwards that I should try to formulate some definite conclusions about the general nature of biography, and in particular the implicit offer many biographers make to explain the inner as well as outer life of other human beings. It was to that issue especially I felt I needed 'some sort of satisfactory mental attitude'.

Having attempted to describe a part of a life appeared a necessary, or at least useful, qualification for an enquiry into life-writing.

Yet the diversity of the form means that personal experience could only ever be moderately representative. For that reason, if for no other, it seemed that I ought in what follows to keep illustration involving Lawrence to a decent minimum. That means that I have had to rely for my other examples on a reading of biographies which is necessarily random since anyone who set out to cover the field in a systematic way would go mad, or die before their task was done. To lessen the impression of randomness, I have come back on several occasions to the same works or authors, favouring coherence at the expense of an inevitable narrowing of the sample.

Most of the biographies from which I have quoted I have read with admiration. Getting your own hands dirty at least allows you to appreciate who does a good job: it takes one to know one who does it better. If, therefore, I am directly critical, or cite some biographers in a critical context, it is usually because I am adopting a specific, diagnostic approach and not concerned with appreciation in a more general sense. Rather than how well they tell a story, use their material or evoke a particular atmosphere, what I am usually trying to discover are certain principles on which biographers habitually proceed.

The search for these principles has necessarily led me towards the kind of difficult issues which intrigue and preoccupy philosophers, although I have not of course treated them as philosophers would. We are not only what we eat but also what we read, and years spent with novels, poems and plays produce very different results from a lifetime in the company of Hume or Hegel. If a philosopher (or an historian) had written this book it would have been quite different. Literary study is itself of course, or has become, a specialism; but rather than to specialists of whatever variety, I address this discussion to the non-specialist in all of us and (what often amounts to the same thing) to other readers of biography. It is aimed principally at those who, like me, have spent years enjoying that comfort of familiarity which an opening chapter on family background can bring and then wondered how the rest of a life could be more than an anti-climax after the absorbing interest of 'childhood' or 'schooldays'. It is meant especially for those who suddenly realised, as I did, that pondering the difference which the new material announced on the dust-jacket had really made was the extent of their critical engagement; or who were able to escape from the grip of the narrative only to the extent that, when things got worse in the way they inevitably do, they had flicked forward surreptitiously for a brief glimpse at the death-bed scene. Of the several reasons I give in my first chapter for the surprising absence of work on the theory or method of biography, an additional one is that the seductions of a well-written life story discourage its readers from questioning the kind of understanding of the subject it offers and how that understanding was achieved.

To answer questions of this kind is the main purpose of this book. In attempting to fulfil it I have incurred debts to a great many people, only some of whom I mention here. I am grateful to Angela Faunch of what is now the 'Document Delivery Centre' of the University of Kent at Canterbury for her patience and industry in procuring inter-Library loans. My colleague Michael Irwin made helpful suggestions on an early draft of my opening chapters and, throughout my whole involvement with the problems raised by the different aspects of life-writing, I have profited greatly from the encouragement and expertise of Michael Sheringham. An invitation to work for two months in the Unit for Studies of Biography and Autobiography at La Trobe University in Melbourne, Australia, allowed me to try out some of my ideas and benefit from the criticism they received; and to John Wiltshire, a member of the English School at La Trobe, I owe special thanks. He read a penultimate draft of my book with great care and prompted me to make many changes. Linda Bree, Peter Brown, Rupert Brown, Grayson Ditchfield, Jan Montefiore and Andrews Reath have on various occasions given me valuable help; and I am grateful (as always) to my two collaborators on the Lawrence biography, John Worthen and Mark Kinkead-Weekes. My greatest debt is expressed in the dedication. That much of the thought in this book goes back to long conversations with Frank Cioffi on explanation in biography will be obvious to anyone who consults the highly condensed and adapted transcript of them which first appeared in *Imitating Art*, a collection of essays I edited in 1993, but which has recently been republished in Cioffi's own *Freud and the Question of Pseudoscience* (Chicago, 1998). Since those first discussions he has continued to guide my steps through the minefield of a topic which, precisely because it has in the past attracted so little serious attention, remains tricky ground for the unwary. If there are occasions on which I have blown myself up, the fault is not his, as anyone who knows us both will be aware.

1

Lives without Theory

Rise early and regularly and read for three hours . . . Read no history, nothing but biography, for that is life without theory.
> (Benjamin Disraeli, *Contarini Fleming*, Pt 1, chap. 3)

THE POPULARITY OF BIOGRAPHY shows no sign of abating. In the *Times Literary Supplement* more space is occupied by reviews of new biographies than of new fiction; if large numbers of celebrated figures could be resurrected, they would be dumbfounded by the frequency with which their lives have been described; and few of us can now imagine how difficult it would be to buy a Christmas present for a relative, of whose taste we were unsure, without that generous provision of biographies on the bookshop shelves in December.

The phenomenon is not without its implications for cultural life. In some cases only a literary biography can send readers back to the subject's writings with renewed interest and curiosity even if, in others, it can also make them feel that, knowing so much about the life, they are dispensed from further or indeed *any* acquaintance with the work. Our times are cynical yet biographies can sometimes offer an inspiring example of how life ought to be lived. More often, they appear to provide their readers with the comfort of believing that those who have achieved distinction in a certain field are not merely as humanly fallible as they are, but much more so.

At a time when the triumph of 'Theory' in the universities has widened the gap between the academic world and the rest of society, biographies represent one of the few remaining points of interaction. Such is the popularity of the form that bulky and highly

detailed lives, composed over a long period, with the Academy principally in mind, can be shorn of their more obviously scholarly
appurtenances, published in a 'trade' form, and left to compete
with the work of professional writers. When the public appetite is
so great, there would be no surprise if the careers of those writers
were partly influenced by it. Only a handful of serious novelists
receive advances which allow them to live comfortably, but lucrative commissions for biographies are by comparison relatively easy
to secure. Although the transformation of Peter Ackroyd from well-
known novelist into excellent biographer may have been entirely
a matter of free will, there is a good chance that it also had some
connections with the free market. Successful though he is, it is
doubtful whether Julian Barnes would now be so well known without
Flaubert's Parrot, that ingenious enquiry into biographical research
which, while it wittily mocked academic pretensions to knowledge
of the past, simultaneously entertained its readers with a fascinating
array of genuine historical information about Flaubert, arranged
in an unusual and stimulating way.

Prominently associated with 'the rise of the novel' in England
was Daniel Defoe who judged it best to send many of his works
into the world thinly disguised as life histories. After his time, the
English novel rose so far and so quickly that its status took away
any need for protective colouring. Accompanying its success have
been countless investigations into the conventions, narrative structures and characteristic features of the novel form. Popular though
biography has become, there has as yet been no comparable interest
in how it 'works': for its readers it has indeed been a rare case
of (as the father of Disraeli's hero puts it) 'life without theory'. Of
recent well-known practitioners only Leon Edel has attempted a
Principia Biographica. From Richard Ellmann onwards the tendency
has been rather to write books that, when they do not consist of
unfinished business, initiate the reader into the behind-the-scenes
secrets of the craft of biography without attempting a sustained
analysis of any element which might be described as fundamental.

Very few monographs on biography – which are not historical
surveys – have appeared, and none of them are particularly satisfactory. Otherwise the field is occupied by collections of essays.
These are often the product of conferences and have the associated strengths and weaknesses. Full of incidental observations of
great interest, it is rare to find in these collections any one theme
steadily pursued. A good many of their contributors, invited to the

conference because they have published successful lives, have neither the temperament nor the interest to reflect on how they did what they did; and for others, however intelligent and well-informed, it is just another conference, not especially central to their concerns.

When the academic body sweats publications at every pore and, in Britain at least, the financial well-being of all institutions of higher education depends more and more on their charge sheets (the number of publications for which they can claim responsibility), the comparative dearth of analytic enquiry into biography is surprising. One possible explanation lies in the announcement, many years ago now, of the 'death of the author'. Even though that news proved on closer examination to have been much exaggerated, and both Barthes and Foucault were themselves later to indulge in biographical enquiry, the notion that authors were mere intersection points for a number of psychological, linguistic or socio-economic systems was hardly an encouragement to study the details of their lives, especially in their more private aspects. Yet the intellectual disapproval this view encouraged, and the consequent lowly status of biography as a genre, have perhaps less to do with the lack of analytic attention it has received than its bewildering diversity: its inevitably heterogeneous nature. If one were attempting to establish some outer, defining limits then one useful rule of thumb might be that the subject of a biography ought no longer to be living. Call no man happy until he is dead, say the Greeks and, although their literature does not always give that impression, they would presumably have agreed that, while a man was still alive, one ought not to call him unhappy either. This means that what offers itself as the 'biography' of a living subject could only ever be an interim report. But removing to one side in this convenient way all those many books which set out to satisfy public curiosity about living figures, the field is still vast. What makes it so diverse is the huge variety of possible subjects: generals and businessmen as well as writers and artists, bishops as well as politicians, wives and sisters of the famous as well as famous women themselves, obscure individuals who never left their native regions or princesses who travelled the world. Both the intrinsic interest of these people, and the kind of evidence which makes it possible to write their lives, are in each case so different that their biographies can seem at first to have very little in common. Yet even within a narrow band (of *literary* biography, for example) the treatment may differ enormously. The heavily researched, 'groaning door-stopper' may be made to look much like the book from an author prac- tised in producing 'lives' every couple of years, but it has probably been written according to very different criteria. There are so many different kinds of biography that it would be foolish to imagine that any enquiry could cover them all without degenerating into a catalogue or list. The real challenge, therefore, is to try to say some- thing about one particular category within the genre which will then have at least some relevance for most, if not all of the others.

*

The paucity of the secondary literature on biography might well be construed in some quarters as a blessing. If there are certain rules or conventions in writing lives which most biographers follow more or less instinctively, how would it help if they were led to reflect more about what they were doing? 'Grand practisers have not the leisure to be analytiques', Aubrey claimed and Beckett has his Molloy say, 'When I try and think riding I lose my balance and fall'.[1] The generally acknowledged predominance of the 'Anglo-Saxon' world in life-writing appears to suggest that there are traditional procedures which have served well in the past, and that there would be no point in even attempting to codify what has flourished so luxuriantly in a world of case law. How biographies work, the habits of enquiry and explanation which so largely determine their form, can seem irrelevant when the publication figures over so many decades (and centuries) demonstrate so resoundingly that they do.

Any general history of biography will tend to mention Plutarch, Suetonius, and various authors of lives of the Saints but, although references are often made to Walton and Aubrey, the two figures most commonly regarded as the 'fathers' of the form in England are Johnson and Boswell. It casts some doubt on how safe it might be for a contemporary biographer to rely on traditional procedures that neither of these writers is a biographer in the modern sense. Johnson's pre-eminence would be widely accepted. It manifests itself in the life of Swift when he is pondering why Queen Anne and her chief minister Harley did not respond with more resolution to loud cries for action from a group of Tories known as the October club:

> The Queen was probably slow because she was afraid, and Harley was slow because he was doubtful: he was a Tory only by necessity, or for con- venience; and, when he had power in his hands, had no settled purpose

for which he should employ it; forced to gratify to a certain degree the Tories who supported him, but unwilling to make his reconcilement to the Whigs utterly desperate, he corresponded at once with the two expectants of the Crown and kept, as has been observed, the succession undetermined. Not knowing what to do, he did nothing; and, with the fate of a double dealer, at last lost his power, but kept his enemies.

Swift seems to have concurred in opinion with the October Club, but it was not in his power to quicken the tardiness of Harley, whom he stimulated as much as he could, but with little effect. He that knows not whither to go is in no haste to move. Harley, who was perhaps not quick by nature, became yet more slow by irresolution; and was content to hear that dilatoriness lamented as natural, which he applauded in himself as politic.[2]

As so often in Johnson, the impression here of understanding – penetrating insight into the motives of another human being – is remarkable; yet, in this respect, his would be a hard act to follow. On more mundane matters, where imitation appears more feasible, he is hardly the ideal model. Except where he has personal knowledge of his subject, the *Lives of the Poets* are for the most part brief commentaries on the better known secondary sources. A modern biographer is supposed to 'research' the subject energetically, and work with original documents or sources; but one of Johnson's attitudes to endeavour of that kind emerges after Boswell had arranged a meeting for him with Lord Marchmont, who had information about Pope. Boswell describes Johnson as declaring that he had no intention of keeping the appointment and reports him as saying, 'If it rained knowledge, I'd hold out my hand; but I would not give myself the trouble of going in quest of it'.[3] The context of this remark suggests that it may have been partly prompted by Boswell's officiousness, and it is a fact that Johnson did later arrange to see Lord Marchmont;[4] yet at the beginning of the life of Swift he displays an indifference to the conventionally accepted duties of writing lives which a modern biographer can only envy. Swift, he points out, 'according to an account said to be written by himself', was born in Dublin. 'According to his own report, as delivered by Pope to Spence', he was born in Leicester so that 'he was contented to be called an Irishman by the Irish; but would occasionally call himself an Englishman'. 'The question', Johnson magisterially concludes, 'may, without much regret, be left in the obscurity in which he delighted to involve it'.[5]

In contradistinction to his great object of study, Boswell boasts of a passion for accuracy in what must be one of its purest forms:

> Were I to detail the books which I have consulted, and the enquiries
> which I have found it necessary to make by various channels, I should
> probably be thought ridiculously ostentatious. Let me only observe, as
> a specimen of my trouble, that I have sometimes been obliged to run
> half over London, in order to fix a date correctly; which, when I had
> accomplished, I well knew would obtain me no praise, though a failure
> would have been to my discredit.[6]

This is how biographers often like to think of themselves: quietly
but doggedly industrious, conscientious, *unappreciated*. Assuming
that, as a researcher, Boswell was as exemplary as he here claims,
there are nevertheless ways in which his *Life of Johnson* is even less
like a modern biography than the *Lives of the Poets*. Although it
covers the whole of Johnson's life, its form alters dramatically from
the moment of Boswell's own meeting with him. At the beginning,
the narrative of his subject's birth in Lichfield, his time at Oxford
and the years of labouring away at the Dictionary in relative obscurity, is conducted in a familiar way; but once Boswell can rely more
exclusively on his records of daily conversations, the onward
momentum slows to a virtual stop, we seem to be in a kind of historic
present, and the nature of our interest changes completely. From
following Johnson's progress from year to year we become involved
in listening to what he had to say from day to day. In general the
all-inclusiveness triumphantly justifies itself, giving readers the feel
of what it was like to be in Johnson's company and demonstrating,
by the very bulk and heterogeneity of the opinions recorded, how
complex he was. Yet although he was hardly averse to passing judgement, Boswell nonetheless presents so much material whose place
in the biographical narrative is self-evidently unclear to him, that
the chief impression left by his book can be of a miscellaneous mass
through which readers have to make their own way. Whatever the
obviously significant degree of dramatic and literary art in the
presentation of particular episodes in Boswell's *Life*, it is hard to
agree with those critics who have praised its coherence. At many of
its most memorable moments, it is more a memoir than a biography and for modern-day writers of lives quite as much a complicated example to follow as the *Lives of the Poets*. For more reasons
than the two I have chosen to emphasise, there is in neither Boswell
nor Johnson the beginnings of a tradition so clear that all subsequent biographers have ever had to do is follow in their footsteps.

Very unlike Boswell are the summarising, well digested and, above
all, even-paced chronological narratives which eventually came to

dominate after his death. As Christopher Ricks has demonstrated,[6] these have often been undervalued and there are many among them that would be the more genuine forerunners of today's biographies, representing a tradition within which the modern practitioner could indeed unselfconsciously operate, if the attitude to the private life they illustrate were not so different from our own. It is their tone more than their shape or method which chiefly distinguishes them, as if their authors had adopted as their unavowed epigraph Wordsworth's thoughts in his essay on epitaphs:

> The character of a deceased friend or beloved kinsman is not seen, no
> – nor ought to be seen, otherwise than as a tree through a tender haze
> or a luminous mist, that spiritualises and beautifies it; . . . Shall we say,
> then, that this is not truth, not a faithful image; and that, accordingly,
> the purposes of commemoration cannot be answered? – It *is* truth, . . .
> hallowed by love – the joint offspring of the worth of the dead and
> the affections of the living![8]

The occasional consequences of this approach were once vividly, if perhaps not very fairly, described by D. H. Lawrence, after he had re-read Lockhart's *Life of Burns* (a poet for whom his own social origins gave him a special affinity). 'Those damned middle-class Lockharts', he complained, 'grew lilies of the valley up their arses to hear them talk.'[9]

Lockhart's *Burns* is pre-Victorian and partly for that reason less prudish than Lawrence's outburst might suggest; but it is also uncharacteristic of biographies in the nineteenth century because it is short. The new and modern form of biography which Lytton Strachey could be said to have inaugurated at the beginning of the twentieth century is a reaction against the excessive length of his predecessors' works, as well as what he judged to be their excessively reverent tone. Strachey took a lower, although not necessarily more complex view of human nature than they had, and he was less inclined to accept that there were certain areas which should never be exposed to public view. More importantly for my purposes, he was also less inclined to believe the subject's own testimony, particularly when it related to the self. In his essay on biographical writing in *The Idler*, Johnson had suggested that 'those relations are . . . commonly of most value in which the writer tells his own story'. This was because,

> The writer of his own life has at least the first qualification of an histo-
> rian, the knowledge of truth; and though it may be plausibly objected
> that his temptations to disguise it are equal to his opportunities of

knowing it, yet I cannot but think that impartiality may be expected with equal confidence from him that relates the passages of his own life, as from him that delivers the transactions of another.[10]

No contemporary biographer could afford to be as cavalier about information as Johnson was; and, since Strachey, very few of them would not have felt discomfort in subscribing to sentiments as confident as these are about the authority of the subject.

One of the difficulties of thinking clearly about biography is that it is often assumed to follow the same procedures and methods as *auto*biography. There are in fact crucial differences between the two forms and, as Johnson implies, their relationship is often antagonistic. Writing the lives of people who have already written their own is a tricky business. In the case of literary figures, although it may be impossible to do better (who is it, after all, who writes the better English?), there is for the modern biographer, less trusting than Johnson, a challenge to at least do differently. At the beginning of his life of Yeats, for example, Roy Foster calls the autobiography which his subject published in 1914, and which deals with the same years he is about to cover, a 'disingenuous masterpiece'. He notes Yeats's tendency to think of his past in terms of 'strictly defined epiphanies', and the way in which his account of the period between 1887 and 1891 was 'constructed to end with the death of Parnell, seen in retrospect as a watershed'. But, Foster comments, 'at the time Parnell figured little in WBY's universe: his idea of a heroic leader was William Morris'. The climax of those four years, he goes on, was 'not the public upheaval of a politician's death, but a more personal apotheosis: the publication of WBY's first book'.[11]

An even more striking example of the modern biographer's sceptical attitude to the subject's own testimony occurs in the first volume of Ray Monk's biography of Bertrand Russell. Shortly before World War I, while he was lecturing in the United States, Russell had an affair with an American named Helen Dudley. He invited her to follow him to England but, when she obligingly did so, more or less abandoned her to her own devices. This callous behaviour Russell attributed in his autobiography to the outbreak of the war which killed his interest in the young woman. 'Half a word fixed upon or near the spot', Thomas Gray once wrote to his friend William Palgrave, 'is worth a cart-load of recollection'.[12] By ignoring the autobiography, and consulting the contemporary record, Monk shows convincingly that the real reason for Russell's behaviour was the renewal, immediately on his return to England, of his passion for Ottoline Morrel. It was *that* and not the outbreak of the war which made Helen Dudley's presence redundant.[13]

In neither of these recent cases have Monk and Foster relied on the impartiality which 'may be expected . . . from him that relates the passages of his own life'. From Johnson's confidence in that impartiality: the reliability of the subject's own testimony, a long road leads, via Strachey, to a contemporary biographer such as Leon Edel who, in his *Principia Biographica*, congratulates the modern world for knowing 'so much more now about behaviour and motivation' (even though it would be hard to find, in the five volumes of his life of Henry James, anything more convincing than Johnson's reflections on Harley). The first duty of the biographer, Edel suggests, is to 'learn to understand man's ways of dreaming, thinking and using his fancy'; and he proposes an 'analytic approach' by which he means the 'kind of analysis which enables us to see through the rationalizations, the postures, the self-delusions and self-deceptions of our subjects'.[14]

Johnson knew that people did not always tell the truth, and that it might sometimes be necessary therefore for biographers to 'see through' them; but he did not conceive that as their first task. What has made a crucial difference in modern times is Freud, or at least a popularly diffused Freudianism. Edel is quite specifically an admirer of Freud but, since Strachey, the Freudian influence has been pervasive, whether or not particular biographers have been aware of it. This has not only meant that subjects' own explanations of their behaviour will usually be regarded with suspicion so that even biographers as fundamentally unFreudian as Foster and Monk will be inclined to believe that the temptation to disguise the truth (consciously or unconsciously) is greater than, rather than equal to, the opportunities for knowing it; but also that motives will often be adduced of which those subjects could almost by definition have had no inkling. In his life of Dickens, for example, Peter Ackroyd conjectures that the birth of a baby brother when Dickens was only two must have inspired 'anxiety and resentment in the sibling's breast'. The death of this brother after only six months could not therefore have been without effect:

> If the infant Charles had harboured resentful or even murderous longings against the supplanter, how effectively they had come home to roost! And how strong the guilt might have been. *Might have been* – that is necessarily the phrase. And yet when the adulthood of Dickens is

considered, with all its evidence that Dickens did indeed suffer from an insidious pressure of irrational guilt, and when all the images of dead infants are picked out of his fiction, it is hard to believe that this six-month episode in the infancy of the novelist did not have some permanent effect upon him.[15]

By consulting the contemporary record, Monk and Foster offer rectifications of their subjects' own accounts of important episodes in their adult lives which one could imagine those subjects being persuaded to accept. Both parties are working broadly within the same idiom so that it is not too fanciful to picture a scene in which Russell felt himself obliged to accede to Monk's tactful, 'But this is surely the *real* reason why you abandoned Helen Dudley?' Although his manner is self-avowedly speculative, Ackroyd suggests an explanation for episodes of irrational guilt in Dickens's adult life which it seems fair to say he would have found baffling. This is not only an example of the biographer knowing differently from his subject, but knowing more. Foreign though it would have been to Johnson, that the child is father of the man was a belief few held more firmly than Dickens, or exemplified in fiction more effectively. But the very early age at which Ackroyd speculates this crucial experience might have taken place, and the particular nature of the emphasis he places on sibling rivalry, sharply distinguish his suggestion from nineteenth century commentaries on the importance of childhood. The combination of those features would make it seem 'Freudian' even for those unfamiliar with the letter to Fleiss in which Freud claimed that the death of his eight-month old brother Julius (when he himself was only nineteen months) left him with a tendency to self-reproach, or the emphasis which sibling rivalry often receives in his writings.[16] Freud helped to induce one of several major discontinuities in the English tradition of life-writing which would make it impossible to claim that any curiosity about present methods is rendered otiose by its smooth and successful development. At no other point before he began to be influential would it have seemed sensible to link the irrational guilt feelings of an adult with the homicidal impulses of a two-year old. If many present-day biographers do in fact set about their tasks instinctively therefore, it will be not so much conventions centuries old which they are following, but guidelines whose origins can be traced back no farther than Strachey and whose present character owes just as much to our present intellectual climate than to the traditions of a well-established literary form.

*

As my illustrations will already have suggested, in this attempt to say something meaningful about biography (without being led into a review of its history), the examples are taken chiefly, although by no means exclusively, from recent *literary* lives. This is a category within the genre that, because of the sources on which it relies, has special features that may make it seem untypical. Since they acquired financial value, there is very often a superabundance of documents relating to the private life of modern figures: letters, diaries and the like which were bought from the owners or their descendants by the great libraries (principally in America). Their availability is as true for politicians as it is for literary men and women, but in the latter case what can be added to the evidence of this private material are the subject's own 'creative' writings. The dangers of working back from these to their author's life have often been rehearsed so that they are now almost as familiar as those of working forward from life to work (the 'biographical fallacy', as it was once called). There are in both procedures the same risks of, for example, crude equivalences between certain characters in a fiction and people its author knew, or too easy assumptions that the emotional states of protagonists were their creators' own. The list of possible perils is long, and they are probably at their most acute when there are obvious parallels between situations in authors' works and in their lives. This is because there is then more chance of ignoring how subtle are the alterations which personal experience undergoes when it enters (as it were) the autonomous world of literary creation. T. S. Eliot famously insisted on the separation between the man who suffers and the mind which creates,[17] and looking at the problem from a quite different perspective, the structuralists and post-structuralists brought him powerful support.

This *de facto* alliance between one highly influential critical orthodoxy and two of its successors has been formidable, yet not formidable enough to persuade most biographers that, in writing the life of a literary figure, the work could or should be ignored. In most countries there are laws still on the statute book which are unenforceable because the great mass of the population choose to disregard them. For the great mass of literary biographers, scrupulously regarding the work of their subjects as irrelevant to their lives would be too great a sacrifice; and they have in any case been able to argue with a fair show of reason that, however complex the relation between art and life might be, the separation between the two can never be absolute; that Eliot may have had a strong vested interest in suggesting that it was; and that at some level art must always be an act of 'self-expression', however much recent theoretical writing has complicated both components of that term.

With material from the creative writings of its subjects, and letters and diaries whose authors tend to exhibit a special gift for self-examination, a distinctive feature of literary biography is thus, not so much these sources themselves, but that it usually offers a reasonably elaborate chronology of thought and feeling in addition to a sequence of events. It describes not merely what happened but the development and succession of states of mind. To a certain degree this is true of most biographies but, because of the nature of the evidence available, it is especially the case in the lives of literary figures. How they felt becomes just as important as what they did. In his excellent biography of George Orwell, Bernard Crick, a political scientist rather than a literary critic, casts a sceptical eye on this aspect of literary lives and refers to the 'affable pretence' of many of their authors that they are able 'to enter into another person's mind'. 'We can only know actual persons', he insists, 'by observing their behaviour in a variety of different situations and through different perspectives'. Noting that Wyndham Lewis had once said that good biographies are like novels, he concludes that 'some good bad biographies appear to be, epistemologically speaking, novels indeed'.[18]

In one respect Crick's position seems unassailable. When biographers give an account of what their subjects thought and felt there is usually no way of proving them right, and every opportunity therefore of accusing them of fiction: making things up. But biography is not the only domain where probability rather than certainty is the order of the day, and where scientific standards of rigour could never apply. 'Our discussion will be adequate if it has as much clearness as the subject-matter admits of, for precision is not to be sought for alike in all discussions', says Aristotle.[19] Readers who pick up a literary biography usually do so in the expectation of learning, not only what the subject did, but also what he or she was like, and few of them are sufficiently behaviourist in inclination to feel that a full answer to the second question could always be inferred from the answer to the first. Discovering what someone is like involves, among many other things, attempting to reconstitute what has been called their internal soliloquy. Crick's stricture against this common practice applies just as forcibly to Johnson's speculations about Harley's motives as it does to Ackroyd's attempts to imagine what Dickens experienced in his third year. Yet it would be very surprising indeed if, in the whole of Crick's life of Orwell, there were no idioms which closely resembled those of Johnson. All biography is a way of thinking about other people and that is a process virtually impossible in our culture without the use of expressions which imply knowledge of their states of mind. What makes literary biography unusual is the assumption of most of its authors that there is privileged access to those states through their subject's creative works.

*

In the epigraph to the first volume of his life of Henry James, Edel quotes James as claiming that, 'To live over other people's lives is nothing unless we live over their perceptions, live over the growth, the change, the varying intensity of the same – since it was *by* these things they themselves lived'. With usually more means at their disposal for following this implied prescription than the authors of soldiers' or politicians' lives, literary biographers dramatise the problem of what can be known about the thoughts and feelings of people from the past. The charge against those of them who are felt to underestimate its complexity, or go too far, is usually the same as Crick's: they have mistaken the form of biography for that of the novel. One way of meeting it is to ride with the punch and ask whether all life-writing is not after all a branch of fiction: not merely because it is full of conjecture about psychological states but also because it is alienated by its essentially literary nature from what is commonly thought of as the truth. This was more or less the position adopted by the author of a monograph on biography, published in 1984, which attempted to harmonise an enquiry into the form with what were then recent developments in theory. In the fifth chapter of *Biography: Fiction, Fact and Form* (apart from the 'Introduction' all the other chapters in this book are historical rather than theoretical in character), Bruce Nadal set out to support his claim that, 'In the composition of biography, fictive rather than historical content dominates as the elements of a life become the elements of a story', and to justify his rebuke to those commentators who have concentrated on 'the accuracy of the materials' rather than 'the form of presentation'. Having previously declared his indebtedness to Hayden White, the name most closely associated with the notion of – to quote the title of one of White's essays –

'The Historical Text as Literary Artefact', he spends most of his chapter exploring in a number of well-known biographies their authors' use of metaphor and metonymy, two of Kenneth Burke's 'four Master Tropes'.[20]

Biographical enquiry is often described as if it were a search for a missing person, buried treasure, a *corpus delecti*. The metaphors used – 'unearthing' new material, for example – suggest that the 'life' of the subject is lying in wait to be discovered. But life stories are of course *created* by biographers from the information at their disposal, and even before this putative process of selection from the available 'facts' (privileging one of their aspects at the expense of many others), interpretation has entered in with initial decisions about the directions in which it would be best to look for them. When it comes to presenting these facts to the reader, it is undoubtedly the case that biographers use many of the same literary devices and methods as novelists (metaphor and metonymy included). To realise this is a useful exercise for people who, when they are reading biographies, believe themselves in direct contact with life as it was lived, less so for those who have always thought life-writing was a literary activity; and that biographies can be analysed in the same way as novels does not prove the two forms are identical. More awareness of the literary devices associated with their composition, the 'aesthetics of biography' as Nadal calls them, may be a useful prophylactic; but it is unlikely to lead to a better, general understanding of their form.

Emphasis on the literary character of biography is usually accompanied (as it is in Nadal) by the assumption that the past is in any case irrecoverable. As far as life-writing is concerned, discussion on that matter is often clouded by the absence of a taxonomy. No one is ever likely to know for certain what went on in Harley's mind when he was faced by the demands of the October club, but where Swift was born is a matter that can be settled definitively. One of the reviewers of *Flaubert's Parrot* rightly praised Julian Barnes for reminding his readers that 'there are questions to which there are no answers';[21] but it is worth noting that the question which is central to the story, and comically emblematic therefore of the past's irretrievability, is not in principle unanswerable. Visiting the hospital in Rouen where Flaubert spent his childhood, the narrator is shown the stuffed parrot which Flaubert supposedly borrowed from the local museum when he was writing *Un Coeur Simple*; but moving on to visit the writer's house at Croisset, he sees another parrot for which the same claim is made. Anxious throughout the action to discover which of these two parrots actually stood on Flaubert's desk, Geoffrey Braithwaite (as the narrator is called) finally discovers that, partly because stuffed parrots were all the rage in the Rouen of the nineteenth century and the local museum therefore kept fifty of them, it has become impossible to know. That is bad luck, but one can easily imagine circumstances in which the authenticity of an item of memorabilia could be established with absolute certainty (should the effort be thought worthwhile!), whereas there are details of Flaubert's inner life about which the biographer can only ever offer more or less convincing conjecture.

Whether biographers are driven back on conjecture because the appropriate evidence for settling an issue no longer exists, or because the questions they are asking could never be answered definitively, would not matter to some. That so much of biography is necessarily conjectural, and that its form is – with equal necessity – always more or less literary, confirm for them the insignificance of the separation between writing lives and writing novels. Yet readers seem to recognise the difference, and so do many writers. When Virginia Woolf published *Orlando* it was described on the title page as 'A Biography', whereas it is in fact an extravagantly fiction-alised portrait of her friend Vita Sackville-West. In her journal, Woolf recorded how easy she found its composition and how much enjoyment it gave her. When on the other hand she came to write a conventional biography (of Roger Fry) her entries were full of complaint. She grumbled continually about the 'drudgery' and 'grind' involved, about everything being 'too detailed, too laid down'; and she complained that she was not able to cut herself free of the facts when 'there they are, contradicting my theories'.[22] It is clear from this contrast that Woolf had taken seriously the imaginary pact all biographers sign with the reader and suffered from the restraint of having to stay within the limits which the information she had gathered suggested. When she began her life of Charlotte Brontë, Elizabeth Gaskell similarly complained to a friend that 'you have to be accurate and keep to the facts; a most difficult thing for a writer of fiction'.[23]

Biographers who, like Woolf and Gaskell, take their trade seriously, are always caught between wanting to retain the interest of their readers and being faithful to the evidence they have collected; they are divided between two objectives very hard to reconcile: telling a good story but not telling fibs. It is no wonder therefore that they sometimes cheat, especially when there is so little danger of reviewers finding them out. The ideal reviewer of a biography has covered the same ground as its author and therefore knows what evidence there is for the thousands of details and explanatory claims it is likely to contain. In the absence of that knowledge, the vast majority have to rely on an impression of trustworthiness derived from how the author interprets information which is displayed in the book itself, and from such matters as tone or the care that has been taken in formulation. These can go a long way, but not perhaps far enough to provide a sufficient deterrent given the temptations to which all biographers are subject when they want to avoid an awkward hiatus in the narrative, or strengthen a particular hypothesis. It is a useful rule of thumb, for example, that two eyewitnesses are required for an episode which is likely to be controversial; but sometimes it is convenient to make do with only one. Witnesses who have proved unreliable on previous occasions may be restored to favour when the biographer has no alternative, and awkward facts that contradict the main drive of the narrative may be omitted when neutralising their effect would take too much space and effort. These are matters in relation to which all biographers are guilty, although some are more guilty than others. Yet the very fact that it appears appropriate to talk of guilt in these matters, or of cheating, seems to illustrate how different life-writing is, despite its many 'fictive' elements, from fiction *tout court*. Biographers certainly 'tell a story' but the circumstances in which the more conscientious among them feel obliged to do so make all the difference.

*

Whether creative work ought ever to be regarded as evidence in the life of a writer, the possibility of identifying correctly other people's states of mind, and the certainly literary as well as supposedly fictive character of biography, are all problems which come up repeatedly when it is discussed. My manner of alluding to them will have suggested where my sympathies lie, but it would seem strange to make them the objects of a pitched battle (skirmishing is another matter) when speculating on the inner states of others is such an ineradicable feature of human existence, so few literary biographers do in fact ignore the subject's writing, and authors of lives who, when they set out on their task, assume they will have the same freedom in the management of their narrative a novelist enjoys, are also very rare. Yet if these issues I have raised are not the key ones, what alternatives are there? One answer is to be found in the remark from the preface to Monk's life of Russell that the point of a biography is 'no more and no less than to understand its subject'.[24] This implies being able to explain to the reader most if not all aspects of that subject's behaviour so that the story of his or her life becomes coherent. As Alan Shelston once put it, 'biography of its nature cannot stop at factual record: instinctively it must move on to explanation and interpretation'.[25] This is true of the form in all its manifestations and it raises the vital question of quite how biographers go about explaining their subjects: the explanatory codes to which they characteristically refer.

Investigating this matter is not of course *necessarily* associated with what gives a biography value, much less with what makes it enjoyable to particular readers. The immediate pleasure some biographies yield is often connected with the choice of subject: an incompetent life of a figure who interests us is always likely to have some appeal whereas we can never be drawn to the lives of others, however well they have been composed. It is to the subject that many reviewers of literary biographies chiefly respond, using their reviews as an opportunity for reassessing a particular writer and taking the selection and arrangement of material with which they have been presented more or less for granted. In doing that they could be said to exploit the biographer from whom many of the details included in the reassessment are usually taken, without any formal acknowledgement. Yet they could also be regarded as the biographer's dupe since the impression which prompts the reassessment must be partly based on those details, many of which could have appeared in a quite different context or not have been included at all. This is very hard to remember when the fallacy to which we are all most prone in thinking about biography is that the unsatisfactoriness of any particular account of a life can be established by reference to the definitive, true version lodged in some heavenly vault.

When reviewers and readers do focus on how a biography has been written, trying to establish what they have enjoyed and valued, it may be difficult for them to make a judgement on the use of evidence, but they can usually appreciate how much energy has gone into its collection. Whether or not the narrative is well managed will be self-evident. Some biographers' English is better than that of others and, when the subject is a writer, it is important that some are better literary critics. One essential duty in the writing of a life is to develop a sense of the period in which the subject flourished, but reading a number of biographies in succession will soon show that the power to evoke the past is very unevenly shared. Although all these factors are important and determine responses, they are hard to investigate on other than an individual, *ad hominem* basis; yet value and enjoyment are also crucially dependent on the biographer's insight and understanding. How would they like this writer, readers might reasonably ask themselves, talking about *them* after they were dead?

With 'insight and understanding' the focus is brought back to the centrality of explanatory method. In his analysis of Harley, Johnson relies on a number of moral axioms (the usual fate of double dealers, what happens to those who cannot decide which way to move), and vernacular psychology: the self-deception that might make us mistake our indecisiveness for political cunning. But Harley is only a bit player in the *Life of Swift*. Had he been its main subject, one might have expected Johnson to enquire more, not only into what made Harley indecisive on a particular occasion, but also what in his past, or in his nature, might have predisposed him to indecision: how far and how justifiably his response to the October Club could be described as characteristic. The ways in which biographers answer questions like these are so much part of our culture that, except in the special case of 'psychobiography', they rarely attract the attention of reviewers. Yet their social importance is considerable and can be gauged by the debates over the motives for certain actions which sometimes take place in the law courts. Interpreting the behaviour of others is an activity to which many more members of society than biographers are committed. There may well be a depressing significance in the fact that the only conveniently simple term in English for talking about other people is gossip. To think, write or talk responsibly about the private affairs of others requires the fulfilment of at least two conditions. One is that we always remain keen to establish that the information we receive is trustworthy: that it comes (for example) from a reliable source. The other, that we have the intelligence and human understanding to draw correct inferences from our information. The ideal gossip is therefore someone who combines the wisdom of Dr Johnson with the assiduity of George Eliot's Casaubon. But this is not a bad description of the ideal biographer also. If the way people talk about each other in any social group is an indication of its health, then so too are the biographies that group most admires.

2

Biography and Explanation

But seeing causes are the chiefest thinges
That should be noted of the story wryters,
That men may learne what endes al causes
                                        bringes
They be vnworthy the name of Croniclers,
That leave them cleane out of their registers.
                              (*The Mirror for Magistrates*, ed. Lily B. Campbell
                                        (Cambridge, 1938), p. 198)

FOR ALL BUT THOSE readers from a culture which is totally alien,
much of the biographical subject's behaviour will be self-
explanatory: only a Martian is likely to wonder why most people in
industrialised societies brush their teeth when they get up in the
morning. Brushing teeth is not however an action which many biographers are keen to record, and the more their narratives lead
them into areas which are unusual, the more they are shot through
with explanatory asides and hints as to this or that episode's
meaning or significance. It follows that the explanatory procedures
biographers employ are usually most clearly evident and open to
inspection when they are dealing with particular traits, recurrent
patterns of behaviour or individual actions which are unusual, or
out of the ordinary. We see best the criteria to which they usually
appeal when they are faced with the abnormal: Van Gogh cutting
off a part of his own ear, Proust deriving sexual excitement from
watching hatpins stuck into rats, or Mozart filling his private correspondence with frequent references to shit and piss. These aspects
of the behaviour of men who in many, if not most, other respects

20

excite admiration are disconcerting, and most biographers would
feel an obligation to respond to the surprise they generate.

Slightly adapting his source (*A Study in Scarlet*), the philosopher
Frank Cioffi has offered a useful paradigm of the effect that explanation can sometimes have in these and similar cases. The occasion
is Dr Watson's meeting on the street with an old friend from
medical school, and the discovery that a certain Sherlock Holmes
is looking for someone with whom he might share lodgings in Baker
Street. Anxious to find lodgings himself, Watson asks what kind of
a person Holmes is. Although the report is broadly favourable, it
does contain hints as to some curious habits. When Watson naturally asks what these are, he is told that the person with whom he
is vaguely contemplating sharing rooms comes to the hospital where
the friend works and . . . beats the cadavers in the dissecting room.
Consternation and surprise are then dissipated, however, when the
friend goes on to explain the apparent abnormality of this behaviour by reference to a passion which in the course of the nineteenth
century had become increasingly respectable: scientific curiosity.
For reasons with which Watson is destined to become very familiar,
Holmes beats the corpses because he wants to discover how long
after death a bruise will form.

It is not always or even usually the case that what at first shocks
can be re-integrated into a system of common assumptions. More
often the effect of an explanation is simply to make comprehen-
sible what was previously baffling: it is the mystery rather than the
oddness which disappears. Yet when what appeared abnormal
becomes normal (as in the Holmes case), there is always the implicit
question of how and why we define those two categories as we do.
Why should a man not beat corpses if that happens to be 'his
thing'? When Charlie Chaplin's second wife sued for divorce,
unusual sexual practices were part of her case against her husband.
'But doesn't', a bemused Chaplin is supposed to have protested,
'*everybody* do that?'.[1] We think we are behaving like other people
until some unhappy social event of this kind disabuses us. It may
be no accident that this last illustration comes from the sexual
realm where it has always been dangerous for biographers to assume
norms, but where recent theoretical writing has now made it virtually impossible to do so. The effect of that work is broadly liberating;
but it might well leave biographers even more confused than they
were before about what needs explaining – quite where in their
subjects' lives there are what some commentators have termed

'narrative gaps'. On the other hand, in compensation for this increased uncertainty, we may now have a clearer idea of why we prefer some biographers to others: it is that their sense of what needs explaining is reasonably co-incident with ours. Everyone must have had the experience of reading a biography where all the things they would really like to know have been left obscure and page after page has been expended on what seems boring or self-evident.

However the concept of abnormality is defined, most biographers are likely to regard Proust's behaviour with the rats as an explanatory challenge.[2] Yet there are of course thousands of features of his or any other life which are less spectacular but which most competent observers would agree also call out for explanation. The number of possible examples here is so great that any choice will seem arbitrary but, in the lives of other prominent literary figures from the earlier part of this century, and taking the matter at its very broadest, one of them would be why, after the success of *Howard's End* in 1910, E. M. Forster did not publish any more novels until *A Passage to India* in 1924, and then no other before his death in 1970. This is an issue which P. N. Furbank treats as more worthy of explanation than, for example, Forster's homosexuality. When he comes to deal with it directly, he cites his subject's own testimony that describing love affairs between men and women when you are homosexual can become tedious implying that, had he been able to publish *Maurice* in 1914, Forster's career might have been different. He suggests, as a second possible explanation, that in any case Forster only ever had in him one novel of which all his works are variations; and thirdly (when it comes to explanation a surprising number of biographers are Trinitarian) he appeals to an essay by Freud entitled 'Those wrecked by success'. Furbank's readers are more likely to feel that these explanations are inadequate to the size of the problem they address than that it has been over-estimated. In their response to another admirable biography – Mark Holloway's life of Norman Douglas – the same readers might well feel that not enough is done to explain why at one moment in his career Douglas is forced to flee one great European capital because of his involvement with a married woman whereas, only a few years later, his fondness for young boys obliges him to escape from another.[3]

What biographers choose to explain is one means of discrimination but another, more important one is provided by how they do the explaining. This was not so much an issue when author and reader both believed that the world was governed by a divine power. Then the subject's behaviour represented either acquiescence in, or rebellion against, the path that power had designated, and the whole of an individual's life was explicable in terms of a providential scheme. Izaac Walton is one of the most pious of English biographers but it is nevertheless significant that in his description of how George Herbert's struggle to come to terms with his priestly vocation was simplified by the death of his two principal patrons at Court, he should refer so instinctively to 'God in whom there is an unseen Chain of Causes'.[4] 'Man's accidents are God's purposes' was the motto which Hawthorne's wife had engraved on the window of her husband's study.[5] When you know who is responsible for order in the world, and the nature of our task here, making sense of a life is not too difficult: the explanatory codes to which the biographer can refer are well defined. Any life conceived within the framework of a single world view is likely to seem coherent. In our time, it is the orthodox Marxist biographer who perhaps comes closest to enjoying the same advantages as those who wrote the lives of the Saints, or who would do if a Marxist biography did not at least imply giving more importance to individual action and experience than a strictly Marxist approach to history could justify.

Biographers with a view of the world sufficiently comprehensive for most aspects of their subject's behaviour to be explicable within it are rare in a secular age. So too are those who, like some psychoanalytic biographers, approach the problem of explanation from a single, well-defined point of view. But if most are haplessly eclectic, willing to take whatever avenue seems best to suit the case, there are nevertheless four broad categories within which many of their biographical explanations can be accommodated. The first and most popular of these is the psychological, which usually shades off at its more technical moments into the psychoanalytic. Psychological explanations take a myriad forms so that cataloguing their different varieties would be an endless task. The least inquisitive of biographers will offer psychological explanations of their subjects' behaviour, by appealing opportunistically to one of the many interpretative systems established this century (if Freud's is by far the most popular, Jung, Adler, Klein, Winnicott and Lacan also have their adherents); or much more usually by invoking one or other of those principles from the common store of vernacular pssychology which Johnson deploys with such power and virtuosity. Explanatory remarks will be scattered throughout their work or at least up until the point where the 'character' of subjects has been established with such certainty that no situation in which they are involved remains a mystery.

Partly, but only partly, because of psychoanalysis, the search for character in biography is very often 'genetic', in the philosophical rather than biological sense. That is because in our day by far the most popular direction in which to look for explanations of human peculiarities is backwards. So much is this the case that Sartre may well have defined the spirit of our age when he said that, '*Une vie, c'est une enfance mise à toutes les sauces*'.[6] The general habit of mind this remark exemplifies is of course traditional and goes back a long way yet, although certain kinds of belief in the crucially determining character of early experience was around well before the Romantics came on the scene, it was above all their doing that looking back to childhood for explanations should now seem second nature to us. Without their efforts, Woodrow Wilson would not have slipped so easily into saying, 'A boy never gets over his boyhood, and never can change those subtle influences which have become a part of him, that were bred in him when he was child'.[7] Wilson is a convenient name to mention in this context in that, after his death, he was the subject of a psychoanalytic biography to which Freud contributed. As I have already suggested in discussing Ackroyd on Dickens, there is much more to Freud than the systematisation of Romantic intuitions, but that is certainly one aspect of his work; and it was he above all who ensured that the area which would receive special biographical scrutiny in the twentieth century was the early relation of subjects with their parents.

A concern with origins is not only characteristic of those who, temporarily or as a matter of either principle or habit, have adopted a psychological approach. The parents of the subject might be interesting to many biographers less for the conflicts they engendered ('Oedipal' or otherwise), than for their supposed genetic inheritance. This is to incorporate into the enquiry physical or organic factors, a procedure especially common or perhaps simply more noticeable when biographers are obliged to consider the effect of illness on their subjects. Although I have chosen in this study to deal separately with the explanation of character in terms of genetic inheritance, and the even more fraught question of how far illness can or should explain behaviour, the two often come together, especially when the illness is a matter of mental derangement or unbalance. 'New research', a newspaper headline once announced, shows that it was an 'inherited condition' which led to Sylvia Plath's suicide.[8] If that is true, then too much analysis of her childhood experiences would seem otiose, as would too minute a reconstruction of the circumstances which led up to her death (including the painful separation from her husband). In reflections on the suicide of Virginia Woolf, Thomas Caramagno has written, 'Ironically, although suicide can seem the most personal of all our life decisions, it can also be the most impersonal for the biology of the brain operates in ways that may seem inhuman'.[9] As I shall try to show, once biology is invoked all the competing determinants appear obliged to take a back seat.

The subjects of biographies are usually outstanding individuals, people who have written, painted or done things which others admire. Only when we see them in a class photograph at school or university might it be brought home to us forcibly that they are also members of social groups. For the most 'literary' and therefore (in this context) most accessible of post-war sociologists, Erving Goffman, 'character' is necessarily a consequence of social interaction.[10] To some extent biographers will acknowledge this. Any author of a life of Plath, for example, could hardly ignore the fierceness of her ambition to write poetry and her intensely competitive relations with other poets (to take only one social group with which she can be associated). These are elements with a bearing on how she behaved which could have been at least as important as her medical or psychological history. A biographer who was ready to take full account of them, however, or accord them the same exclusivity of attention a sociologist might, would be unusual. One reason for this is that the documents with which the biographer of Plath tends to work are her own poems, letters and diaries. This makes any account of her life subject-centred in a way which is inimical to a classic sociological approach. Since Plath is the illustration here it is worth noting that one of the founding texts in sociology is Emile Durkheim's study of suicide. As Caramagno notes, no action seems at first sight more deeply personal than the decision to kill oneself, but some students of Plath clearly believe that she was the helpless victim of her genes or driven, if perhaps less helplessly, by psychological difficulties from her early life. The originality of Durkheim was to show that not only could the group of individuals most likely to commit suicide be established from statistical evidence, but also both the place where, and the time when they would do it. This was because suicide, which seems so personal, was no less a social act than voting in an election (one of those apparently private decisions the consequences of which are now routinely predicted with accuracy). Each social group, Durkheim claimed, had a collective tendency towards suicide from which individual tendencies derived. 'Today', he wrote, in another of sociology's master texts, 'most of our ideas and tendencies are not developed by ourselves, but come to us from outside'; and he elaborated on the thought in the following paragraph: 'We are, then, dupes of an illusion which makes us think that we have ourselves developed what is imposed upon us from outside'.[11]

Reviewing the different ways in which she might have approached the biography of Virginia Woolf, Hermione Lee noted that it would have been possible to 'start with Bloomsbury, fixing [Woolf] inside her social and intellectual group'.[12] In describing the various people who made up what is known as Bloomsbury, Lee is excellent; but, through the copious diaries and correspondence, she remains sufficiently close to her subject's point of view never to suggest that what Woolf became, her 'character', was a consequence of her group affiliations. The portrait she offers is entirely different from what is likely to have been the result had Woolf herself ever attempted a biography of her cousin, Herbert Fisher:

> Father . . . laid immense stress upon school reports; upon scholarships; triposes and fellowships. The male Fishers went through those hoops to perfection. They won all the prizes, all the honours. What, I asked myself, when I read Herbert Fisher's autobiography the other day, would Herbert have been without Winchester, New College and the Cabinet? What would have been his shape had he not been stamped and moulded by that great patriarchal machine? Every one of our male relations was shot into that machine at the age of ten and emerged at sixty a Head Master, an Admiral, a Cabinet Minister, a Warden of a college. It is impossible to think of them as natural human beings as it is to think of a carthorse galloping wild maned and unshod over the pampas.[13]

The horse which gallops wild maned and unshod over the pampas stands for that mythical human being uncontaminated by social groups and institutions. Woolf implies that in the society of her day, dominated as it was by the 'great patriarchal machine', upper middle-class women had more chance of remaining 'natural human beings' than upper middle-class men, and that all that one could or might want to know about Fisher was synonymous with knowledge of it.

In his biography of Flaubert (*The Family Idiot*), Sartre makes a similar point to Woolf's when he is describing how Gustave's elder brother, Achille, was destined from birth to be his father's successor as the chief surgeon in Rouen. He became in consequence, Sartre writes,

> A relative being, inessential and timid, who never determined what he would be *from within*, but always in terms of the external model he had been given and wanted always to follow ... there was nothing in him which was not imposed *from without*, nothing that expressed his original spontaneity.

A few pages earlier Sartre had explained that the terms in which he had chosen to analyse Achille would not be suitable for anyone in whom thought which was originally 'stubborn, original, active, became *creative*'.[14] Woolf might well have used this distinction to explain why a biographical approach appropriate to her cousin would not have been apt in her case. Yet a sociologist could reply that what is sauce for the gander is also sauce for the goose, and that social conditioning acts on the gifted as well as the dull. Glenn Gould is reported to have asked himself whether he would have become a musician had he not been born into a musical family, and, taking the family as the primary social group, there is no reason why even Mozart could not be imagined making the same enquiry.

*

The three categories of biographical explanation very roughly sketched above are broadly deterministic: they assume that people behave in a certain way for reasons beyond either their mental or physical control. In a fourth category, far more authority is accorded the subject and what they do is regarded as much more a consequence of choice. Plath may after all have decided to commit suicide for long pondered reasons we are called upon to respect. This insistence on the freedom individuals have to fashion how they live and – in the case of suicide – how they die, is spectacularly evident when Sartre in his book on Baudelaire insists that, after the trauma of his mother's remarriage, the poet *himself* determined the kind of person he wanted to be. The line of reasoning he adopts eventually prompts him to suggest that even the syphilis which led to Baudelaire's miserable death was not an unfortunate accident but a matter of existential choice.[15] Totally innocent of existentialism, the eighteenth-century scholar Frederick Pottle made a similar point when, in his biography of Boswell, he suggested that his subject's recklessly acquired venereal diseases were one of the methods he had for imposing suffering on his flesh, that they represented a 'conscience-soothing acceptance of punishment'.[16] Here, however, one can begin to see the path which leads to explanation in terms of unconscious motivation whereas the main feature of this fourth category is the willingness of its exponents to challenge the sciences of human behaviour, so hugely influential in our time, and interpret human conduct as the more or (in Sartre's case) less straightforward consequence of an individual's power of choice.

How these four approaches to making sense of a life might be invoked can be illustrated by considering D. H. Lawrence's famous rages, and the tendency he had in them to hit his wife. To call Lawrence a wife-beater would be inaccurate since that phrase implies regularity of abuse and could not sufficiently take into account that, in this case, the victim was capable of physical retaliation and would on occasions beat her husband back. Yet Lawrence's attacks on Frieda were sufficiently frequent and violent to shock many of their friends. It is of course open to biographers to pass them by as unremarkable ('Doesn't *everybody* do that?'), but most of them would feel some need to explain. Given Lawrence's well-known and well-documented attachment to his mother: the way his feelings progressed from passionate devotion to bitter resentment at the responsibility he felt she bore for the person he had become, and adding to that his simultaneous need and repudiation of Frieda Lawrence as a mother substitute, the psychological approach might seem particularly promising. Yet in his last years Lawrence suffered from tuberculosis and, as I shall show later, that disease was often associated in his time with ungovernable rage. When he hit Frieda, the chief responsibility could therefore be assigned to the bacillus which was undermining his system rather than to any psychological legacy from his childhood. A sociological explanation seems less obviously available until one remembers that Lawrence is very unusual among famous writers in having had a working-class childhood. In his own portrayal of it, the mining culture of Nottinghamshire was one in which husbands were expected to dominate their wives and domestic violence was by no means uncommon. As Lawrence moved from adoring his mother to a retrospective idealisation of his father, it could be that a desire to emulate what he took to be appropriately manly behaviour had an influence on his conduct.

The fourth possibility is to see that conduct as a manifestation of a philosophy of openness which both Lawrence and his wife had adopted early in their married life. He had been brought up by his mother to be genteel and 'nice', and no one can be either of those things without a good deal of repression of feeling. In Frieda he met someone who had been taught by one of Freud's early disciples, Otto Gross, that all repression was wrong. She helped him to shed his inhibitions in material circumstances which were ideal for that purpose, whatever other drawbacks they might have had. In the early days, when they were not yet married and Frieda was still very much the wife who had abandoned a husband and three children, the Lawrences were social outcasts moving periodically from place to place and never subject to the pressure to conform to any settled, social group of which they formed a part. If they 'belonged' anywhere after their marriage it was with a small section of London Bohemia whose notions of normal behaviour were unusually liberal. As a writer moreover, Lawrence did not have to submit to all the conformities of a workplace in order to earn his living. These freedoms provided an ideal context for the spontaneous expression of feeling and both Lawrence and Frieda made obedience to true feeling the cornerstone of their moral system. Anything that was genuinely felt could not *by definition* be wrong. Lawrence inveighs frequently against the evils of repression in his letters. Being a choleric man himself, he understood very well that his position implied an acceptance of all that was violent and aggressive in human nature; but he would have said with Blake, 'Sooner murder an infant in its cradle than nurse unacted desires'. This would be on the grounds that desires which are nursed rather than acted upon directly are certain to manifest themselves in insidiously perverse ways. Once one took into account the views of both the Lawrences on repression, then one could argue that there was far more involved in their famous quarrels, plate-throwing, etc. than bad temper. Lawrence's role in the abnormality of these clashes, which must on occasions have been followed or accompanied by violence, can certainly be explained in terms of physical or psychological forces beyond his control; they can be interpreted in relation to the social context in which he grew up; but they might just as well be seen as the determined acting-out of a philosophy of life which had been quite consciously adopted.

By no means all of the biographical subject's character and behaviour can be interpreted in terms of these four categories. This is an area in which it would be futile to expect neatness and, in any case, when it is a question of a particular action – even such an extreme one as striking one's wife – the circumstances may be all one needs. Certain psychologists have referred in the past to the 'fundamental attribution error' which is defined as 'a systematic tendency to underestimate the extent to which the behaviour of others is affected by situational forces and to overestimate the extent to which it expresses enduring personal characteristics'.[17] Put more simply: that a specific act is repeated does not make it characteristic. How many glasses of wine does someone have to knock over before they can be designated as careless? Each episode might have a context which makes it unique.

The more unusual the circumstances which contribute to that context, the more important they are. Using a strange image, Mandelstam once claimed that, after the Russian Revolution, individuals were cast out of their biographies like billiard balls from their pockets by large impersonal forces.[18] It seems obviously true that the more extreme the external circumstances are, the more they are likely to explain. In times of crisis, questions of individual motivation tend to become less urgent and the crisis itself may be enough to account for why people act as they do. This may nonetheless bring one back to the four categories in that, for biographers whose interests are sociological, one feature of a crisis is that it reveals to the uninitiated what habitually prevails: destroys the myth that we are determined by what goes on inside rather than out.

For some people, Mandlestam's 'large impersonal forces' could be taken as analogous to the grand passions which affect most if not all human beings. Arguing that the biography of any individual, however obscure, could have its value, Dr Johnson wrote: 'We are all prompted by the same motives, all deceived by the same fallacies, all animated by hope, obstructed by danger, entangled by desire, seduced by pleasure'.[19] This might well be so but the *degree* to which we are deceived, animated, obstructed, entangled and seduced is different in each case and may well need explaining. The common declaration that an individual cannot be persuaded into performing a certain action for either love or money reveals how powerful and all-embracing these two motives are felt to be. Yet different people clearly manifest sexual desire in different ways and although, since the collapse of socialism, money makes the world go round even more than it used to, its effect is by no means uniform.

Biographers could often be accused of paying insufficient attention to money: of being betrayed by its lack of glamour as a motive into underestimating its explanatory power. Reading a biography of Voltaire which had been sent him, D. H. Lawrence told a friend that he thought the author cunning and underhand for not explaining how, at Lawrence's own age, Voltaire came to have 'an *income* of £3,000'.[20] The influence of money on all our lives is very great, and determines all kinds of choices. As professional biographers are likely to know better than their colleagues who work in universities, it can profoundly influence the shape of a literary career. Sir Walter Scott's is not the only life which would be incomprehensible without taking it into account. Yet one does not have to be an enthusiast for the way Freud traced the origins of our attitudes to money back to toilet training in order to realise that those attitudes can be complex. Everybody wants to make a decent living but the definition of 'decent' can vary wildly according to expectations and the life-style to which people are accustomed. For some, money is so clearly the signifier of success that to earn less than a rival is painful; whereas for others earning more money is an attempt to achieve a 'security' which has very little to do with financial affairs. Distinctions of this variety abound. Only perhaps when a starving man needs money in order to buy his next meal does it become the kind of overwhelmingly influential external factor which, like the Russian Revolution for Mandelstam, encourages us to dispense with normal methods of analysis.

*

When they are preparing the record of a particular episode or period, biographers usually read all the documents they can: letters and diaries of the subject and of close friends or associates, descriptions of an area or of the historical context, works of fiction that contain obvious transpositions, and anything else that seems relevant. ('Poor Herbert Horne', Reggie Turner is reported to have said of a fellow expatriate in Florence who during the 1920s laboured away at his biography of Botticelli, 'Poring over washing bills and always a shirt missing').[21] Once notes from this material have been accumulated, but also of course, as they are *being* accumulated, biographers have to invoke principles of organisation that will allow them to decide the order in which the material should be presented, and which items are best juxtaposed with others. One of these principles is undoubtedly literary effect but although biographers are indeed faced with a variety of aesthetic choices (this metaphor, that metonymy), many of their governing principles are also associated with explanation. This is because the more sense actions appear to make, the more readable an account of them is likely to be. As they scrutinise their material, biographers seek to identify the gradually evolving or suddenly discovered explanatory frameworks into which this or that item best fits. That at least is very often the case, but all this talk of explanation might seem strange to some when the passages of explicit explanatory comment in quite a few lives are sparse and when, for most of the time, the impression these biographies make is less of narrative than of what might be called chronicle: a record of events.

James Clifford has suggested that the 'new cultural configuration' first defined by Coleridge in 1810 as 'the age of personality' means that people are inclined to 'strain after an unlivable identity. The desired unity', he goes on

> can at least be known vicariously, through the reading of biographies. But this very demand to deliver a self, ensures that its rendering of the person will emphasize closure and progress towards individuality, rather than openness and discontinuity.[22]

There are, perhaps, some biographers who have ideological reasons for favouring discontinuity and avoiding the search for coherence, who deliberately and self-consciously present their material in a disordered state as an insurance against the mind's propensity to impose distorting patterns; but there are many more for whom the depiction of a unified self is simply not a very interesting aim to pursue. The range of attitudes to life-writing is very broad with, at one extreme, those who are reluctant to include any detail which does not obviously fit while, at the other, there are those for whom a particular detail has such a strong, 'intrinsic' interest that its lack of significance for the narrative as a whole is of no account. Dr Johnson belonged very firmly to the first category, complaining that he could not see what advantage posterity received from 'the only circumstance by which Tickell has distinguished Addison from the rest of mankind, the irregularity of his pulse'; and that he did not feel he had been overpaid for the time spent reading a life of Malherbe,

> by being enabled to relate, after the learned biographer, that Malherbe had two predominant opinions; one that the looseness of a single woman might destroy all her boast of ancient descent, the other that the French beggars made use very improperly and barbarously of the phrase *noble gentleman*, because either word included the sense of both.

In the same number of the *Rambler* in which he makes this sarcastic protest against triviality, Johnson calls Sallust 'the great master of nature' for not having omitted to remark in his account of Cataline 'that his walk was now quick and again slow, as an indication of a mind revolving something with violent commotion'.[23] Because what it tells us about Cataline's mind justifies for Johnson the description of his way of walking, he would have found himself approving of Aubrey (not the biographer one would think of as his most natural ally) when he writes of Thomas Fuller that he 'was of a middle stature; strong sett; curled haire; a very working head, in so much that, walking and meditating before dinner, he would eate up a penny loafe, not knowing that he did it'.[24]

Less intellectually rigorous than Johnson, and with fewer anxieties that what he wrote might prove gratuitous, Boswell is often prepared to record a detail which has struck him, even when its point is not obvious. 'This reminds me', he remarks at one well-known moment,

> of the ludicrous account which [Johnson] gave Mr. Langton, of the despicable state of a young Gentleman of good family. 'Sir, when I heard of him last, he was running about town shooting cats'. And then in a sort of kindly reverie, he bethought himself of his own favourite cat, and said, 'But Hodge shan't be shot: no, no, Hodge shall not be shot'.[25]

Ultimately assimilable although this anecdote must of course be, it is hard at first to know what to make of it; yet Nabokov (who used it as the epigraph to *Pale Fire*) cannot be the only reader of Boswell's *Life* who was glad to find the passage there. The detail allows us to visualise Johnson in an unfamiliar light, and prompts the recollection that Virginia Woolf wondered whether Boswell was possessed of 'some madness' which 'let him see in sudden incongruous flashes, as the scene shifted round him, how strange it all was'.[26] Its appeal may be precisely that of any particular remark or action which appears to lie outside any immediately available explanatory framework. Peter Ackroyd is one of the most resolutely interpretative of modern biographers but he achieves a similar effect as Boswell when he describes Dickens dancing the hornpipe.[27] If we reflected on the significance of episodes of that kind, we might wonder why they needed to be included; but if we are in fact able to distinguish them from what is genuinely mindless detail, then sudden vivid glimpses which bring the subject to life before us are invaluable.

One great master of these glimpses is the Aubrey improbably imagined a moment ago as enjoying the approval of Dr Johnson (not often in the *Brief Lives* is there either an implicit or explicit rationale for the information they provide). Apart from his power of expression – considerably enhanced by what for most twentieth-century readers are the oddities of his seventeenth-century prose – the secret of Aubrey's powerful appeal lies partly with his editors. As the most well known of them (Oliver Lawson Dick) pointed out, some of Aubrey's favourite stories are repeated as many as seven times in his papers. By eliminating repetition, and including in a long introduction many of the best phrases from the almost 300 lives excluded from his edition (which contains only 134), Dick is able to display Aubrey's gift for the arresting detail to great advantage. The impression would be very different for anyone who read through the Aubrey material in the libraries. Yet even Dick's reader-friendly presentation of the biographical parts of this material ('ruthlessly rearranged') suggests that the title it is usually given is less apt than Aubrey's own *Minutes of Lives*.[28] There must be some doubt whether it is always useful to call Aubrey a biographer when the only two details of substance which he provides for Sir Everard Digby, for example, are that he was 'one of the handsomest men of his time' and that, when he was executed for his part in the Gunpowder Plot and the executioner ripped out his heart with, 'Here is the heart of a Traytor', he is 'credibly reported' to have replied, 'Thou liest!'[29] (a useful indication this, perhaps, of the very limited extent to which anyone who has ever published a book which is harshly reviewed has the right of reply). Aubrey's general attitude to biographical information emerges clearly in his introduction to what he has to say about Thomas Hobbes, more authentically a 'brief life' than anything else he wrote. 'Men thinke', he remarks,

> because every body remembers a memorable accident shortly after 'tis donne, 'twill never be forgotten, which for want of registring, at last is drowned in Oblivion; which reflection haz been a hint that by my meanes Antiquities have been reskued and preserved (I myselfe now inclining to be Ancient) – or else utterly lost and forgotten.

He had intended, he goes on, to remove everything that was superfluous from his life of Hobbes but friends had told him to let it all stand, 'for though to soome at present it might appeare too triviale; yet hereafter 'twould not be scorned but passe for Antiquity'.[30] Boswell defends the inclusiveness of his life of Johnson on the grounds that any detail relating to such a great man is worth recording, and he implies that what may not seem significant in his time could do so later. It is not only Aubrey's vocabulary which makes one want to say that his attitude is, in the best sense, more purely antiquarian. Whatever its eventual value or significance, *any* record of the past is always in his view worth preserving. Inclusive and antiquarian are the adjectives one might associate with biographers at Aubrey's end of the spectrum while at Johnson's they are interpretative and *ex*clusive (however long their books might turn out to be!).

*

No modern biographer is antiquarian in Aubrey's sense but among those who tend towards inclusiveness, and are not notably interpretative, a good example might be Norman Sherry. There is in the first volume of his life of Graham Greene, for example, a disinterested enthusiasm for information which is infectious, and no one in recent times has displayed more energy of enquiry. Yet of course, quite unlike Aubrey, Sherry knows how to fashion what he has discovered into a long, compelling story in which many details with no direct relevance to the life of his subject can be considered as contributing successfully to a period atmosphere. To write at such length of Greene's first thirty-five years without being stodgy is a great achievement, although it is true that Sherry has the advantage of a subject whose peculiarities were almost as striking as his talents. Not many Englishmen of his time, from an impeccably conventional middle-class background, were psychoanalysed during their schooldays, played Russian Roulette on several occasions while they were students, or combined to quite the same excessive extent an often cynical and opportunistic view of the world with an unusually fervid romanticism. It was the intensity of Greene's romantic attachment to the Catholic woman who eventually became his first wife which lay behind his conversion to Roman Catholicism, but the long dreamed of marriage to Vivien Dayrell-Browning did not prevent him from suddenly deciding to undertake an exceptionally arduous as well as dangerous trek through Liberia (then one of the most unexplored and 'primitive' of African states). Ambiguous though the origins of his commitment to his new religion were, it was partly his concern with the persecution of Catholic priests which led him, some time later, to undertake an almost equally difficult journey through the remoter parts of Southern Mexico. Sherry brings his subject back to England from Mexico in May 1939 and ends his 725 page account of this first part of Greene's life with:

> In London, the telephones were cut off, the anti-aircraft guns set up on the Common, and trenches were being dug. Air Raid Wardens had been appointed and Air Raid Posts set up in anticipation of the onslaught of German bombers. In spite of Neville Chamberlain's attempts to avert it, war was inevitable – and Greene would welcome it, in spite of the disruption it was to cause. It would be a new experience, another way of escape.[31]

To return to those distinctions offered at the beginning of this chapter, this is a response which could reasonably be described as abnormal. Sherry's narrative takes away any surprise his subject's welcoming of World War II might cause a reader, but it could hardly be said to explain it.

That Greene remains something of a mystery could be a consequence of what makes volume 1 of his life unusual, and *sui generis* in this enquiry: that he was still alive when it was published (he died two years later at the age of eighty six). But there are signs in volume 1 that it is more a matter of biographical temperament. At one point, for example, Sherry quotes highly elaborate accounts by Greene of two of his dreams, but then passes briskly on to his next topic with virtually no comment. This may indicate no more than a justifiable impatience with dream interpretation, but it seems significant in combination with Sherry's treatment of another of Greene's letters in which he tells his fiancée that major episodes in his life, up until his meeting with her, had been determined by rivalry with his brother Raymond. It was because Raymond won prizes at school for verse, Greene claims, that he wrote it too ('I never succeeded in winning any prizes . . . but then . . . I began to make money on it, so felt one up there'). When Raymond became a 'first class mountaineer', Greene felt he had to find ways of emulating him by undertaking dangerous journeys, and he says it was the way his brother risked his life in climbing mountains which made him take up 'the revolver trick' (Russian roulette). To this challenging interpretation of his own behaviour, the biographer's only response is 'Perhaps he was right'; yet nothing which appears previously in the volume would lead one to believe that Sherry really thought he was.[32] Like the account of the dreams, this self-analysis seems to owe its appearance in the biography to the inclusive principle on which Sherry operates; but it does not attract his curiosity in anything like the same degree as what are literally day-to-day details in his absorbing accounts of Greene's treks through Liberia and Mexico.

In the sense in which I have tried to define the term, Sherry is no Johnsonian; but it would nevertheless be quite wrong to say that he always describes and never explains. The conclusion to his first volume is provided by not only the outbreak of war but also a description of the experiences which led to the writing of *The Power and the Glory*. In his account of this novel, Sherry is as uninhibited as he has been previously in making connections between personal experience and fictional characters or episodes, and he feels confident that during his own researches in Mexico he was able to identify correctly the single models for the police lieutenant who pursues the 'whiskey priest', and the *mestizo* who betrays him. He has already found this scenario of sadistic persecutor, half-willing victim and Judas figure in several of Greene's previous writings, and traced it back to a period in his subject's boyhood when he was bullied at school. Even Sherry is unable to discover all the details of this episode but it appears to have involved a boy called Carter, who would prick Greene with dividers, and his henchman Wheeler who made friendly overtures in order later to betray him. That their victim happened also to be their headmaster's son made his situation especially difficult and the effect of their bullying, whatever the precise form it took, led Greene to make several half-hearted attempts at suicide and then run away from home (it was this last step which led his parents to send him off to London to be psychoanalysed). When he describes these events Sherry claims that they 'wrenched Graham's nature out of true', and suggests that Carter 'with his inexplicable cruelties, his nihilism, his ability to feign innocence, put Greene on to his fundamental theme, the nature of Good and Evil and the conflict between them'.[33] He illustrates this last point with proleptic glimpses of Greene's future writings using certain extracts, with that circular logic to which all biographers are prone, as a way both of showing the effect of early experience and attempting to clarify its lost details. For him, the Carter episode crucially determined Greene's outlook on life as well as the way he wrote. His return to it in his concluding discussion of the protagonists in *The Power and the Glory* suggests that, although the attitude to explanation among modern biographers may differ markedly, none of them ignore it; and that any enquiry into its nature will always therefore have some degree of general validity. Explanation is after all a part of form so that, for Sherry, tracing the sufferings of the whiskey priest directly back to those of Greene at school is a little like running a steel pole throughout the length of a fine old Victorian warehouse and then bolting it to the outside walls in case they should show signs of bulging out. More of a chronicler than most other contemporary biographers, there are exigencies in the management of a narrative as long as his which mean that he could never write as Aubrey often does and leave explanation entirely out of account.

3

Ancestors

People often say that writing about the Settlements is irrelevant
learning, but we think we can better meet the criticism of foreigners,
when they accuse us of being descended from slaves or scoundrels,
if we know for certain the truth about our ancestry. And for those
who want to know ancient lore and how to trace genealogies, it's
better to start at the beginning than to come in at the middle.
  (*Book of the Icelandic Settlements* (Thórdarbók version), trans.
  Hermann Pálson and Paul Edwards (Winnipeg, 1938), p. 6)

A REMARKABLE NUMBER OF BIOGRAPHIES begin with an account
of the subject's more or less remote ancestors. This seems as
necessary an introduction to the biographer's relation with the
reader as 'How do you do?', and often it is about as meaningful.
What intellectual benefit do we after all derive from being told that
the subject's great great grandfather was a yeoman farmer in Sussex,
or a small manufacturer in Yorkshire? The evidence that many
people like to know these things about themselves is overwhelming,
so there is a fair presumption they like to hear them about others.
But how do they make any difference to understanding? In many
cases, one could exchange the yeoman farmer from one biography
with the small manufacturer from another and no reader would
feel the difference.

The custom is to accompany these introductory genealogies with
a family tree, like the one in John Richardson's splendid life of
Picasso. It is in the nature of the case that this includes no yeoman
farmers from Sussex, but instead Richardson traces Picasso's lineage
to a 'fifteenth century knight of legendary courage', Juan De León

(d.1481).[1] There is no good reason for thinking that the line Richardson traces is dubious, but neither is there a better one for believing it would matter if it were.

It is not very difficult to see why this habit of biographers should be so instinctive and ingrained. As the Bible sufficiently tells us, as well as all our early literature, lineage was always a vitally important element of European culture. A sixteenth-century woodcut shows the dying Emperor Maximilian I listening to a reading of his family tree.[2] Given his condition, one would have thought he might have been more interested in where he was going than where he came from; but for all the centuries before the emergence of some kind of political influence for the 'common man', ancestry was a topic of absorbing interest. Crucially linked to the inheritance of titles and property, it also became associated with notions of character. In the English context, for example, there was, and still is, the idea of blood which is 'blue' and which is always at risk of being contaminated by other kinds, especially those of the distinctly 'bad' variety.

These ancient prejudices in which 'blood' figures so largely are part of the reason why so many biographies begin as they do, but they would not still be so powerfully operative without the support they received in the nineteenth century. It was above all then that vague notions of what we owe to our ancestors were bolstered by a burgeoning science of inheritance. The 'Reflections' which Herbert Spencer appended to his autobiography in 1893 are mainly concerned with explaining his character in terms of his mother and father, but at one point he claims that, in addition to small hands, he has inherited from his grandfather the faculty for exposition, a tendency towards fault-finding, a lack of respect for established authority and an absence of moral fear. All this, he explains, in a remark more Lamarckian than the Darwinism with which he is popularly associated would lead one to expect, because his grandfather was a teacher.[3]

In general, if not in this particular instance, Spencer's remarks are representative of a naively exuberant biological determinism: the confidence that science had provided, or would shortly provide, all the answers to the mysteries of character. Less than twenty years before, Francis Galton had begun his road to the devising and championing of eugenics with *Hereditary Genius*, a book in which, by concentration on a number of highly successful English families, he offered the current intellectual aristocracy the means of legitimising itself in ways very similar to those which it was traditional for the aristocracy proper to employ. One needs to bear in mind this background, as well as his own social origins, to understand why in 1922 D. H. Lawrence should have insisted in *Fantasia of the Unconscious* that at each birth something totally new is created:

> The quality of individuality cannot be derived. The new individual, in his singleness of self, is a perfectly new whole. He is not a permutation and combination of old elements, transferred through the parents. No, he is something underived and utterly unprecedented, unique, a new soul.[4]

Scientifically rather than metaphorically speaking this is not true, but when one considers that, by Lawrence's time, the mechanisms of inheritance had turned out to be far more complicated than was imagined in the late nineteenth century, and add to that the complexity, which ought always to have been perceived, of the interaction between inherited attributes and environment, then there are distinct advantages in choosing to begin with a clean sheet. As far as *remote* ancestors are concerned, for example, the difficulty biographers might have in saying anything both usefully and accurately explanatory means that they would often be better off saying nothing at all.

The danger of approaching the question of character via ancestors is illustrated by Spencer when he attributes not only his small hands to his grandfather but also his tendency to find fault. Daily experience shows that we inherit physical features and mannerisms from our forbears, but to move from there to moral or intellectual attributes is difficult for many reasons, almost the least of which is the absence of a norm. What is it that distinguishes a helpfully critical intelligence from that tendency to fault-finding which Spencer identified in himself? More crucially, how are that villainous trick of an eye and that foolish hanging of the nether lip, by which Falstaff claims Henry IV would recognise Hal as his son, to be equated with cowardice or a fondness for music? When Darwin turned his mind to the processes of inheritance he assumed they must take place through the medium of the blood. As George A. Miller put it, in one of the standard histories of psychology from the 1960s, 'Blood was too much a part of the everyday language of kinship for anyone to assume it was completely irrelevant to the hereditary mechanism'. But of course it was. Miller's book is interesting because it contains potted biographies of leading figures in the early days of psychology, one of whom was Pavlov. He was the grandson of a peasant and, in Miller's view, this meant that the 'almost fanatic devotion to pure science and to experimental research' which Pavlov showed 'was supported by the energy and simplicity of a Russian peasant'.[5] The dubiousness of this statement is evident enough. Were all Russian peasants at the beginning of the nineteenth century (Pavlov was born in 1849) energetic and simple, and if they were why did their progeny not all do as well as Pavlov? More pertinently, how are energy and simplicity transferred; is there a gene for each or is a claim being made here for the power of example? In itself, what Miller says is so familiar, so characteristic of what is said every day in hundreds of biographies, that to single out his phrases might appear gratuitous. There seems no more fairness in quoting him than there is in repeating the claim of a recent biographer of Woolf that, 'Although Virginia did not know her Stephen ancestors, she inherited her Stephen great-grandfather's powerful way with words, her grandmother's sense of humour, and her grandfather's tendency towards depression'.[6] These statements are par for the biographical course, but the special interest of Miller lies in the way his explanation of Pavlov's success can co-habit with shrewdly critical accounts of the mistakes nineteenth-century scientists made in thinking about inheritance. What his example shows is that even when a mind unusually well informed on the topic of heredity moves from an expository, critical mode into a biographical one, then the traditional paradigms take over and exert their remarkable power.

How powerful in fact they are, even for minds which are highly sophisticated, can be illustrated further from Ackroyd's *Dickens*. The origins of the Dickens family, he writes, are unknown. Claims have been made for a Dickens family from Babbington, Staffordshire, 'who were lords of the manor of Churchill from 1437 until 1656', but they would be hard to substantiate. Ackroyd prefers those of a family with the same name which had 'first lived in Derbyshire but who were memorialised frequently in London records of the seventeenth and eighteenth centuries'. The reason he offers for giving the preference to them is that,

> if there is to be origin for Dickens, it is perhaps more appropriate to look for it here in generations of Londoners. Surely the image of the city which Dickens creates comes from sources as deep as himself, as deep as his own inheritance?[7]

Dickens is indeed one of the great poets of London but that hardly seems a good reason for rejecting one unsubstantiated claim for the honour of being his forbears, which happens to come from the country, in favour of another claim, equally unsubstantiated, which comes from the town. He writes so well about London life that the sources of creativity he displays in doing so are no doubt as 'deep as himself'; but why should that makes us believe that he inherited the capacity for his London writing from forbears in the eighteenth century? 'If there is to be an origin for Dickens ... ', Ackroyd writes. At this price, he would clearly be better without one.

When genetics did become properly scientific, it was chiefly due to the rediscovery of Gregor Mendel whose experiments tended to direct the attention of the non-scientific public towards the importance of grandparents in the inheriting process. Ackroyd seems to be reflecting this tendency when he writes,

> There is no doubt that, in the lives of writers, the shadows of a grand-father or grandmother (most potent even when they are not clearly discerned) can be seen lying across the paths they follow. It is as if the peculiar chemistry of genius sometimes skips a generation, as if it is the nature of the grandparents which really accounts for the temperament and even behaviour of the one who comes after them.

Both Dickens' paternal grandparents, Ackroyd explains, were servants and he finds it noteworthy that William Dickens, who died 'long before' the birth of his grandson, was a butler because the characters in the novels are 'always being ... observed by butlers'. More importantly, he believes that Dickens inherited his thrift, conscientiousness and administrative ability from his grandfather William. His paternal grandmother was also 'trusted and competent' but more significant is the reputation she had as a 'fluent storyteller'. 'Towards the end of her life,' Ackroyd reports, 'she gave her grandson a fat old silver watch which had belonged to her husband, but it is also possible that he inherited much more interesting gifts from her'.[8]

The gifts Ackroyd describes Dickens as receiving from his grandparents on the maternal side were less immediately beneficial. Two years before he was born, his mother's father was found guilty of embezzling from the Navel Pay Office and had to flee to the Isle of Man. 'The problems of class', Ackroyd concludes,

> had surfaced with his paternal grandparents, the servants, and now criminality – specifically criminality tied to the misuse of money – also marked those around him. Is it not appropriate, then, that the major themes within his novels lie in the making and spending of money, and the effect that this pursuit can have on families? Certain themes, it seems, run in the blood.[9]

If all Ackroyd were saying here is that knowledge of his grandfather's difficulties had an influence on Dickens' writing, it would be unexceptionable. But the context is genetic inheritance and the specific claim that his maternal grandfather's experience somehow 'ran in the blood', like the thrift of his grandfather on his father's side. 'Thrift' is such a relatively unspecific notion that whether or not it is derived from a grandfather hardly seems to have much significance. Themes of 'the making and spending of money, and the effect this pursuit can have on families' are hardly more specific so that only if there were some causal relation, strict enough to be worth mentioning, between embezzling grandfathers and novels in which these themes occur, would it be worth looking at the authors of hundreds of other Victorian novels that concern themselves with money to see whether they also had grandfathers who took money which was not theirs.

*

In giving his readers the genealogies and causal connections convention leads them to expect, Ackroyd employs idioms that suggest a degree of intellectual play; but there are other biographers much more solemnly committed to pinning responsibility on their subjects' ancestors. What makes this so often pointless is not the character of the enterprise itself but its extreme difficulty. Although it may one day be possible to offer individuals a printout which shows the genetic origin of all their predispositions, this will not happen tomorrow; and it seems foolhardy therefore for biographers to be driven by habit into tasks that are necessarily beyond their competence.

There is nevertheless one, very extensive category of cases where lineage might certainly need to be investigated. This is where a subject's knowledge of his or her forbears has had an important influence on the sense of self. 'John Hawthorne, the famous judge at the Salem witch trials . . . and his father, William Hawthorne', Edwin Haviland Miller writes, 'were the founders of the family in the New World and awesome Puritan patriarchs of Salem with whom Hawthorne conversed for a lifetime in an attempt to prove himself worthy of their praise'.[10] A much less troubled version of the attitudes individuals might have towards their ancestors is illustrated by Robert Graves at the beginning of *Goodbye to All That.*

My passport gives my nationality as 'British subject'. Here I might parody Marcus Aurelius, who begins his *Golden Book* with the various ancestors and relatives to whom he owes the virtues of a worthy Roman Emperor: explaining why I am not a Roman Emperor or even, except on occasions, an English gentleman. My mother's father's family, the von Rankes, were Saxon country parsons, not anciently noble. Leopold von Ranke, the first modern historian, my great-uncle, introduced the 'von'. I owe something to him. He wrote, to the scandal of his contemporaries: 'I am a historian before I am a Christian; my object is simply to find out how things actually occurred,' and when discussing Michelet the French historian: 'He wrote history in a style in which the truth could not be told'. That Thomas Carlyle decried him as 'Dry-as-Dust' is no discredit. To Heinrich von Ranke, my grandfather, I owe my clumsy largeness, my endurance, energy, seriousness, and my thick hair.[11]

At the beginning of this passage Graves gives the impression that he might be someone who does not take lineage seriously – he will 'parody' the way Marcus Aurelius derives all his virtues from his ancestors; but by the time of 'thick hair' it is clear that he does. If he is not a fully fledged English gentleman, he is a German one as the phrase 'not anciently noble' sufficiently indicates to anyone who might have failed to pick up the significance of the 'von'. When he comes to express what he owes to his great uncle, he might be taken to mean that it is only what anyone else might owe who happened to open Leopold von Ranke's books. But that interpretation would be very strained in the context and is belied by the final phrase about the legacy of Heinrich von Ranke. There Graves is like Herbert Spencer in being able to move effortlessly between two attributes which belong to entirely different categories: seriousness and thick hair.

Because Graves's notion of what he had inherited from his ancestors was part of his 'character', a biographer would be obliged to pay it some attention. The more socially prominent the ancestors were, the stronger this kind of obligation is likely to be. As Miranda Seymour makes clear, being an aristocrat was not a negligible feature of Lady Ottoline Morrell's life.[12] For Cyril Connolly, on the other hand, what made ancestry so important was that, even though his mother could claim descent from Irish aristocracy, he was not just a mite better connected. Had his blood been in fact bluer, Jeremy Lewis makes clear, in his entertaining biography, Connolly might not have felt, when he was once staying in Sardinia close to Princess Margaret and Lord Snowdon, that it was like 'being in the Garden of Eden without seeing God'; or opened himself to being described as looking, after he had finally been introduced to the Princess and was able to join her in a swimming pool, 'like a blissful hippo'.[13]

Bertrand Russell's ancestry was too distinguished for him to have shared any of Connolly's anxieties. According to Ray Monk, he was proud to belong to the Whig tradition of his nineteenth-century ancestors (in the century before they seemed to have been rather less public-spirited), and awareness of them 'shaped much of his thinking about his place in the world and about politics in general'. Since he was to develop his family's tradition in an evermore liberal and 'progressive' direction, it is mildly surprising to learn that as a young man he 'knew the biographies of all sixteen of his great-great-grandparents', and that he had a strong interest in heraldry. But the real significance of his lineage became evident after he had left his first wife and was living (on and off) with Dora Black. At a certain point in the relationship, Russell began desperately to feel that he wanted children. She had no objection but, 'new woman' as she was, did not feel that issue had any connection with the question of marriage. If Russell nevertheless persuaded her into matrimony against her better judgement, it was because any son of his who was illegitimate could not inherit a title. As Monk puts it, 'The thought that she might one day be a countess might have meant nothing to Dora, but the thought that his son might one day be an earl meant a great deal to Russell'.[14] Here is one important effect of lineage quite different from inheriting this or that characteristic from a grandfather.

The psychological effect of lineage on the subject might seem particularly important in the case of someone such as Virginia Woolf, or Virginia Stephen as she was before her marriage. Born into a remarkable network of familial relations in the English civil service and educational establishment, she could claim kinship with a large number of highly successful and influential individuals. Several of the families to which these individuals belonged had first become associated at the time of the movement against the Slave Trade, at the beginning of the nineteenth century, and were known as the Clapham sect. Virginia Stephen and her sister Vanessa prided themselves on having broken clear of the family networks but it has sometimes been observed that, with its commitment to social progress and its exclusiveness, the 'Bloomsbury' group which they were so influential in forming was a Clapham sect of the twentieth century. Yet if that is true then the significance will be as much sociological as genealogical: less a matter of inheritance than a tendency of all coteries to display the same characteristics.

More potentially important than the familial networks is what Virginia Stephen might have felt she had to live up to. What after all would it feel like to have been a member of a family cited by Galton as evidence for 'hereditary genius'? From Hermione Lee's account, it would seem that in fact Woolf dealt with her lineage much as thousands of others have whose ancestors were far less distinguished. Only half as a joke (that is) she constructed for herself a private myth in which her more rational qualities could be attributed to her father's line – Scottish Calvinist farmers before their success in England – and her volatile, emotional side could be traced back to a great grandmother who was a French aristocrat, Adeline De l'Etang. What justifies calling this notion of how her nature was composed mythological, is its reliance on common stereotypes associated with the Scots and French. (In a more obvious reliance on them, Edmund Wilson once noted that Lady Wilde's maiden name of Elgee was a corruption of Algiati and warned, 'Oscar's Italian blood should be taken into account in considering his theatrical instincts and his appetite for the ornate').[15] Woolf's faith in this myth would certainly justify some enquiry into her ancestry, but perhaps not so very much given that it is her beliefs which matter here and not actualities. Yet once biographers have been bitten by the genealogical bug, it is hard for them to remember where their chief responsibilities lie. Here, for example, is Noel Annan in a book on Woolf's father which, although it announces itself as 'a critical study . . . rather than a biography', certainly begins in a biographical mode:

> Sir Leslie Stephen is the brother of Sir Fitzjames Stephen, the eminent jurist and Anglo-Indian administrator, and the uncle of the young parodist J. K. Stephen and of Katherine Stephen, Principal of Newnham College. The Venns and Diceys, both celebrated academic families, are his first cousins, and his Stephen collaterals excel in the law. Sir Leslie marries firstly a daughter of Thackeray and secondly a Jackson. Julia Jackson, who has Vaughans and Princeps as uncles, is a niece of Lady Somers and Mrs. Cameron the photographer, and is the aunt of H. A. L. Fisher, Cabinet Minister and Warden of New College, and of Mrs. F. W. Maitland, wife of the historian, who later marries Sir Francis Darwin. The daughters of Sir Leslie's second marriage are Vanessa, the wife of Clive Bell, and Virginia, the wife of Leonard Woolf; the sons are Thoby and Adrian. Adrian marries Karin Costelloe, the niece of Logan Pearsall Smith and of Alys, first wife of Bertrand Russell; she is also the sister of Ray Strachey and the step-daughter of Bernard Berenson.[16]

This is Stephen's genealogy as it manifests itself synchronically at a certain point in time. The essay in which Annan first reflected in public on it is called 'The Intellectual Aristocracy' and contains page after page in this vein. That it begins, 'Family connections are part of the poetry of history'[17] will cause some readers to remember the description of Dr Johnson's poetic drama *Irene* as being in the blankest of blank verse. Annan seems to deny in this essay that his interest is Galtonian (or like Havelock Ellis's, who also wrote a study of genius), but it is difficult to know how then it ought to be described. For the passage quoted above to yield any sociological significance, we would need to have the names of all those relatives and descendants not mentioned so that we could consider whether the percentage of distinguished people was unusual. We would need to ask also what Annan's criterion for distinction is (how is a 'parodist' to be compared to those who 'excel in the law?'), and whether the ratio of successful to 'unsuccessful' individuals is similar to that for comparable groups in England, and other countries with a similar social structure. The information offered could no doubt lead to conclusions about the nature of English society in recent times, were it properly presented; but it is doubtful whether it could ever have much biographical importance in a study of Leslie Stephen. In that context, the most obvious rationale for its appearance would be that there are always people who like to hear these things, and people who enjoy telling them. It is as if, in the families of both groups, there were ancestors who insisted on reading to their dazed offspring those long sections in the Bible about who begat whom; that the offspring adapted to that particular difficulty by developing a narcotic pleasure in such narratives; and that this capacity was then passed on to their descendants as an acquired characteristic.

*

There is a danger of being inappropriately and therefore comically severe in dealing with this question of origins. When George Miller claims that in his devotion to science Pavlov was supported by the energy and simplicity of a Russian peasant, it is not really fair to ask whether all nineteenth-century Russian peasants got up early in the morning; and neither ought we to expect that all the authors of English nineteenth-century novels which dealt with the making and spending of money had a peculating maternal grandfather like

Dickens. We are not dealing here with *laws* of causal connection but working in an area where exceptions can be readily admitted. Biography is not a scientific discipline; but then neither should it be one in which anything goes. If Miller had traced back Pavlov's persistence in his research to an energetic grandfather who happened to have been a peasant he would have made more sense, although 'energy' would still then have been a term which is unhelpfully vague. In Ackroyd's case, it is not the causal agent (Dickens's maternal grandfather) which is indeterminate but the supposed effect, and since there are very few nineteenth-century English novels which do *not* deal with 'the making and spending of money, and the effect this pursuit can have on families', the role played in their composition by literary convention has to be considered. Certainly, as Ackroyd would be the first to recognise, quite why Dickens wrote a novel such as *Our Mutual Friend* in the way he did, is not and could not be a question with a single answer.

Freud's writings are sometimes defended against their critics on the grounds of narrative coherence: the various details in any given case are (it is claimed) fitted together in such a neat way that anyone who disagreed with how they had been interpreted would be committed to finding one that was better. Yet this move to less recognisably scientific ground does not mean that there are not still criteria to be met. No one could demand that whatever biographers wanted to say about their subject's more distant forbears should be scientifically verifiable; but it ought to have at least the same circumstantiality and convincingness as analogous claims in any competent *Bildungsroman* of the nineteenth century. It is doubtful whether it often does. Frequently, the references of biographers to ancestors have about the same convincingness as Hobbes's attribution of his 'extraordinary Timorousness' to (as Aubrey puts it) 'his Mother's dread of the Spanish invasion in 88, she being then with child of him'; or the notion which Joseph Merrick, the 'elephant man', himself entertained that his physical deformities were the result of his mother having been frightened by an elephant when she was carrying him.[18]

These two claims about the importance of what happens to pregnant women before a child is born are a special form of the argument from inheritance. That they are nonsensical in content rather than in form is shown by recent discussions about the dangers of pregnant women smoking. In many respects, biology is indeed destiny but, in the present state of knowledge, that is true in such general ways that only exceptionally can its truth have genuine biographical significance. Only after a child is actually born, does it begin to seem demonstrable (rather than merely indisputable) that its mother, and its parents generally, shape its life. There are more ways than Freud's for demonstrating why that should be so. In his *Search for a Method* Sartre wittily complains of certain Marxists that they write as if we were all born at the same time that we receive our first pay packet: 'They have forgotten their own childhoods'. In his view, the family is a microcosm where the social and economic forces which shape the subject's character are first brought to bear. 'If Flaubert reasons and feels as a bourgeois', he writes, illustrating how much his notion of choice narrowed after the essay on Baudelaire, 'it is because he has been made such at a period when he could not even comprehend the meaning of the gestures and the roles which were imposed on him'.[19] Yet although children grow up emulating or reacting against the models provided by their already socialised parents, most of those parents would be only too eager to recognise that the often unexpected results of the social 'education' which (consciously or unconsciously) they provide cannot wholly be accounted for by mechanisms of this kind, however refined and sophisticated the analysis of them may become. They are obliged to acknowledge, that is, that there are factors at work which are not at all social. Sartre is exceptional among biographers in the extent to which he deliberately seeks to minimise these genetic factors; but the problem for the others lies in saying something sensible on that topic. In his 1991 Reith lectures on *The Language of the Genes*, Steve Jones usefully demonstrated that accurate knowledge of genetic mechanisms is very recent, and energetically disposed of a number of potent myths. At the same time he inadvertently illustrated, in one passage, how wide the gap can be between scientific fact and the kind of understanding of human behaviour to which the biographer characteristically aspires.

The importance of genetics makes most impression on a lay public in the study of inherited diseases: 'About one child in thirty born in Britain has an inborn error of some kind and about a third of all hospital admissions of young children involve a genetic disease', Jones writes, in a striking illustration of how crucial ancestry can in fact be. These diseases are easiest to study when their victims are prominent people since we are likely to know much more about the British royal family, for example, than the forbears of the couple next door. Partly because of her family's prominence, we know that one of Queen Victoria's legacies to her descendants was haemophilia (the reluctance of the blood to clot). Affecting males more often than females, this legacy can easily be traced to its most famous sufferer, Alexis the son of Tsar Nicholas of Russia, whose wife was one of Victoria's granddaughters. 'Some suggest', Jones comments, 'that one reason for Rasputin's malign influence on the Russian court was his ability to calm the unfortunate Alexis'.[20]

Well before Victoria's time, it is possible that the British royal family was afflicted with another inherited disease. In a later chapter I will suggest how difficult it is to diagnose the illnesses of those long dead, but a book to give hope to all who try is Ida Macalpine and Richard Hunter's remarkable *George III and the Mad-Business*. Their exposition of why they believe that, in his recurrent bouts of alarming behaviour, George III was not suffering from insanity in the usual sense, but from an inherited defect in body chemistry that leads to 'an abnormal accumulation of toxic chemical substances which damage the nervous system',[21] is as cogent and as meticulously documented as one can imagine a historical enquiry of this kind ever being. It would, however, be more of a model to follow if the subject Macalpine and Hunter chose had not provided them with advantages which are peculiarly rare. It is not only that kings are always likely to be observed with more care and attention than anyone else. The acute constitutional crisis which George III's illness provoked (who could assume the authority to declare that, since he was unfit to rule, his son should take over?) meant that minute documentary records of his state from day to day were produced and then scrutinised by parliamentary committees. His doctors may, in modern terms, have observed him poorly because they did not know what they were looking for; but they nevertheless left behind a huge mass of evidence from which Macalpine and Hunter could draw conclusions. That the particular disorder or disease which these two writers felt sure they had identified moreover (porphyria) is in fact hereditary, meant that they could confirm their initial suspicions by tracing its symptoms in George III's successors.

Yet with all these advantages, as well as their formidable expertise and presentational skills, it is important that Macalpine and Hunter were not able to convince every specialist that their diagnosis was correct. The reviewer of their book in the *British Journal of Psychiatry*, for example, referred back to the 'long and sometimes acrimonious correspondence' which earlier articles by them on George III's supposed porphyria had sparked off in the *British Medical Journal*; reminded his readers that one of the specialists involved had said that he would be 'prepared to eat his hat if the authors' case was substantiated'; and then ended his review by scornfully suggesting that the excellence of several parts of *George III and the Mad-Business* made it 'all the more regrettable that the authors ever took that course in biochemistry without tears'.[22] What is clear from this and other responses is that the suggestions of Macalpine and Hunter began a controversy which is by no means settled. Assuming that it is, Steve Jones points out that George's doctors had noticed the king's urine was of a port wine colour 'which is now known to be characteristic of the disease. One of the King's less successful appointments', he immediately and abruptly continues, 'was that of his Prime Minister, Lord North, who was largely responsible for the loss of the American colonies'. Picking up his reference to the influence of Rasputin over the Tsar's son, he then concludes, in a staggering illustration of how heredity ought *not* to be invoked in biographical study: 'It is odd to reflect that both the Russian and the American Revolutions may have resulted from accidents to royal DNA'.[23]

George Miller explains clearly why nineteenth-century English biologists were wrong about inheritance but cannot resist deriving Pavlov's dogged research habits from a peasant grandfather. Jones exposes many, more recent misunderstandings of the topic but then offers, for two of the most important and complex events in Western history, genetic explanations which are hard to take seriously. Unlike Miller, Jones is not emphasising here how a particular genetic characteristic was acquired (where it came from), but what difference it made. His speculation is of a general historical rather than biographical nature but the second is implied by the first, and the idea that Lord North was somehow 'responsible' for the American revolution is no more of a gross simplification than the notion that George III's porphyria led him to choose North as prime minister. If that *was* a bad decision, then there is a sense in which George's genetic make-up must certainly have played a part in inclining him to take it. What makes that truth worse than useless is that it might give the illusion of increased understanding. Aspects of the genetic make-up of any biographical subject must always be influential in everything he or she does but except in unusual cases, such as porphyria, they are hard to identify; and even when they are identified, the degree to which they acted in concert with social, environmental or other factors will be hard to estimate. Our genes largely determine our physical and perhaps even our psychological make-up, but they are not responsible for every decision we make; or if they are, the road which connects them to the effects of those decisions is so long and winding, and intersects at so many different points with other roads, that it is rarely worth taking. Certainly it seems a bit hard that, through his appointment of North, the genes of George III should have to take the blame for the loss of the American colonies.

'My soul', Somerset Maugham once claimed,

> would have been quite different if I had not stammered or if I had been four or five inches taller: I am slightly prognathous; in my child-hood they did not know that this could be remedied by a gold band worn while the jaw is still malleable; if they had, my countenance would have borne a different cast, the reaction towards me of my fellows would have been different and therefore my disposition, my attitude to them, would have been different too. But what sort of thing is this soul that can be modified by a dental apparatus?[24]

What sort of thing indeed? Leaving aside here how far modern biographers might feel Maugham was qualified to pronounce on his own soul, as well as the question of whether stammering ought to have been implicitly placed in the same category as height, an unsympathetic summary of his claims might be: 'If I had been a different person, I would have had a different life'. Yet it is not impossible to imagine particular situations when one or other of the genetic disadvantages Maugham complains of proved crucially influential. 'I like Willie very much', someone to whom he was violently attracted might one day have said, 'except that he is *too short*'. Height is of course dependent on environmental factors as well as ancestry but this is not the case for a protruding jaw, and Maugham's parents' ignorance of the gold band makes that as much a case of biological destiny as the most famous of 'accidents to royal DNA', the Hapsburg chin. From the way Steve Jones deals with George III's supposed porphyria, and Alexis Romanov's haemophilia, one could anticipate he would approach this genetic misfortune in the same spirit as Pascal did Cleopatra's nose: 'had it been shorter, the whole face of the world would have changed'.[25] It was a necessary condition of Antony's death that Cleopatra should be attractive to him and a well-formed nose might well have been a necessary condition of her attractiveness. In what was likely to have been an antithetical way, the Hapsburg chin may have had effects on the private lives of its bearers which also had implications for 'history' in general. Yet if it did, conscientious biographers would be hard put to describe them. Attractiveness (my imagined episode from the life of Maugham notwithstanding) is in itself a complex phenomenon, rarely dependent on a single feature, and the causal chains which can be supposed to lead from its immediate to its more remote consequences are highly complex also. Cleopatra's nose, the Hapsburg chin and Maugham's jaw are highly specific genetic features, and therefore easier to deal with than Hobbes's 'timorousness' or Pavlov's 'energy'; but it is much harder to define what contribution they should make to an explanation of their owners' lives than Maugham's remarks suggest (was it his actual countenance which determined how people approached him, for example, or the attitude he adopted because of the way he thought he looked?). For a biographer of Joseph Merrick, on the other hand, genetic inheritance is a simpler matter with an importance impossible to ignore.

Whether or not Merrick's mother encountered an elephant when she was pregnant, her influence on him before he was born was – like that of his father, grandparents and other contributors to his genetic make-up – immense, and a powerful reminder that the significance of genetic inheritance for biographers can sometimes be a more obvious and straightforward matter than I have been suggesting it is here. In more normal circumstances however, what makes the influence of the mother so important after, rather than before a birth, is the likelihood of daily contact. The frequent involvement most parents have with their offspring means that the insoluble question of nature versus nurture does not have to be broached (as it might well be when biographers are arguing for a direct effect on the subject of more remote ancestors). It can be ignored because the end result is always a combination of both according to a ratio which no biographer can be expected to work out. John Richardson presents no evidence that the legendary courage of Juan De León ever mattered to Picasso, but that his father was an art teacher and an indifferent painter certainly did. This is true whether or not one believes that it was José Ruiz Blasco himself (as Picasso's father was called) who bequeathed an initial capacity for painting to his son. Whatever the genetic origin of Picasso's gifts, what seems certain and verifiable is that it was the struggle to emulate and surpass his father which led him to perfect them.

Nothing anyone can say is likely to inhibit some biographers from using forbears to explain aspects of their subjects' character. The route is so well trodden that neither the absence of sufficient information nor the lack of an appropriate expertise will prevent its being taken. Deriving our close friends' characteristics from what we know of their parents or grandparents is in any case such a common feature of casual conversation that we expect to find it in biographies, and may be disappointed when it is not there. Yet as Johnson said, when he advised Boswell to clear his mind of cant, there ought to be a difference between what we say and think:

> You tell a man, 'I am sorry you had such bad weather the last day of your journey, and were so wet.' You don't care sixpence whether he is wet or dry. You may *talk* in this manner; it is a mode of talking in society: but don't *think* foolishly.[26]

As far as ancestors are concerned there is, from the Johnsonian if not the Aubrey point of view, such a powerful tradition of foolish thought that it is hard to say anything without slipping into it.

4

Primal Scenes

A childhood impression is often responsible for the bent or the character of a whole life. I have been told that Merimée was a man created uniquely by the fear of appearing ridiculous, and that the origin of that fear was this: that when he was a child he was scolded; and on leaving the room he heard his parents laugh at the blubbering face he made during the reprimand. He swore that no-one would ever laugh at him again, and he kept his word maintaining a harsh, curt exterior which has now become part of his profoundest nature.
(*The Goncourt Journals: 1851–1870*, trans. Lewis Galantière
(New York, 1958), p. 178)

'PRIMAL SCENE' IS A term first used by Freud in what one of his editors describes as 'no doubt the most important of his case histories': 'From the History of an Infantile Neurosis' (more commonly known as 'The Wolf Man').[1] It refers to an episode when, at the age of one and a half, the patient was sleeping in his parents' room and woke to observe them copulating. His memory of this moment is not direct but ingeniously 'constructed' by Freud as he interprets a dream which the patient does remember having had when he was nearly four. In this, he was lying in his bed when a window suddenly opened and he saw a number of animals with wolf-like features sitting in the branches of a tree outside. Via a highly complicated associative chain, one item of which is the patient's memory of being terrified by an illustration in a fairy story which showed a wolf in an upright position, one foot forward, claws stretched out and ears pricked, Freud infers that when the child saw his parents copulating it must have been with his father standing up and his mother bending over so that he could penetrate her

56

from behind. Apart from seeming to explain why his patient should be incapable of sexual intercourse other than in the *a tergo* position, this conjecture has the advantage for his interpretative intentions of having allowed the child a clear view of the female genitals. According to Freud, the perception that women do not have penises is a a major element in any young boy's development of the castration complex, the workings of which are evident for him in the 'big tails like foxes' of the wolves in the dream. In a characteristic move, these are interpreted as compensations for the boy's feared loss of his own 'tail'.

It would be a wholly exceptional biographer to whom a primal scene in its true, Freudian sense was available. For those significant, determining moments in childhood which, from Wordsworth's 'spots of time' on, we have been more and more led to expect, biographers have frequently to rely in the first instance on their subjects. It is the subject who will have remembered a particular episode, in the way the Wolf Man could not and, in many cases, already pointed to its significance.[2] In the first volume of his autobiography, for example, Compton Mackenzie described a moment when he was six years old which seemed to him in retrospect crucial. Both his parents were actors and, from the child's point of view, all too rarely present. They had however arranged to be at home for a week at Easter and, on the family's last night together, were allowing all three of their children to stay up until the unprecedented hour of eight o'clock. But at seven, friends arrived to invite the parents out to dinner. Mackenzie describes the 'agony of apprehension' in which he listened to his mother's protests that this was after all her children's last night being overcome and how, after he had been given a sovereign by the male member of the couple carrying her and his father off, he went upstairs and threw the coin out of his bedroom window. Having read some Freud, he is very anxious to deny that there was any 'Oedipal' element in his distress, by which he means only that he has no memory of being jealous of his father or of ever having had to compete with him for his mother's attentions. What the episode made him conclude, he says, 'not in so many words exactly of course, but with the equivalent surge of emotion', was:

> 'You can never again in life afford to depend on the love of somebody, you must always be prepared henceforth to be disappointed, and then if you are disappointed you will be able to bear it because you knew that it might happen.'

Mackenzie explains that he has used this episode in his autobiographical novel *Sinister Street*, but 'much changed in background to suit a piece of fiction'.[3] For one of his contemporaries' more celebrated key episode from childhood, fiction is all we have. The young narrator's desire for his mother's goodnight kiss, on which the whole enormous edifice of *A la recherche du temps perdu* could be said to rest, was first described by Proust in *Jean Santeuil*. There (along with many other differences), the visitor who inhibits the young boy from openly seeking his mother's attention, is not Swann but the local doctor; there is no role for the grandmother or the various aunts; and the young boy, equally anxious in both versions that his mother should kiss him goodnight, calls down to her from his bedroom window when she is in the garden, rather than ambushing her on the landing as she is coming to bed. The significance which Proust attributes to the boy's triumph over his mother's efforts to make him less dependent is however very similar in the two cases. What she says in both versions to excuse her yielding allows him to feel that his nervous anxieties are not after all his fault, and prepares the way for his appreciation of the advantages of being ill. But in addition, Proust famously insists, it prevents the development of a strong and healthy will.[4]

The difficulty biographers have when they come to deal with episodes like these two is that so much of the work has already been done for them. In his life of Mackenzie, Andro Linklater attempts to 'deconstruct' the key episode, or turning-point, by claiming that it must have had its predecessors. Yet without the opportunity to question the subject that an analyst would enjoy, he cannot be certain what these were. However much he would like to show that a biographer is no mere reporter by challenging Mackenzie's belief that this was the episode that really mattered, he is hardly in a very strong position to do so; and when it comes to interpreting its significance, he turns out to have very few cards to play also. The emotional strategy which Mackenzie describes himself as determining upon once his mother had been taken off, is a familiar solution to a very familiar problem. The realisation that the loving maternal presence cannot always be relied upon might well be associated with the refusal of some people to commit themselves fully to any relationship in later life in order to protect themselves from future disappointment. Linklater repeats this reading but, feeling the need to make his own contribution, adds that 'desire for a maternal affection ... never satisfied in childhood' marked all Mackenzie's most important relationships with women in adult life, as did an unyielding self-control which 'only rarely broke, and then with catastrophic consequences'. Thus it was not only disappointment against which the child was protecting himself with his strategy but a 'chaos of profoundly destructive emotions'. Most of this gloss could be inferred from what Mackenzie himself says so that the only genuine addition to the subject's own explanation is the claim that in later life he looked in women for 'maternal affection'. Whether or not this could be said to be true of a majority of men, it is such a common description of them that there seems no pressing reason why it should be associated with the sharp particularities of this specific moment in Mackenzie's life.[5]

In dealing with the goodnight kiss, George Painter is bolder although not necessarily more convincing that Linklater. He initially accepts it as the 'most important event in Proust's life', one that caused 'irrevocable harm'; but this was because it showed that 'love is doomed and happiness does not exist'. The 'more matter-of-fact' account in *Jean Santeuil* he takes as probably containing the 'literal truth', in contrast to the 'symbolic truth' of *A la recherche*; and he is able to show both that the episode must have taken place in the Prousts' house in Auteuil rather than in Combray (Illiers), and that when in the later version the narrator's mother reads George Sand's *François le Champi* to her son, having yielded to his efforts to bring her to his bedroom, one specific episode from Proust's childhood is being combined with another. But biographer's pride prompts him to add to these useful details a paragraph in which he justifies his decision to read the episode *against* its author. Having described it on the previous page as the most important event in Proust's life, he now decides that to call it 'the most important trauma . . . would be to over-simplify'. Like Linklater, he assumes there must have been 'innumerable similar events' and even suggests it could be a 'screen memory' (although in Freud's account of such things, screen memories are distinguished by the apparent triviality or unimportance of their content). For Painter, Proust's own reading of the goodnight kiss is 'not quite adequate' because its true crux is to be found in the mother's initial refusal rather than her final capitulation. However much comfort she might have eventually brought on this and subsequent occasions, her son would 'always hate her' for her initial denial of him on the evening of the doctor's (or Swann's) visit. To say of a man very warmly attached to his mother that he hated her is safe enough because all intense relations have their moments of hatred; but to take that as the principal significance of the story Proust tells seems arbitrary when nothing in the story itself supports such a reading. One can easily imagine an analyst working back to hatred from the story's details (eliciting in the process a host of other memories), and triumphantly taking all the many declarations of love in both its versions as proofs of the contrary; but although Painter does not have that luxury he seems nevertheless to have adopted as axiomatic the analyst's belief that no one can analyse himself, even when he is the most subtly introspective figure in modern literature. Beyond the 'open resentment' against his mother which he claims Proust displays in *Jean Santeuil*, Painter offers no reason why we should prefer his interpretation of events to his subject's, but seems instead to be applying models of human development from the general psychoanalytic store (particularly those that relate to homosexuals and their mothers). Proust is now the only authority for the events in the garden in Auteuil; he is not the only authority for their meanings, which could of course be multiple and contradictory; but successfully to brush him aside as 'not quite adequate' would take more eloquence and intellectual power than Painter displays.[6] Yet as Linklater shows to a much less egregious degree, what are biographers for if they cannot improve on their subjects' own testimony?

Those two accounts remind one of Dr Johnson's remark that the first qualification of a historian is the knowledge of truth. Only Mackenzie knew what he felt when his parents went out to dinner and who else but Proust could be privy to what it meant to him that his mother should kiss him goodnight. In the process of interpreting those early feelings there may be all manner of distortion, but how are their biographers to discover its character and extent? After Yeats had described in his autobiography his response to the death of Parnell, and Russell had explained in his why he was no longer interested in Helen Dudley, once she had arrived in England, Foster and Monk successfully demonstrated that their subjects were not to be trusted by juxtaposing with the later accounts letters written at the time. But children of Mackenzie and Proust's age at the period when the episodes they describe took place do not usually write letters or keep diaries. That makes it so much more difficult for biographers to indulge in their profession's characteristic, yet wholly legitimate habit of biting the hand that feeds.

It is not of course always a question of conflict or antagonism. Some biographers calmly accept their subjects' accounts of their development while others feel they can do without their coopera-tion. For reasons which are self-evident, Brenda Maddox falls into this latter category when she is speculating on how D. H. Lawrence was affected by the imminent birth of his sister:

> For Lawrence, with his wheezy chest, streaming nose and fragile hold on life, his mother's pregnancy when he was just over a year old (especially if she were still nursing him at the time) might have been sufficiently life-threatening to account for his murderous rage against women that later filled his work. He undoubtedly bore the brunt too of her exhaustion. His lifelong passion for washing and scrubbing, accompanied by a guilty delight in the dark smells and crevices of the body, may reflect the pressure to be 'clean' put on the elder of two babies by a mother who had to do all the family laundry by hand.[7]

Some readers might want to come to Lawrence's rescue here by suggesting that, if there is murderous rage against women in his works, it could hardly be said to 'fill' them; that no one who knew him thought there was anything in the nature of a 'lifelong passion' about the enthusiasm with which he scrubbed the floors of houses he rented; and that even if there were evidence for believing that he delighted in the 'dark smells and crevices of the body' (which is doubtful), there would still be little justification for calling such a delight 'guilty'. But the accuracy of Maddox's speculations, where 'may' and 'might' co-exist uneasily with 'undoubtedly', are less the issue here than the general approach they exemplify. That is typical of a great deal of modern biography in being only vaguely 'Freudian'. What principally distinguishes it from that of those nineteenth-century predecessors for whom the early years also provided the key to adulthood is Maddox's allusion to the lasting effect of toilet training on later life. Like Painter's reference to the episode of the goodnight kiss being a potential 'screen memory', it is this which signals most clearly the psychoanalytic affiliation. Because it is highly unlikely that there could ever have been a moment when Lawrence said to himself, 'I realise now that the anger I have always felt against women derives from that time before I was one year old when my mother was pregnant with my sister', Maddox is in one way closer to Freud than Painter in that the episodes she is dealing with involve unconscious ideation (Lawrence's access to them would have been no more direct than the Wolf Man's to the scene of his parents copulating). In another way, however, she is much, much farther in that she is applying to the chronology of the Lawrence family life a familiar model of psychoanalytic causation with scant regard for corroboration. The apparent fit between cause and effect is obtained by largely imagining the first (Mrs Lawrence's behaviour towards her son during his first year), and then seriously mis-reporting what serves as the second. By interrogating their subjects' own testimony, Painter and Linklater are by contrast more in the position of analysts and their patients, listening to what their subjects have to say and then trying to show what it *really* means. But that is very hard indeed when the subject can no longer respond to further enquiry.

In their very different ways, Linklater, Painter and Maddox illustrate how difficult it is to take a broadly psychoanalytic direction without access to its most characteristic method (free association). Biographers have certain advantages over analysts: they are usually dealing with the whole of a life and, hard though general enquiry will be where children are involved, they are not limited to the oral testimony of their subjects. Yet not to be able to ask their subjects questions, and to be deprived therefore of all the new material which the *process* of analysis throws up, is a crippling drawback. So severe is it that one would think there would be general agreement on the inadvisability of psychoanalytic analysis when no means are available for supporting its conclusions. That would however be difficult to achieve when the founding father of psychoanalysis set the standard for irresponsible speculation in his biographical study of Leonardo da Vinci. It becomes hard to claim that Maddox did not have enough information for her mildly psychoanalytic interpretation of Lawrence's childhood when what is known about his earliest days immeasurably outstrips anything Freud could discover about da Vinci's, and when her analysis is not after all based, as a major part of Freud's is, on a mistranslation of a crucial word in the most significant extant document. To the extent that Freud's essay is a model for later attempts to associate with early childhood the supposedly more enigmatic aspects of a subject's life (Leonardo's failure to complete many of the paintings he began and the diversion of his energies from painting into scientific research), or of their work (the traditional puzzle of the Mona Lisa smile and the fact that Leonardo depicts the Virgin and his mother as women of a similar age), it has a lot to answer for.[8] If gold rust, as Chaucer says, what shall iron do?

*

62

The supposed significance of childhood experience cannot always be reduced to key moments. There is wide agreement that when, with his father's imprisonment for debt, the young Dickens was obliged to work in a blacking factory, it had a lasting effect on his future life and career; but there seems to have been no one episode there with any special importance. In 'Such, Such were the Joys' Orwell records in exceptionally vivid terms being caned by the headmaster of his preparatory school for wetting his bed. Yet as that text makes clear, it was not only this one incident which he felt had marked him but his whole experience between the ages of eight and thirteen at 'Crossgates'. Even if he had not explicitly said so, the very vividness of the account would indicate that he regarded his whole period there as formative. The force of the writing has in the past tempted at least one critic to assume that Orwell's schooldays 'explain' *Nineteen Eighty-Four* much better that his responses to Stalin or the Nazis. 'Whether he knew it or not,' wrote Anthony West, 'what he did in *Nineteen Eighty-Four* was to send everybody in England to an enormous "Crossgates" (St Cyprian's) to be as miserable as he had been . . . Only the existence of a hidden wound can account for such remorseless pessimism'.[9] This view is partly endorsed in Michael Sheldon's 1991 biography. 'Not many critics', he claims, 'have been willing to see how firmly rooted (*Nineteen Eight-Four*) is in Orwell's past'. The bullying he experienced at St Cyprian's cannot, according to Sheldon, be discounted as an influence on the novel; and he compares the young Orwell's relationship with its headmistress to that between Winston Smith and Big Brother.[10]

The attempt Bernard Crick had made, in his biography of Orwell (the first version of which appeared ten years before Sheldon's), to discourage this kind of speculation has a special interest because it is also a general protest against what he feels is the psychoanalytically inspired habit of always explaining adult behaviour in terms of childhood experience. 'Confident assertions that there was a trauma that marked and warped him for life,' he protests,

> somehow *explaining* (often explaining away) the most uncomfortable parts of his future writing, have become a commonplace of critical writing on Orwell; but they are highly speculative, often attempts to use psychological explanations to short-cut a slow and detailed examination of his adult experiences, some of which may have affected his adult beliefs. Those who are confident that they can find a psychological 'hidden' wound in the young Eric and then locate *Nineteen*

Eighty-Four on the map as a version of St. Cyprian's, as if the vision of totalitarianism arose from prep-school terror and suffering, may be disguising their own lack of perception of the political horrors that Orwell said were under their own noses, far more dangerous, dramatic and objective, in their shared contemporary world of the 1930s and 1940s.[11]

West's error, it might be said, lay in attributing too exclusive an importance to Orwell's time at prep school. In dealing with it, Crick's irritation leads him into an attempt to undermine the authority and status of 'Such, Such were the Joys' which seems to me misguided. His first move is to reproduce a number of the twenty-two examples which survive from the weekly letter that, over his four years at St Cyprian's, Orwell was required to write to his mother. None of these, Crick rightly points out, are indicative of a boy in a traumatised state. Yet neither do they show one who was particularly happy and, as Crick himself half admits, their value as evidence is destroyed by our knowledge that they were overseen and corrected by the couple who ran the school. That censorship apart, Orwell himself explains in 'Such, Such were the Joys' why he felt that it would have been impossible for him to complain to his parents.

Thanks to not only Orwell but two other ex-pupils, Cyril Connolly and Gavin Maxwell, St Cyprian's has become one of the best known prep schools in English literature. Nothing Crick quotes from the various descriptions we now have of it convincingly contradicts 'Such, Such were the Joys', although attitudes to its various features do of course vary considerably. A passionate defender of the school was Henry Longhurst, who later became a golfing correspondent, but his attempts at refutation are so fatuous that they act instead as confirmation: with friends like him (Crick rightly observes) St Cyprian's did not need detractors. He takes more comfort from 'a very eminent Old St. Cyprianite' who littered his copy of 'Such, Such were the Joys' with fierce disagreements. Admitting that there was a bed-wetter who was publically beaten, this ex-pupil insists that it was not Orwell thereby encouraging Crick to ask 'why should not a polemical essayist transpose events for dramatic effect?'[12] But this is merely to set the potentially fallible memory of one person against the potentially fallible memory of another and, in any case, unless Crick means to imply that Orwell was never beaten, it is important that the beatings described at the beginning of 'Such, Such were the Joys' were private, not public.

Even more unavailing than his reliance on his 'Old Cyprianite' is the way Crick seizes on a phrase from Orwell's account of his second and more serious beating which followed immediately on from the first, after he had been overheard telling his friends, as he came out of the headmaster's room, that the first had not hurt. 'This time', Orwell writes, 'Sambo laid on in real earnest. He continued for a length of time that frightened and astonished me – about five minutes, it seemed . . . '.[13] Ignoring the difference between real and subjective time, and trying also to ignore Orwell's obviously deliberate 'seemed', Crick goes to some lengths to demonstrate that the headmaster cannot in fact have continued his beating for five whole minutes ('that would have been as bad as a naval flogging at the Nore or Spithead, and would have put the victim in the infirmary for days'); and then feels justified in warning the 'innocent reader' against accepting 'as gospel what is more likely to be either semi-fictional polemic against such real abuses of authority, or else in part fantasy'.[14]

These uncharacteristically weak efforts to challenge the reliability of 'Such, Such were the Joys' are important because they are all working towards an attempt by Crick to question its literary *genre*. It is not so much 'pure autobiography', he suggests, as 'a polemical short story written in the first person and drawn from experience'. Failing to establish any part of it as patently and deliberately fictional however, he is obliged to fall back on what has always been a traditional objection to any autobiographical narrative. The effect of the second beating, Orwell writes, was to make him feel that sin was not necessarily something you did but rather something that happened to you. He does not want to claim that this idea flashed into his mind 'under the blows of Sambo's cane'; he must have had glimpses of it before: 'But at any rate this was the great abiding lesson of my boyhood: that I was in a world where it was *not possible* for me to be good'.[15] 'This is, indeed,' Crick comments,

> the world of a totalitarian state, truly of *Nineteen Eighty-Four*. But it is also the reflection of a mature writer. Was it possible for any boy of eight to have thought that? Could Orwell really have thought that he thought it then? Which is more plausible: that he is here untypically exposing the roots of his own psychology, or that he is transfiguring imaginatively aspects of his early experiences into what was soon to become the helplessness of Winston Smith?[16]

Although the final rhetorical question is far from clear, it seems to accuse Orwell of projecting back on to his childhood feelings which he was developing, not in any direct relation with his own experience, but with that of a fictional character. The evidence for that charge is associated with a complaint that could just as well apply to Mackenzie, Proust or any of the other figures previously discussed. At eight years old, Crick feels, Orwell was too young to have the feelings the 'mature writer' attributes to him: he contests, that is, Orwell's efforts to find words for feelings which, as a boy, he could either never have had or (more generously) would have been too inarticulate to express.

If *What Maisie Knew* were an autobiography, then that might well have been a legitimate criticism of Henry James; but Orwell's description of the eight year old's state, which he takes care to hedge round with qualifications, and which seems far too familiar to justify the reference to 'the world of a totalitarian state', appears wholly plausible. That is perhaps a matter of opinion. What is not is that Crick has saddled himself with a false distinction from which only confusion can arise. He appears to feel that opposing fiction on one side is 'pure autobiography' on the other, and he associates the second with what he calls 'literal truth', without explaining how an individual's memories of his or her childhood could ever be 'literally true'. In most autobiographical records of childhood there will be episodes the details of which are accurate and others which are mis-remembered; but almost inevitably their authors will take up an attitude to both which is personal and subjective. Even more inevitably, they will rely for their records on language which must, to some degree, be the repository of what they have experienced between the period when the episode took place and the moment they decided to describe it. These unavoidable conditions of autobiography will make it seem 'impure' only to those who mistakenly believe in some supposedly 'objective' alternative.

The letters Orwell wrote home from St Cyprian's, Crick says, ought to make people have second thoughts about 'accepting as literal rather than figurative truth [his] later account of the great terror of first term at prep school'; and he concludes that although 'Such, Such were the Joys' 'seems truthful . . . it is not literally accurate, and [Orwell's] account of his own relationship with [St Cyprians], of its effect on him, is either semi-fictional or heavily over-drawn'.[17] Orwell may have mis-remembered certain details of the personnel, buildings and organisation of St Cyprian's (although Crick can produce no convincing evidence that he did), but these elements are so closely associated with his individual response to them that to contrast this with some putative account which was 'literally true' makes no sense. If Crick really believed that 'Such, Such were the Joys' was fictional, semi or otherwise, why does he rely on it for most of the details in his chapter on St Cyprian's; and why is he able to say, on the last page of that chapter, that Orwell's 'experiences at prep school prepared him to reject imperialism when he went to Burma and to side with the underdog, for ever afterwards, with empathy and understanding'?[18] This is tacitly to admit that the account of the experiences in 'Such, Such Were the Joys' must be broadly accurate, and at the same time to accept Orwell's own interpretation of them. Crick could easily have done both these things more explicitly without in any way endorsing the significance Anthony West attributes to Orwell's childhood experience. Laudable as his effort is to swim against a fashionable tide and insist that there are episodes in later life which are just as significant, and sometimes more significant, than anything that happens to us in childhood, his attempt to show that in 'Such, Such were the Joys' Orwell did not set out to record his experiences of prep school as accurately as he could, but was instead more concerned with telling a 'story' in the fictional sense, is a failure. If that text is indeed full of fiction, moreover, a 'story' in which many of the details are deliberately invented, then the implications for his biographical enterprise are ones which Crick has not begun to meet.

Biographers can of course identify their subjects as fabricators and choose to dismiss out of hand most of the testimony they provide. This is broadly the approach of Kenneth S. Lynn, for example, in his debunking biography of Ernest Hemingway; and it is probably the one which has to be adopted by anyone now writing the life of a figure such as Frank Harris. Like Harris, Ford Maddox Ford was also someone who, in describing his own experiences, had what Alan Judd has called a 'contempt for facts'. In his biography of Ford, Judd justifies not having annotated his text as 'scholarship necessarily demands' on the grounds that he wanted to write a book in which the spirit of a subject who was never 'detained by a footnote or checked by a reference' could be at ease. Noting that Ford's account of receiving his first letter from Conrad may well have been false, he claims it nevertheless preserves an 'essential truth'; and on the impossibility of discovering whether he did have an affair with his wife's sister, Judd comments: 'Lacking some undiscovered box of letters, we shall have to wait for a novel about Ford – which would be his true biography, revealing by Fordian truth – to tell us'.[19] Claims like this make one feel that it would be a help in all discussions of biography if the word 'truth' could be proscribed. Without denying a gifted novelist can sometimes offer more insight into certain historical figures than their biographers, one has to ask why, if Judd is so impressed by essential or Fordian truth, he should have bothered to add his own narrative of a life to Ford's own numerous autobiographical writings. Subjects who deliberately and – in the cases of Ford and Harris – cheerfully fabricate, and can be discovered doing so on occasions sufficiently numerous for them to be regarded as fundamentally untrustworthy, pose many more problems for the biographer than he allows. They form a special category it would need a specially allocated space to describe. Yet it is not one into which Orwell, or any of the other biographical subjects mentioned in this chapter, fall. When Orwell can be shown to mislead, it is much more because of the accidents inherent in all autobiographical writing than by design. This is some comfort given the extreme difficulty of demonstrating, as far as the early years are concerned, where and how his account is false. These were the important things that happened to me in childhood, says the introspective and articulate subject, and this is what I believe they meant. Freud would not have been worth his fee had he not been able to contest both parts of this statement; but without free association and all the other tools of the therapeutic method, biographers can usually only challenge the second, and what they say is restricted by their dependence on their subjects for the details of the first.

More often than not, there is no direct access to the past. When children record an experience immediately after it has occurred they may not have enough understanding to be coherent, and when adults look back there are grave risks of distortion and the imposition of inappropriate meanings. What an experience was and meant – the two are hard to disentangle – can never be objectively determined in the way in which we can know (or discover) the hour at which the sun rose on a certain day in the past. There can, therefore, be no norm against which the inaccuracy of competing accounts can be measured. The consequence of this is not that all biography is fiction, just as the consequence of discovering that something can never be known for certain is not necessarily an irresponsible relativism. It is rather a question of greater or lesser probabilities, or what might be termed 'relative plausibility'.[20] This is true in general but also on the specific issue of whether the subject's record of his or her own experience could ever be accurate. Dr Johnson was no doubt too trusting, but since Freud's influence has made itself felt it could be said that biographers have been too much inclined to assume that their subjects are always wrong. This is in part because of the psychoanalytic axiom that patients cannot analyse themselves which I have already mentioned, to which Freud himself is the only (if rather glaring) exception, and which follows logically from the belief that the difficulties that bring patients to analysts in the first place arise from conflicts which are unconscious. The unease Linklater and Painter manifest in dealing with their subjects' self-analyses reflects the success Freud had in convincing many people that a conscious recollection could only ever be a starting-point.

If a man claims that his fear of water derives from an incident in childhood when he nearly drowned, it would seem perverse to deny that he knew what he was talking about. That there may be occasions when individuals have the epistemic authority to state correctly why they became as they are, is, however, a much debated and highly complicated issue; yet whether Mackenzie and Proust knew what they were talking about is fortunately less important here than how their biographers could decide that question one way or the other. The difficulties of doing so become apparent in Crick's attempts to demonstrate that 'Such, Such were the Joys' is unreliable. But as significant as the failure of these attempts is the admirable motive for them. Rightly protesting against those critics who move directly back from *Nineteen Eighty-Four* to St Cyprian's, as if there had been no intervening life experience, Crick would have sympathised with a reviewer of the penultimate volume of Edel's biography of James who complained that its author was 'so intent on fastening James's feelings and behaviour to the distant past, interpreting any story to which his history has risen in terms of ground floor and basement . . . that he skips every floor in between'. The same reviewer went on to note the paradox that, although the intervening floors are skipped as far as interpretation is concerned, they are nonetheless described at great length.[21] When the correct answer to a sum can always be anticipated, he implies, in a shrewd criticism of the more extreme members of the 'back-to-childhood' school, why bother to give all the figures?

*

The advantages which the analyst, in negotiation with the patient, has over biographers dealing with their subjects seem obvious enough; yet several of their problems are similar. For both parties, this question of why what matters should be restricted to single moments or episodes can be acute. Orwell takes care not to associate too closely his second beating with the 'abiding lesson' of his boyhood, thoughtfully aware that what would be convenient for narrative structure may not be a faithful record. On inspection, the childhood moment is often susceptible to dissolution like that other great structuring device of biographical or autobiographical narrative, the 'turning-point' in adult life. There are genuine turning-points, like the swimmer breaking a leg a week before the Olympics; but when it is a question of psychological development or process, they can often be drained of their dramatic force. Michael Sheringham, for example, by merging the moment of illumination into its immediate past and future, and by demonstrating how much there is of narrative convention in its presentation, has skilfully shown that St Augustine's conversion was not as sudden and dramatic as he makes it seem in his *Confessions*.[22] Many a determining moment in childhood can no doubt be 'deconstructed' in a similar way. It may be that a friend could have persuaded Compton Mackenzie that his account of his mother's desertion of him on the last day of the Easter holiday was an arbitrarily chosen representative of a movement from utter reliance to a position of semi-independence which is always gradual, as well as quasi-universal. Yet it may be also that the child did have that sudden sense of betrayal on the evening in question, and that the memory of it was genuinely pathogenic. It does not necessarily count against this assumption that, if he did, it makes for a better story. Freud's case histories would be much duller without the reconstruction of childhood experience as a series of dramatic episodes. The question for both the biographer and the analyst is neverthless whether psychological development is always accurately represented by such moments. Might Proust's narrator still have been the weak-willed individual he represents himself as being if his parents had not indulged him on that fateful night which loomed so large in his memory?

There are several different, dramatic moments in the Wolf Man case history but the one that is assumed to matter most is the first, so that it is 'primal' in both senses of the word. By attributing his patient's crucial experience to the time when he was only one and a half Freud protected himself from being out-flanked (except of course by later advocates of the birth trauma); but in doing so he raised the problem of quite what a child of one and a half could make of seeing his parents copulating, *a tergo* or otherwise. The question is therefore not merely: why always childhood? but also: why early childhood rather than later? The answer is that it can always be claimed that responses to an experience in later life would not have been as they were (so severe or determining, for example) had not the ground already been prepared by responses which came earlier. In his life of Russell, Ray Monk was faced with an account in the *Autobiography* of a moment which his subject claimed changed his life for ever. Although he notes that Russell was 'fond – perhaps over-fond – of presenting his life as a series of epiphanies, many of which, one suspects, were overplayed by him in later life for the sake of lending drama to the facts of his life', he establishes that in this case the significance of the episode was at least not a retrospective discovery, but proclaimed by Russell in a letter written only two days after it occurred. He and his wife Alys had gone to hear Gilbert Murray reading from his new translation of *The Hippolytus* and returned to the home of the Whiteheads, where they were both staying, to find Mrs Whitehead 'undergoing an unusually severe bout of pain' (she suffered from what was later cruelly diagnosed as 'pseudo-angina'). The realisation of not being able to do anything for her overwhelmed Russell with 'the sense of the solitude of each human soul' and converted him, he claims, into 'a completely different person'. Among the many remarkable effects he attributes to this experience is that 'from having been an Imperialist, I became during those five minutes a pro-Boer and a Pacifist'.[23]

Monk is able to make all this clearer by pointing out that, at the time, Russell was in love with Mrs Whitehead, a detail not unsurprisingly glossed over in the autobiographical account; and by suggesting that listening to *The Hippolytus*, with its tale of guilty passion, and being 'profoundly stirred by the beauty of the poetry', would have put Russell in a particularly receptive state of mind. But the detail which most interests him concerns the Whiteheads' two year old son Eric who had not previously attracted Russell's interest, but whom he now took by the hand and led out of the room to prevent him troubling his mother: 'He came willingly, and felt at home with me. From that day to his death in the War in 1918, we were close friends'. This boy, Monk notes, was almost exactly the age Russell had been when his own mother died. His 'deep sense of identification with the boy was surely not uncon-nected with this', he writes, 'especially when one considers that the loneliness, the solitude that was the subject of Russell's pre-occupations during his "conversion" was, in his case, the direct result of the death of his mother'. For Monk, 'There is a sense in [Russell's] descriptions of those extraordinary five minutes of a great unleashing of hitherto repressed feelings'. According to him therefore, and for reasons of which Russell himself remained unaware, the meaning of the Whitehead episode lay as much in the past as the present.[24] Whether or not it did, and forgetting for the moment the practical difficulties, the biographer nearly always has this option of taking one step further back in time, however much earlier in a life than Russell's vision of Evelyn Whitehead a significant episode might have occurred. There is a potential logical bind here, a play of infinite regress, which Freud partially avoids in the Wolf Man case by having a patient whose determining expe-rience took place so early.

Virginia Woolf recorded that she was sexually abused by her half-brother, George Duckworth, when she was in her late teens. Would the presumed effect have been so devastating had she not also (again, according to her own report) been sexually abused by her other half-brother, Gerald, when she was six? The obvious truth is that individuals respond to significant experiences in later life in a way which must to some extent be determined by what has happened to them previously. The crucial question is the extent. When many soldiers in World War I succumbed to what became known as the 'war neuroses', it was open to the new science of psychoanalysis to explore their childhood experiences and thus speculate on why *they* had become ill while others had not. But there was often not much point in that when the reasons for their illness were so evident in the life of a soldier during the war and the cooperation it received from early difficulties in childhood was so clearly not what most mattered. Why look for the cause of Wilfred Owen's final breakdown, for example, in early conflicts, and espe-cially in early conflicts of a sexual nature, when it occurred, as a recent historian of these matters puts it, 'after he had spent several days in an isolated forward position with the maimed and dismem-bered body of a fellow officer lying alongside him'.[25] A later experience may well be linked to an earlier one but that does not mean that the latter always has pathogenic as well as chronological priority. In our time, the effect of a mother's death in early life acts like one of Dr Johnson's moral axioms and cannot be denied: it will always prove more than a match, in explanatory terms, for seeing a person one loves in pain and not being able to do anything about it. But one can imagine less serious misfortunes the memory or effects of which would have proved negligible without some greater disaster in later life. In those cases it would seem strange for the biographer (or the analyst) to begin explaining the present by reference to the past.

Whether to concentrate on single episodes or on processes, and how far back into childhood it is either appropriate or possible to go: these are problems common to analysts and biographers. But the greatest difficulty they both encounter when dealing with child-hood experience is to decide whether, or in what proportions they are dealing with historical events or fantasy. This is what so exercises Crick, and it ought to exercise Painter more than it does because both Proust's accounts of the goodnight kiss are self-avowedly fictional. Hermione Lee takes a Crick line in being sceptical about Gerald Duckworth's supposed abuse of his half-sister when she was six, claiming that 'there were many more long-term, problematic, and influential features in her childhood than this'; and that the treatment she received from George Duckworth later in her life was 'much more damaging' to her.[26] This is to accept implicitly what elsewhere Lee occasionally doubts: that Woolf's reports can be relied upon; but in her investigation of quite what George might have done to his half-sister, she displays an admirable scrupulosity. With great care she reviews all Woolf's references to the occasions when George would come into her bedroom after having accompanied her to some social occasion and then, according to one of these references, help her to undress, lie on her bed, and fondle her. This was when Woolf was in at least her late teens so that the significance of the crucial phrase Lee's enquiry eventually throws up, however peculiarly apt it may be to the problems of dealing with *childhood* experiences, is clearly not limited to them. Having concluded from all the references that it is impossible to know quite what George Duckworth did to Virginia Woolf – whether it was in fact fondling or something much more serious – Lee claims that 'what matters most in this story is what Virginia Woolf made out of what happened'.[27]

This is an approach sometimes adopted by Freudian revisionists against those inclined to feel that some of the early experiences attributed to patients in the case histories stretch credulity too far.

In the special instance of the Wolf Man – special because Freud often concedes that the primal scene is his own supposition – he himself sometimes seems willing to take the view that whether his patient did actually see his parents copulating is perhaps not so important. Responding in notes to Jung's scepticism, he suggests that the Wolf Man may have woken up to see his parents in their white underclothes (it is important that in the dream the wolves are white), but then grafted on to the memory of this moment an experience he later had of seeing two dogs copulating.[28] This is a concession he feels obliged to make, but in general, in this and the other case histories, Freud is extremely reluctant to give up the idea that he is dealing with historical events (however distorted or incomplete a picture we might later be able to have of them). In some ways this is strange. The birth of psychoanalysis is notoriously linked to the time when Freud decided that the neuroses of his patients were not associated with real sexual abuse suffered in their childhood, but with sexual fantasies. It was not that a father had slept with his daughter (for example), but that the daughter had unconsciously wanted him to. But if that were in fact the case, why should the analyst be so concerned with *genuine* episodes from the woman's early life? Whatever the answer to this question (and no one even vaguely familiar with the area could doubt that Freudians would be without one), it is clear that Freud himself remained committed to discovering as much reliable information about his patients' past as possible, and that his method would collapse without such a commitment. There is after all an awkwardness for analysts, whose sole criterion is narrative coherence, in having to explain to their patients that whether what they were about to discuss was true or false had no real importance.

Biographers who explained to their readers that they were not interested in what had actually happened to their subjects, only in what those subjects had made of what they knew or imagined had happened, would be in an equally difficult position. Or rather their position would be more difficult because biography is so much more clearly than psychoanalysis a branch of history. Its aim is not the subject's cure but an accurate record of that subject's life. Moreover, if we want to understand the 'character' of someone like Woolf it must be very important to know whether (for example) she fantasised sexual abuse or actually suffered it. How she responded to what did or did not take place cannot be more important than the real or supposed events when the two are so interconnected. The putative incidents which concern Lee most belong to a period when Woolf was already a young woman. The difficulty she has in establishing their true character can be taken as a sign of how much harder it is to know what happened to people, the further back in their lives one delves. But one thing does not become less important than another simply because it is much more difficult, or perhaps in certain cases impossible, to know. All this is bad news for modern biographers who live in a culture where childhood is so commonly assumed to hold the key to understanding and where, as Crick complains, the effect of adult experience tends to be marginalised. 'In the lost boyhood of Judas', the poet George Russell ('AE') once wrote, 'Christ was betrayed'; and on a more popular, less serious level crooners in the 1940s and 1950s used to sing: 'You must have been a beautiful baby/'Cos, Baby, look at you now'.[29] But who could know what Judas was like as a boy, and whatever did happen to those family snapshots?

5

Body Matters

I left no calling for this idle trade,
No duty broke, no father disobey'd.
The Muse but serve'd to ease some friend, not Wife,
To help me thro' this long disease, my Life, . . .
      (Alexander Pope, *Epistle to Dr Arbuthnot*, in *Poetical Works*
      (Oxford, 1966))

ONLY THE VERY FORTUNATE have no experience of illness. Some people can never be described as healthy while others encounter illness in mid-stream. There are those who, having always thought of themselves as well, are proved on later investigation to have been mistaken. Our dealings with disease are complex, so that what biographers are to make of it, and how it can and should be invoked to explain a subject's behaviour, are complex matters also.

Most immediately accessible to enquiry would seem to be the effect on the subject of the *knowledge* of being ill. How different would Dostoevsky's life have been without the continual threat of his epilepsy, or Pope's had he felt himself to be a healthy man? These are not easy questions to answer. Reviewing a new biography of Baudelaire at the end of 1944, George Orwell complained that its author never once mentioned his subject's syphilis:

> This is not merely a piece of scandal: it is a point upon which any biographer of Baudelaire must make up his mind. For the nature of the disease has a bearing not only on the poet's mental condition during the last year but on his whole attitude to life.[1]

Orwell's chief concern here appears to be with what it feels like to have syphilis: its psychological implications, and he rightly implies that no account of Baudelaire could be adequate that did not take that issue into account. But what precise weight ought his biographer to have given it? Towards the beginning of his excellent biography of Oscar Wilde, Richard Ellmann remarks, in a footnote, that he has come to believe Wilde contracted syphilis while he was a student in Oxford: 'I am convinced that Wilde had syphilis and that conviction is central to my conception of Wilde's character and my interpretation of many things in his later life'.[2] Yet in the rest of Ellmann's biography, syphilis is hardly mentioned. It is invoked just once as an explanatory factor but in a thematic analysis of Wilde's plays and not (for example) in the account of how Wilde changed from being bisexual to entirely homosexual. On a psychological level it is not hard to imagine how syphilis could have been important here. What kind of resentment against women might a man who has caught syphilis from a prostitute harbour; or, more generally, and bearing in mind the rashness which Wilde occasionally exhibited, not least in his decision to prosecute Queensberry, how might someone's behaviour be affected if they have frequently in mind the thought, 'I have a fatal disease and may not live long'? The issue is not whether these speculations have any value, but how syphilis can be 'central' to a conception of Wilde's character when it is accorded no role in his life's major episodes.

The most convenient way to study how subjects are affected by knowledge of illness would seem to be to focus on those moments (if there are any) when they first learn they have a fatal disease. With our thirst for drama, we tend to expect people to be quite different after they have received the news and illness to then become a major determinant in all they do. Certain practical consequences would seem to be inevitable: the settling of affairs, the abandonment of projects, or the withdrawal from familiar activities; but less certain is how radically altered what Orwell calls the 'whole attitude to life' is likely to be.

One of the writers who most encourages us to think of our lives in terms of dramatic turning-points is Rousseau. In the sixth book of his *Confessions* he describes the morning when, feeling no worse than usual, he was suddenly assailed by a loud buzzing in his ears and the beating of blood in his arteries. What finally convinced him he was doomed, and had very little time to live, was his inability to sleep. From being a *grand dormeur* he was transformed into an insomniac. 'Not being able to prolong my life,' Rousseau writes, 'I

determined to profit all I could from the little that was left to me';
and he goes on to describe how, although the buzzing has never
left him, and the attack has meant that he has never again been
able to sleep well, making the most of life is what he has been
doing for the thirty years since it occurred.[3]

If we believe Rousseau (and thousands wouldn't), a radical
change of life came about because of the sudden realisation of a
supposed fatal illness. In retrospect, it must have seemed to
Rousseau himself, but even more to his friends, like a patently false
alarm; but many people do not need even that to decide that they
are going to make the most of life. Catherine Carswell was five years
older than D. H. Lawrence but remembered him commenting,
when she was once bewailing how unproductive her own life had
been in comparison with his, that the time she had left was after
all much longer than any he could expect.[4] She concluded from
this that Lawrence was driven forward by an ever-present feeling
that he would die young, which might well be true even if it was
not the threat of tuberculosis which provided the impetus. In an
early letter to a friend he confidently asserted he was 'not consumptive – the type as they say. I'm not really afraid of consumption, I
don't know why – I don't think I shall ever die of *that*';[5] and he
continued to maintain this belief in the mid 1920s, when the signs
of tuberculosis had become unmistakable. He lived his last years as
if he were subject to nothing more than recurrent bronchial trouble,
bothersome but not life-threatening, so that to look for the effects
on his behaviour of a sudden or indeed gradual realisation of fatal
illness might seem a waste of time. Yet as several commentators have
pointed out, many of the places in which Lawrence stayed during
those last years were particularly recommended for TB sufferers so
that it is possible to suggest that a secret, or perhaps not consciously
avowed understanding of his true condition was crucially influential on his movements, if on nothing else.

As his symptoms grew worse in the late 1920s, Lawrence began to
feel that, although he was in no immediate danger, he had nonetheless damaged his health in a fruitless effort to convey important
truths to the English-speaking world; and he regretted in his own
character what in *Women in Love* Ursula had described as Birkin's
'*salvator mundi* touch'.[6] In a remarkable re-writing of the Resur-
rection, initially published as 'The Man Who Died', he described
how when the Jesus figure came back to life, he denounced the
futility of his 'mission' and resolved from then on to take life as it

came, forgetting all plans for the future and concentrating instead on the satisfactions of the everyday and the natural beauties of his immediate environment. It is clear from his letters that, after one of his periodic bouts of illness, this is a resolution Lawrence himself also made, but its effects were short lived. Before long, he was once again deep in composition, and then embroiled in what turned out to be a crusade for ensuring that the consequences (*Lady Chatterley's Lover*) reached as many people as possible, in defiance of English and American censorship. It is not easy to change one's 'nature': to alter radically one's habits and patterns of behaviour. Knowledge of illness will always make a difference (if rarely to the extent Rousseau claims it did for him), but in cases where the illness is more or less life-long, as it seems to have been for Pope, it is hard to say what the differences might have been because ill-health is all the subject has ever known. Where illness dramatically supervenes, on the other hand, as it does for most of us, there are many occasions when 'character' is so well established that the difference the knowledge makes might be no more than superficial. There are no doubt lives where the relation between the subject's either gradual or sudden awareness of being seriously ill and his or her 'attitude to life' is plain; but in a surprising number of them, even this most apparently straightforward of the biographer's dealings with disease can prove tricky.

*

Like Rousseau, Florence Nightingale also became convinced at a relatively early moment in her life that her days were numbered (she lived to be ninety). For the biographer, her case raises the issue of those illnesses whose origin may well be psychological rather than organic. Many, if not all, the physical symptoms she endured were perhaps genuine but George Pickering has argued that, like Darwin, she became a chronic invalid chiefly in order to avoid conventional social obligations and thus be able to continue her life's work (reform of the British War Office). This diagnosis has been challenged, as has a similar one in the case of Darwin. Both these figures spent a long period abroad and it has been suggested that both returned to England with debilitating, long-term illnesses which the medical science of the time would have found it difficult to detect. In Florence Nightingale's case the culprit would have been brucellosis, or 'Crimean Fever', and in Darwin's, Chagas's disease, which is a consequence of being bitten by 'the *Benchuca* (*Triatoma Infestans*), the great black bug of the Pampas'.[7]

Much of what Pickering says to refute these organicist explanations seems reasonable, but the way he presents his own case poses grave problems. Dismissive of Freud, he has a disablingly simple view of the 'psychoneuroses' which he feels explain the invalidism of both Darwin and Florence Nightingale. Following Pavlov, he defines psychoneurosis as the result of conflicts the victim can neither escape nor resolve, and he takes as his chief model a condition first diagnosed during the American Civil War and known as Da Costa's syndrome. For Pickering, the symptoms of heart pains, breathlessness, sweating or giddiness which are associated with this condition were generated in soldiers by a conflict between having to do their duty and fear of being shot. The trouble is that there is nothing in the account Pickering gives of Darwin, whose troubles were in any case gastro-intestinal, which could correspond to this second item. His wife and family were unusually accommodating and he had no need to earn his living so that, without a far more sophisticated account of the workings of unconscious or half-conscious motives – in connection (for example) with how subversive he felt his intellectual enquiries might prove – it is hard to see why Darwin could not have become a Victorian eccentric recluse without burdening himself with a number of painful physical symptoms. In the narrative Pickering offers (and there are other, more convincing accounts of how being ill was an advantage to Darwin), these are less obviously what facilitated his work on evolution than interruptions which hampered its progress.

The case of Florence Nightingale is different. She appears to have had a demanding, intrusive family and, as a woman in Victorian England, was much more susceptible to social obligations than a man might have been. For her, the retreat into illness does appear to have been an effective method for clearing enough space and time to live life as she chose. ('A married woman', she once wrote, in her autobiographical essay *Cassandra*, 'was heard to wish that she could break a limb that she might have a little time to herself'.)[8] Pickering's account nonetheless leaves the reader with a series of unanswered questions. The occasions he describes when falling ill appears to have been Nightingale's method for defeating the insistence of mother and sister that they should live with her in London are perfectly intelligible since (as in Da Costa's syndrome) illness is then a direct response to an immediate threat.

But without an appeal to some such agency as the Freudian unconscious (that improbably cunning campaigner), it is hard to explain
why she persisted in being ill when the threat was removed, and
the advantages illness brought were less tangible and only explicable in terms of some general, rationally conceived scheme of how
she preferred to live her life. Freud's unconscious is quite often
depicted by him as capable of complicated, long-term reasoning.
Those depictions are problematic, but Pickering has not even
considered whether similar powers ought to be accorded to his
psychoneuroses. The question is highly significant. In a newspaper
report on the latest research to support the idea that Florence
Nightingale suffered from brucellosis, James Le Fanu refers to biographers who have interpreted her illness as 'a sophisticated form
of malingering'.[9] An organic disorder acquits her of that charge;
so also would a Freudian interpretation of her behaviour which
alleged that all her motives were unconscious. Pickering's 'psychoneurosis' explains certain crises in her medical history but not the
'strategy' of the illness as a whole. As a result, he fails to clarify
what attitudes to Florence Nightingale's chronic invalidism we
ought to take up. As readers of her life, do we chiefly sympathise
with her as a victim, or offer silent tributes to her nerve and cunning? How difficult these questions are can be illustrated by the
lack of consensus in our day on what is now usually known as
'chronic fatigue syndrome'.

In Pickering's view, the illnesses from which both Charles Darwin
and Florence Nightingale suffered were 'creative' (*Creative Malady*
is the title of his book). Without them we would have had neither
the *Origin of Species* nor important reforms in the British War Office.
This notion of the benefits of disease, in its symbiotic relation to
creative endeavour, had already been developed in a more elaborate and sophisticated form by George Painter in his description
of Proust's first asthma attack:

> On the way back [from the Bois de Boulogne] he was seized by a fit
> of suffocation, and seemed on the point of dying before the eyes of
> his terrified father. His lifelong disease of asthma had begun. Medically
> speaking, his malady was involuntary and genuine; but asthma, we are
> told, is often closely linked to unconscious conflicts and desires, and
> for Proust it was to be, though a dread master, a faithful servant . . .
> Other great writers, Flaubert and Dostoevsky, suffered from epilepsy,
> which stood in an inseparable and partly causal relation to their art.
> Asthma was Proust's epilepsy. In early years it was a mark of his differ-
> ence from others, his appeal for love, his refuge from duties which

were foreign to his still unconscious purpose; and in later life it helped him to withdraw from the world and to produce a work '*de si longue haleine*'. Meanwhile, however, he was only a little boy choking and writhing in the scented air under the green leaves, in the deadly garden of spring.[10]

In his *Golden Codgers* Richard Ellmann has analysed this passage admirably, although with an irony which is perhaps gentler than it deserves.[11] In this context, the first important point is Painter's reluctant acknowledgement that the allergy which provoked Proust's asthma attack was a genuine medical condition. He could have been a young boy far less anxious to secure his mother's love and attention, one with quite different 'unconscious conflicts and desires', and still found himself 'choking and writhing in the scented air'. The process Painter implies is therefore one where Proust learned to draw a number of important advantages from his illness, perhaps to the extent that in later life he would have been at something of a loss without it. When Pickering writes about Darwin or Florence Nightingale he is inclined to suggest that their psychoneuroses directly provoked their physical symptoms; but this way of making a virtue of necessity is much more familiar to us. For Painter, it explains why asthma stood in a 'partly causal relation to [Proust's] art'. On the evidence he here most clearly provides all this means is exactly what Pickering claims illness meant for Darwin and Florence Nightingale: because of his asthma it was easier for Proust than it might have been to devote himself to what he really wanted to do, even in a period when what he really wanted to do was a 'still unconscious purpose' – a phrase standing in here for what, in an earlier biographical tradition, would have been called Proust's 'destiny'.

This is the only clear consequence of illness in Painter's passage but there are strong hints, as there are also in Pickering, that he would also like it to signify something more interesting, less practical. The shortness of breath asthma brings is implicitly contrasted by him with Proust's later ability to write a book which is, in the best possible sense, and distorting the meaning of the French a little, exceptionally long-winded ('*de si longue haleine*'); and there is a suggestion that this is not only a question of compensatory mechanisms since a contribution to its quality is presumably an individuality illness has emphasised – Proust's 'difference from others'. Without endorsing them directly, Painter is working here in the slip-stream of two remarkably influential paradigms in biographers' treatment of illness. One of these is that there is some natural connection between the pathological and the creative: that no person who is completely 'healthy' is likely to do important work. The second, lingering on even in writers who would disclaim any interest in religion, is that there is a providential scheme which ensures that the severest of afflictions are likely to bring their compensations.

Although both these paradigms are apparent in Pickering and Painter, as well as in many other biographers, they can also be conveniently illustrated in the work of Oliver Sacks, whose case histories often take the form of mini-biographies. *In The Man Who Mistook his Wife for a Hat,* for example, Sacks describes a visit to an unfortunate 'Dr P' whose neurological impairment leads him to mis-recognitions as severe and ludicrous as the one described in the title. As Sacks is leaving, Dr P's wife shows him a series of paintings by her husband which in her view illustrate an 'artistic development' from realism to abstraction. Sack's first response is to think that the paintings are rather 'a tragic pathological exhibit' which reveal only too clearly the progress of Dr P's disorder, and which 'belonged to neurology, not art'; but with his usual buoyant optimism he then reflects that this judgement might be wrong, and that what they could illustrate instead is the 'collusion between the powers of pathology and creation':

> Perhaps, in his cubist period, there might have been both artistic and pathological development, colluding to engender an original form; for as he lost the concrete, so he might have gained in the abstract, developing a greater sensitivity to all the structural elements of line, boundary, contour – an almost Picasso-like power to see, and equally depict, those abstract organisations embedded in, and normally lost in, the concrete.[12]

Here is that association between art and sickness we inherit from the Romantics, but also the idea that Dr P had not been so cursed after all: that his affliction had brought its advantages. For biographers the two paradigms often have the effect of taking the edge off the obligation to decide the precise degree to which their subjects were affected by illness: although Nature takes away with one hand she gives with the other, and whoever heard of a writer or artist who was 'normal'. Yet what is convenient for the purposes of explanation is not necessarily accurate and, although a Proust without asthma is hard to conceive (without asthma he would not *be* Proust), there ought to be some discomfort in according that disorder too much credit for his success. If he can be imagined as thinking, towards the end of his life, that things had after all turned out quite well, there would, it seems to me, be a good deal of danger in imputing to him the idea that it had all been for the best. Certainly that is not a view which fellow sufferers from asthma, who did not happen to write *A la recherche du temps perdu*, could be relied upon to endorse. They might not only ask why the Providence which supposedly ensured that the maladies of Proust and Dr P should be creative was looking the other way when their cases came up for review, but also be much more inclined than others to speculate on what these two might have achieved *without* being ill.

*

The organic basis of Dr P's difficulties was established by x-rays and admits of no contradiction. The putative psychological determinants in the illnesses of Darwin, Florence Nightingale and Proust complicate biographers' lives and might give their readers the false impression that matters are necessarily simpler when psychology is eschewed. Mozart's marked fondness for scatological references, especially in letters he wrote to a young cousin, was revealed in only comparatively recent times. Had the feelings it provoked not been so disconcertingly different from those aroused in most people by the piano concertos or the *Requiem*, it might not have attracted much notice. A psychological explanation is not hard to imagine, similar in type (for example) to Erik Erikson's suggestion that the preoccupation of Martin Luther with excrement could be traced back to the beatings on his buttocks which he received as a child.[13] Yet there are also ways in which psychology can be ignored altogether. Relying partly on accounts of his nervous mannerisms, some commentators have concluded that Mozart suffered from Tourette's syndrome, a condition characterised by uncontrollable tics and also on occasions 'copralalia': the medical term for the inability of the syndrome's sufferers to stop themselves blurting out obscene words in wholly inappropriate social contexts. In the specialist literature, Tourette's syndrome is described as a strictly neurological disorder and researchers insist that 'carefully controlled studies' have provided little support for a psychological aetiology.[14] By attributing to Mozart this rare condition, his admirers can acquit him of whatever moral blame they might be inclined to attach to his obscenities; but at this distance in time the attribution is necessarily hazardous, and whether deciding that he was sick rather than cheerfully foul-mouthed helps them to think of the *Requiem* in exactly the same way as they always used to, is a moot point.

The issue of strictly organic illness is no clearer with regard to another famous figure from the eighteenth century. It is generally accepted that during his final voyage of exploration Captain Cook's behaviour was radically different from what it had been on his previous two. Whereas before he had been a relatively mild disciplinarian, he was now savage in his treatment of an unruly crew, and savage too in his infliction of punishment on the native peoples who broke his rules. Moody and irresolute he seems to have lost that fine judgement which had distinguished him in the past. In a closely argued article, chiefly concerned with the degree of credit Cook ought to receive in any account of the eventual defeat of scurvy, Sir James Watt has suggested that the explanation for the change was organic. He deduces from the recorded symptoms that Cook suffered from a parasitic infection of the intestines which, in addition to causing a blockage, interfered with the absorption of the B complex of vitamins. 'By concentrating on vitamin C deficiency', he complains, in a reference to the interest in scurvy, 'historians may have ignored for too long the serious effects on decision-making resulting from vitamin B deficiencies, which could help to explain some otherwise inexplicable actions of great naval commanders'.[15]

The medical diagnoses of Mozart and Cook have been hotly disputed, especially that of Cook where there is a sensitive political context. ('A more pathetic attempt to exonerate Cook from responsibility for his actions', writes Gananath Obeyesekere, in reference to James Watt's speculations, 'could scarcely be imagined'.)[16] What both chiefly illustrate is the extreme difficulty of discovering which illnesses people suffered from once they are long dead. Accurate diagnosis is a difficult enough operation in the living but the more years that have past the more likelihood there is of records having been destroyed, and of those records which do survive unhelpfully reflecting a medical practice which, in comparison with ours, was unscientific. The difficulty is clear in Ralph Colp's detailed review of all the different explanations for Darwin's invalidism which had been put forward before he published his own book;[17] but it can even be illustrated in someone as close to being our contemporary as D. H. Lawrence. Although he himself never once acknowledged it, no one would now dispute that tuberculosis was the disease from which Lawrence suffered for at least the last five years of his life. The problem is not therefore what ailed Lawrence but when tuberculosis first declared itself; and there has always been a tendency among commentators to push back its onset as early as possible so that it can then be more conveniently invoked in explanations of his behaviour. Yet practically the only written evidence for the disease before 1925 is a passage in David Garnett's *Golden Echo*, published in 1954, in which he excuses the Lawrence of 1913 for lacking 'the instincts of a gentleman' in his treatment of Frieda, on the grounds that he was ill.

> Once I caught sight of one of Frieda's handkerchiefs, marked with a coronet in the corner, crumpled in Lawrence's hand, after a fit of coughing and spotted with bright arterial blood – and I felt a new tenderness for him and readiness to forgive his bad moods.[18]

Many of us spit blood from time to time but it might take a sharp eye to recognise immediately where it comes from and what has caused it to appear. 'Bright arterial blood' act as code words during this period for tuberculosis, but no one in 1913 confirms Garnett's diagnosis. Two years before, when Lawrence was suffering from the illness which led to his giving up his career as a schoolteacher, and which was diagnosed as double pneumonia, he had a sputum test that proved negative. 'The report concerning the expectoration', wrote his sister, 'was very satisfactory. No germs were discovered and since then both lungs have almost completely cleared up'.[19] Against the idea that Lawrence developed TB early in his life is also the remarkable capacity for physical exertion which he periodically demonstrated before 1925. After that date, but especially after the major haemorrhage he suffered in Florence in July 1927, he found it impossible to walk long distances, he coughed persistently, and he panted if he had to go uphill. Tuberculosis prevented him from leading a normal life. Before it, there were times when he walked, or rode, or threw himself into manual work to a degree which many would have found completely exhausting, if not impossible.

It is dangerous to begin thinking of Lawrence as a victim of TB before 1924; but it is impossible to be sure that he was not. The negative sputum test which Lawrence had at the end of 1911 would seem to dispose of claims that he was a consumptive from that early date; but as Brenda Maddox has pointed out, sputum tests were never entirely reliable in Lawrence's time, either because all the stringent conditions which would make them so now were not fulfilled, or reliability required that they should be repeated at frequent intervals. As for his periodic demonstrations of physical energy, these are not at all inconsistent with the peculiarities of pulmonary tuberculosis. A person could well develop an infection and then recover without the disease ever having been identified. Any symptoms they had would be of a kind easy to associate by their doctor with less life-threatening conditions such as influenza or bronchitis. This is the phenomenon known as spontaneous remission, the only evidence for which would be a scar on the lung. If the x-rays which were taken of Lawrence's chest by the doctors from Mexico City's American hospital in March 1925 still existed, we might know for certain whether any of his illnesses before 1924 were in fact tubercular in origin. But in the absence of those, certain diagnosis becomes impossible, especially because of the often slow pace of TB's development, and the very different degrees of a sufferer's resistance. Lawrence died in March 1930, when the x-ray machine was becoming increasingly familiar, scientific tests of blood, sputum and other bodily fluids were common, and only a few years remained before the discovery of the drugs which would hold out a prospect of eliminating tuberculosis for ever. His is a recognisably modern world. If there is nevertheless no way of being certain of his state of health before 1924, what chance is there of being more than dubiously speculative about the illnesses of Darwin, Florence Nightingale, Mozart or Cook? The spectacular success of the Danish doctor who, in 1968, was able to conclude from a plaster cast of the skull of Robert Bruce that the cause of the Scottish king's death, more than five centuries before, had been leprosy, is an exception to the rule; and even there, although the diagnosis may be certain, there must still be some doubt whether the object on which it was performed had been correctly identified.[20]

*

Concentrating on the organic rarely solves a biographer's problems because there is so often a lack of adequate information. At least as serious as that difficulty, however, is the problem of what symptoms can be associated with different illnesses, as well as what the different effect of those illnesses would have been on different people (once a specific disorder has declared itself, a gifted commentator on the relation between medecine and literature has recently put it, it has a tendency to 'radiate out along the cracks and fault-lines of a particular life').[21] Establishing that Cook suffered from vitamin B deficiency is not the same as establishing the degree to which he suffered, or the effects it had. Of course, when investigators start with very unusual particular effects (Mozart's 'copralalia'), and work back to a disease, their life becomes comparatively easy; but just as often they are faced with the task of discovering not only what disease their subjects suffered from, but what physical differences it made. The challenge Ellmann fails to meet in Oscar Wilde's case turns out therefore to be double. Not only, that is, does he do little to show how the knowledge of the syphilis which he regards as central to Wilde's character affected Wilde's attitudes, but he has nothing to say regarding the physiological effects of the syphilis itself. Who can blame him? We all tend to feel that in cases where people have a serious disease they are changed by it; but, partly because illnesses affect different individuals so differently, there are not many guidelines as to how we can go about explaining those changes. In a review of various books on Wilde, including a biography by Hesketh Pearson, Edmund Wilson once half-committed himself to the notion that Wilde was 'haunted through his adult life by an uncured syphilitic infection', used it to explain why Wilde stopped having sexual relations with his wife, and invited readers to consider *The Picture of Dorian Gray* 'with the *Spirochaeta pallida* in mind' ('in the end . . . the horror breaks out'). All this was, however, in a casual journalistic mode: to work out suggestions of that kind in any detail would be a different matter; and in any cases there is nothing in Wilson's wording to mark the distinction between what Wilde felt about his syphilis and what it may have done to him, irrespective of how he felt.[22]

Someone who once attempted a detailed examination of this second issue – not in relation to Wilde but to Nietzsche – was the Swiss philosopher Karl Jaspers. For the ten years before his death in 1900 Nietzsche was insane, a sufferer from what is generally assumed to have been the third stage of syphilis. The question Jaspers asked is what account a biographer ought to take of illness before madness supervened. He observed that in 1879 illness 'procured for Nietzsche the desired liberation from his office [a university post] through retirement', although this was in his view in no way a 'neurosis of expediency' (the kind of breakdown writers like Pickering would later ascribe to Darwin and Florence

Nightingale): the illness was 'deep-seated and rooted in the physical, its external consequences were merely incidental'. He suggested also that, insofar as Nietzsche's various disorders often prevented him from working, they may have made a contribution to 'the aphoristic style which prevails in his publications after 1876' (just as the short, aphoristic poems which Lawrence wrote in his last two years – his 'pansies' – can be related to the state of his health in that period). But the crucial issue with which Jaspers wants to deal is whether the remarkable change observable in Nietzsche's life and work at the beginning of the 1880s ought to be associated in any way with what he calls a 'biological factor'. 'It seems as though', he writes,

> the transformation in Nietzsche's thinking and experiencing, beginning in 1880 and continuing into the year 1888, is such that the effect of the biological factor, the immediacy of vision in his new manner of experiencing, and the new philosophical substance stand to each other in a relation of undeniable identity.

This is expressed with the characeristic care of a philosopher, but it leaves open precisely what the relation was between the biological factor on the one hand and both the new philosophical substance and the immediacy of vision on the other. In his next paragraph Jaspers edges closer to an answer with, 'The "sick factors" – if we can so designate the unknown biological factor – ... may even have made possible what otherwise would not have eventuated'. The effect of this is then strengthened when, having noted that in the period after 1880 'stylistic blunders seem to spring from the same ground as that on which the unheard-of becomes expressible', Jaspers remarks,

> What at first impresses one as accidental and strange may suddenly appear as the most profound truth or the meaningful strangeness of the exceptional. The spirit imparts meaning even to the insanity, and so permeates the insane notes that they become indispensable to the work.

Having acknowledged in passing the contradictory effects of illness however, it is logical that when Jaspers comes to summarise the two approaches which need to be adopted in considering 'the relation of Nietzsche's sickness to his work' (and presumably also therefore to his life), one involves the removal from it 'of those flaws which can be regarded as accidental disturbances resulting from illness', and the other an 'increasingly mythical envisioning of a total reality in which the illness seems to become a moment of positive meaning, of consummate expression of being, of unmediated revelation of something that otherwise would remain inaccessible'.[23]

The providential paradigm is not here fully endorsed, but neither is it abandoned completely. Illness is both a good and bad thing, and the problem is that readers of Nietzsche's work are left entirely free to discriminate one case from the other. They are implicitly invited to act like bad textual editors and make decisions about particular passages according to taste rather than any firm principles which would allow them to decide how the positive effects of syphilis are to be distinguished from its negative consequences. Jaspers is sure that, in the decade before an 'organic brain disorder' caused Nietzsche to collapse into insanity, an encroaching syphilis made a vital difference; but the terms in which he describes that difference mean that it would be very difficult to arrive at a consensus as to what precisely it was.

Most biographers are concerned to trace the effects of illness on their subjects' lives (in particular their conduct or behaviour). Yet Jasper's attempt to find them in the work as well is familiar and puts him in the same general category as the critic who, much more ambitiously, has tried to relate individual poems which Sylvia Plath wrote in her last months to those days when she was suffering from pre-menstrual tension.[24] In the search for precisions of that kind, whether (to rely again on the traditional distinction) they relate to work or to life, it does not help that so many illnesses or disorders have symptoms which are both loosely defined and not at all exclusive. Tight, one-to-one correspondences between a disease and a symptom are uncommon and, when quite specific symptoms are confidently attributed to a particular disease, they often have more to do with folklore than medical science. Although syphilis certainly has its folklore symptoms, tuberculosis is also a prime example of a disease with very widely accepted effects on behaviour for which there is no scientific justification. Commonly regarded as especially prevalent among those of refined literary sensibility – a view easily disposed of by statistics (far more plumbers were afflicted than poets) – it was felt to make its sufferers unnaturally concerned with sex, and render them unusually susceptible to sudden bursts of violent anger.

This last view is the one David Garnett is illustrating in his remarks above on D. H. Lawrence's treatment of his wife. The pain or discomfort of any illness is of course unlikely to improve the temper; but what is usually meant in remarks like Garnett's is irritability of an unusual kind, and certainly the record of Lawrence's life is punctuated by spectacular explosions. When Katherine Mansfield began to suffer from TB she said that it allowed her to understand the propensity to sudden bursts of anger which she had observed in Lawrence in 1916; and Paul Delany, writing only a relatively short time ago, put the matter in a nutshell when he referred to Lawrence's 'tubercular rages'.[25] The trouble is that evidence for Lawrence's rages goes back a long way so that irritability becomes a device for driving the diagnosis of TB further and further into the past: where there is TB there will be rage so that where there is rage there must be TB. As I have noted before, because they are so often obliged to work with insufficient evidence, this kind of circularity is common among biographers. When he wrote about Lawrence, Richard Garnett found a neat way of avoiding it by referring to his 'consumptive temperament'.[26] With this concept, tuberculosis becomes an explanation, not for particular aspects of behaviour but the whole person. The shift is similar to the one Michel Foucault documented so copiously between ascribing to an individual certain practices and characterising him as 'homosexual'. If we have the intellectual decency to forgo it, then doubts about the tubercular origin of Lawrence's rages during the war must come from the general consensus that, from about 1926, when we can be certain that he had TB, he was *on the whole* a much gentler person than he had been before. This objection can be surmounted if TB is conceived as a disease of different stages with specific effects appropriate to each. But these need to be properly described by biographers if they are to say anything useful.

The question of stages is also relevant to whether TB made Lawrence more concerned with sex than he might otherwise have been. In 1935 Curtis Brown, Lawrence's agent and someone who, unlike David Garnett, had no axe to grind, wrote:

> Lawrence was not, I am convinced, an erotomaniac. In various delightful talks with him on all sorts of subjects, *that* subject never once presented itself. But it is likely that his tuberculosis, with its well-known bearing on sex impulses, may have led his eye unusually often to that subject; and once focussed on it, we had a *Lady Chatterley's Lover.*[27]

The notion that tuberculosis makes the sufferer more sexually active and interested is so prevalent that one is forced to wonder where it comes from (of Aubrey Beardsley's death Yeats reported that 'sexual desire under the pressure of disease became insatiable').[28]

Certainly in the nineteenth and early twentieth centuries sex and TB are frequently associated, often as part of that culpabilisation of the sick person which Susan Sontag has written about so well. That thousands of young people, only intermittently unwell, were cooped up together in sanatoria may also have helped to propagate the myth. For Curtis Brown the bearing of TB on the sexual impulses is 'well-known'. He accepts the view that Lawrence was only tubercular towards the end of this life and that his illness gave rise to *Lady Chatterley's Lover*. But Lawrence was called 'sex-obsessed' from the beginning of his career so that there is every reason for thinking of his last novel as part of a gradually evolving process rather than as some sudden product of one specific cause. Moreover, although Curtis Brown adduces TB as the reason for a suddenly increased interest in sex which led to *Lady Chatterley's Lover*, we may also need to remember that it is very frequently cited as the cause of the impotence from which Lawrence suffered in his last years. There is of course no necessary contradiction between sexual obsession and impotence (although Lawrence himself usually refers to the latter as the 'failure of desire'); nor is there any reason why the same cause should not have effects which are contradictory, or which manifest themselves differently at different stages. There is no knock-down, logical method of proving that Curtis Brown, or indeed Garnett and Paul Delany, are simply wrong in the effects they attribute to tuberculosis in Lawrence's case. But one can become uncomfortable at seeing it called upon to do so much interpretative work, especially when the scientific evidence is nonexistent. There is no proven relation between tuberculosis on the one hand and either sexual obsession or bad temper on the other; and neither is it 'obvious' (as Edmund Wilson claimed it was in his review of the books on Wilde) that Baudelaire's 'morose disaffection' and the 'desperate pessimism' of Maupassant were 'the shadows of the syphilitic doom in the days when the disease was incurable'.[29] Whether one interprets Wilson as meaning that the shadows were cast by these writers' awareness of being ill, or the disease itself, the confidence of this last claim is as unfounded as that of Delany and Curtis Brown in their references to tuberculosis.

*

In addition to the difficulty of diagnosing the complaints of those long dead, allowing for the different ways different people respond to being ill, and establishing the connections between particular diseases and particular effects, there is another, less obvious factor which helps to explain why biographers so often find if hard to evaluate the significance of their subjects' illnesses. This is that a medical explanation has a tendency to invade all the available interpretative space. Most of us recognise why this should be so from our own experience. Once a person has fallen seriously ill every feature of their behaviour which strikes an observer as abnormal tends to be attributed to their disease. Charles Lamb writes charmingly of the 'regal solitude' of the sick bed and the way in which 'supreme selfishness' is inculcated upon its occupant as 'his only duty';[30] but an equally common experience is of an increase in social responsibility. When the sick receive visits in hospital they are obliged to make a special social effort at the very time when tiredness and pain are likely to make that difficult; and this unfairness is then compounded by the fact that they can do nothing unusual without its being seen as an effect of disease. Sickness drastically restricts their physical freedom whereupon their freedom in the moral sense is curtailed because they are no longer free agents in the minds of other people.

Illness is a sharp reminder that we are first and foremost bodies, and in one view of the matter *only* that. As a result, it not only tends to provoke the marginalisation of other kinds of explanation but also a sudden shift into a different way of thinking and talking: an alternative discourse. Biographers are usually only led to think of the body as a crucial determinant when it is diseased but are 'we' not always synonymous with its state? Great advances were made at the beginning of this century in endocrinology. One eventual consequence was a number of books like *The Glands of Destiny: A Study of Personality* by Ivo Geikie-Cobb, a doctor fashionable enough to be consulted by Cyril Connolly's wealthy first wife in the early 1930s. In his section on Napoleon this author argues that 'the gland which ruled the man who ruled Europe was the pituitary'; and that 'the early physical and mental decline suggest that this gland had ceased to supply those hormones which made it possible for the Corsican notary's son to become Emperor of the French'. He concludes by wondering whether the fluctuations in the size of the pituitary might not explain 'the meteoric rise and fall of . . . the world's most interesting character'.[31] This treatement of issues that I raised at the end of Chapter 3 is comically inadequate, but that there are important connections between glandular function and behaviour which deeper knowledge might reveal seems undeniable; and although James Watt is an infinitely more sophisticated thinker than Geikie-Cobb, he puts himself in broadly the same camp when he suggests that Cook's probable vitamin B deficiency may have led, not to a rash or pains in a particular part of his body, but poor decision-making. That causal leap strikes a blow for physical determinism which is a highly problematic issue for biographers (not least because it threatens to put many of them out of business). So knotty are the problems in this area that the way they decide to talk about the illness of their subjects often seems less a matter of an approach and vocabulary imposed by the material, than of arbitrary choice.

Given all the difficulties conscientious biographers encounter when their subjects are ill, or suffer from life-long diseases, it is tempting to feel that Boswell's solution was after all the best. Acknowledging that Johnson had once told an acquaintance that there were times when he was 'so languid and inefficient, that he could not distinguish the hour upon the town clock', and conjecturing that this may have been the consequence of some 'defect in his nervous system, that inexplicable part of our frame', Boswell went on,

> But let not little men triumph upon knowing that Johnson was an HYPOCHONDRIACK, was subject to what the learned, philosophical, and pious Dr. Cheyne has so well treated under the title of 'The English Malady'. Though he suffered severely from it, he was not therefore degraded. The powers of his great mind might be troubled, and their full exercise suspended at times; but the mind itself was ever entire.[32]

The chief aim here is to prevent the reader from thinking less well of Johnson because he was often in a disturbed state; but the passage serves the incidental purpose of acquitting Boswell of any responsibility for evaluating the significance of Johnson's illness. It is the difficulty of that task which makes the decisiveness of the passage so appealing. Even in its own terms however, the satisfaction it provides could only ever be momentary. If Johnson's great mind was often troubled, and its full exercise sometimes suspended, in what sense could it have been *ever* entire? His illness cannot be neatly separated from his life and work but must always have been part and parcel of both, as the syphilis of Baudelaire and Nietzsche, or the tuberculosis of Lawrence, were part and parcel of theirs. That the connections are difficult to establish does not itself make them any less important, just as the frequent inaccessibility of childhood experience does not mean that its significance is any the less. In both areas, greater awareness of the problems is likely to lead to abandon and despair only in those biographers whose expectations of the form are too high, and who forget that its inevitable inadequacies are shared by several alternative and more systematised methods for the understanding of other human beings. The emphasis on difficulty in both this and the two previous chapters would have been misplaced if it were taken to imply that what troubles biographers does not also trouble everyone else.

*

Note: when the evidence used to calculate the effects of illness is not only the behaviour of subjects but also their creative works, the intrinsic difficulty of that enterprise, and the uncertainty of its results, can only be an encouragement to those advocates (mentioned in my first chapter) of the Eliotic separation between the suffering man and the creative mind. 'Generally speaking', Jaspers writes, in his discussion of Nietzsche, 'the value of a creation may be regarded and judged only in terms of its spiritual substance; the underlying causal factors are irrelevant to the value of the product'; and he goes on, 'A speech will not be regarded as either worse or better when it becomes known that the speaker customarily drinks a bottle of wine beforehand in order to free himself from inhibitions'.[33] This is quite true, but drinking wine before making a speech is hardly representative of all the possible antecedents to action or utterance; and although some of these may not matter to us, there will be others that do. For a few people's sense of both man and work, it will be important whether Mozart's penchant for obscenities can be attributed to Tourette's syndrome; but if it could be established that tuberculosis makes its victims obsessed with sex, then there might be many more who would find it hard to disassociate that illness from their responses to *Lady Chatterley's Lover*. There are no general rules here but, in any case, if 'underlying causal factors' *are* so irrelevant, it is hard to see why Jaspers should have devoted so much time and intellectual energy to an attempt to evaluate the importance of Nietzsche's syphilis for his work. In *Keepers of the Flame*, Ian Hamilton describes how, after several more suitable recipients had refused the Burns's papers, they were given to a Liverpool doctor who had hardly known the poet, and who happened to be a specialist in alcohol abuse. In the biography this doctor then based on them, he concluded that the likely cause of Burns' death was not only drink but also venereal disease. For many of his admirers the outrage this information provoked also disturbed their sense of the poetry. A hundred years later another doctor reviewed the evidence and concluded that the cause of death was rheumatic fever. As Hamilton puts it: 'At long last the Burns Clubs could admire their hero without reservation. The author of "O, my luv's like a red, red rose" did not die of syphilis'.[34] This is an excessively, perhaps even distressingly simple illustration of a phenomenon that takes many varied and subtle forms; but whether or not 'underlying casual factors' ought to be relevant to 'the value of the product', it is a demonstrable fact that in many, if not most, people's minds they often are. One of the characters in Jane Austen's 'Sanditon' warmly praises Burns's poetry. 'I have read several of Burns's poems with great delight', the heroine responds, and then adds in words which might have been addressed directly to the New Critics or certain of the Post-Structuralists, 'but I am not poetic enough to separate a Man's Poetry entirely from his Character; and poor Burns's known Irregularities, greatly interrupt my enjoyment of his Lines'.[35] It may be that people ought to be sufficiently poetic to separate authors from their works *entirely* but, taking 'Character' here to include illness, there are many who are like Charlotte in not being able to do so. Were that not the case, the problem for literary biographers of identifying organic factors correctly, and the even greater one of calculating their effects, would be less acute.

6

The Sociological Imagination

> It is by means of the sociological imagination that men now hope
> to grasp what is going on in the world, and to understand what is
> happening in themselves as minute points of the intersections of
> biography and history within society.
>
> (C. Wright Mills, *The Sociological Imagination*
> (New York, 1959), p. 7)

A recent life of the English cricketer Wally Hammond was subtitled
'The Reasons Why'. What needed to be explained was why almost
all the people who met Hammond in his later years found him
so singularly disagreeable. According to his biographer, the explanation lay in the mercury injections he was obliged to take for
his syphilis. But, complained the reviewer of the book in the *Times
Literary Supplement,* do we really need 'a chemical explanation for
an unpleasant temperament?'; and even if we do, would not
Hammond's 'daily heavy drinking' serve equally well? This was to
oppose one organicist explanation with another, but the reviewer
was in fact the partisan of a quite different approach. It was, he
pointed out, only for a brief period that Hammond was recognised
as 'the greatest cricketer in the world' so that 'the brooding discon-
tent of the decline is adequately (if less sensationally) explicable
as a reaction to the loss of that stature'.[1]

It would be hard to over-estimate the effect on people's behaviour of how they are regarded within the various social groups to
which they belong and, for many sociologists, over-estimation would
in any case be impossible given the exclusive importance they attach
to social affiliation. In the wake of Durkheim's pioneer work on

suicide, his followers were bound to go further in attempts to 'collec-
tivise' what we are accustomed to think of as essentially private
phenomena. Even our memories of the past, Maurice Halbwachs
ingeniously argued, are not exclusively our own: 'one remembers
something only by adopting the perspective of one or more social
groups, and by placing oneself again in one or more currents of
collective thought'; and on the same page he conveniently defined
what was, and to some extent still is the classic sociological approach:

> when a man returns home unaccompanied, there is no doubt that for
> some time 'he has been alone', according to our current methods of
> expression. But his solitude was only apparent because, even during
> that period, the nature of his social being provided the explanation
> for his thoughts and acts, and he did not cease for a moment to be
> enclosed within a social group.[2]

Armed with perceptions of this kind Halbwachs considered
Stendhal's very first memory of his childhood in the *Life of Henry
Brulard*. He was, Stendhal recalled, in the middle of a meadow with
a twenty-five year old female cousin when she asked him to kiss
her ('*Embrasse-moi, Henri*'). Not wanting to do so, made angry by
the request, and with the recumbent cousin's cheek at the height
of his mouth, he bit her hard. I can still visualise the episode, he
writes (doing Halbwachs's work for him), 'but no doubt because
it was immediately transformed into a crime and I was reminded
of it constantly thereafter'.[3] His first memory, that is, must inevitably
have been held in common with his family group and have come
to constitute for both him and them a social act. Freud believed
that many early memories became the victims of repression, and
physiologists have speculated on the age at which the physical capac-
ities of infants would allow them to experience what could later
provide material for memories. In contradistinction to both,
Halbwachs claims, 'If we are not able to recall our earliest childhood it is because our impressions have nothing to which they can
attach themselves while we are still not social beings'.[4]

In spite of its title, the *Life of Henry Brulard* is of course an
autobiography. Holding promise of relevance to more strictly
biographical issues is *Biography and Society: The Life History Approach
in the Social Sciences*, a collection of essays edited by Daniel Bertaux
and published in 1981. In the first of these the Italian sociologist
Franco Ferrarotti reminds his reader of the danger for any valid
sociological method of taking as the point of departure a 'given
social atom', and that it is not the individual that ought to be

regarded as primary but families, co-workers, neighbours, classmates and other small social groups. The illusion to guard against in Ferrarotti's view is that it is the individual who is the founder of 'the social' rather than its sophisticated product, and he concludes with what may well seem a truism within the field of social science but which must strike anyone outside it as a challenging paradox: 'Much theoretical work must be undertaken, which will one day permit us to take that passage from the most simple to the most complex, the passage from group biography to the biography of the individual'.[5]

The shelves of the bookshops would seem evidence enough that, before tackling individual lives, biographers have not cared to wait for the theoretical work to which Ferrarotti alludes; and the degree of concern they have traditionally shown for what might be loosely termed the 'social dimension' varies considerably. For reasons which will be evident, the influence of the group on adult life is likely to figure much more prominently in the life of a politician (for example) than in that of a writer. Yet if literary biographers were to imagine that they could remedy their shortcomings by intensive study of what 'biography' means to sociologists they would be sadly mistaken. For non-specialists a title such as *Biography and Society* is misleading. The sociological community has always been divided between those 'nomothetists', who disdain the study of individual lives because it can never yield information which has a general application, and partisans of the 'idiographic' approach. It is for the latter only that biography has any meaning but, as Rom Harré has demonstrated in his description of the De Waele method ('the only systematic life-course psychology so far developed'),[6] that meaning is highly specialised. One of the conventional criteria for establishing the scientific credentials of a particular form of enquiry is whether its results allow us to predict accurately what will happen in the future. In one sense, biographers are often involved in prediction in that their accounts of what subjects did in a certain situation are often based, not on any direct knowledge, but on knowing how they behaved in previous situations which were similar. They rely on a supposed understanding of the subject's 'character' up to that point in his or her life in order to fill the narrative gap. De Waele's enquiries were predictive in a more straightforward sense in that his subjects were a number of murderers in a Brussels jail whose 'biographies' were the means which he felt would allow him to predict those of them it would be safe to release on parole.

According to Harré, there are three phases to the construction of a biography in the De Waele method. The first begins when the subject is required to prepare an autobiography. This text is then divided into a number of chronological phases ('time slices'), each one of which is offered to individual members of a team of investigators ('let us suppose that there are six'). It is the task of these investigators to reconstruct a whole biography from their particular slice 'using common-sense social and psychological knowledge'. Each investigator next 'negotiates' with his colleagues, and then with the subject, in order that they should produce together an agreed version of the latter's life history. In the second phase of the construction, the same procedures are followed except that the investigators are different and the subject's autobiography is now divided, not into time but theme slices: 'work, education, relations with the opposite sex, and so on'. When these processes have also produced an agreed biography 'the time reconstruction and the theme reconstruction are finally brought together'. As if this were not enough, the agreed biography is then analysed for 'a whole range of situations which are felt by the participant to be problematic or to have involved some sort of conflict'. Episodes formally isomorphic with these situations are then devised which the participant is expected to re-live, without being told which of the events in his past the artificial problem and conflict situations are supposed to replicate. 'The results of this role-playing phase of the investigation are then combined with the agreed biography to produce the final document, the prisoner's "life"'.[7]

Harré's brief summary cannot do complete justice to the complexities of the De Waele method, as he himself has described it, nor answer all the questions it raises (in what ways is the subject supposed to re-live his past? what is the 'common-sense social and psychological knowledge' on which the investigators are meant to rely?); but it will be sufficient to indicate how huge the gulf is between this kind of work and biography as it is usually understood. The differences are many but two are essential. The first concerns the method's heavy dependence on what is usually the oral testimony of the subjects themselves. A very modest amount of investigation reveals that when sociologists or social psychologists talk about biography they usually mean autobiography or, to employ the formulation of Harré, '(auto)biography'. In the literary camp, where biographers prefer their subjects dead, that could be regarded as at the very least a potentially damaging confusion of genres. The second difference is closely related to the first. It is evident that in spite of their stress on individuals, Harré and De Waele are really interested in a whole *class* of subjects; but it is never quite clear from Harré's account whether the purpose of the method is the recovery of genuine (i.e. reasonably true) life histories for members of this class or the creation in them of socially advantageous states of mind. The method has the practical purpose of predicting which of the convicts are least likely to re-offend; but in that case the accuracy of the details any particular criminal gives of his past might seem less important than the concrete results of the rehabilitation process to which he is subjected. Unless the investigators believe, along with certain psychoanalysts of the old school, that no improvement is possible without discovering what *actually* happened in the past, then (like the authors of the 'Lives of the Saints') they are bound to be less concerned with truth than with social efficacy. Their practical aims mean that they are not really interested in biography (which is a misnomer), nor indeed in history, but in an extraordinarily labour-intensive form of psychotherapy. More awareness of what it might mean to recognise fully that writers and artists are also social beings may well be desirable among their biographers, but the De Waele method suggests that not much help is likely to come to them from those formally engaged in 'biography' in the social sciences.

*

Even in literary biography, there are cases where the crucial importance of the social groups to which the subject belongs cannot be ignored. Early in his life of Pope, Maynard Mack notes that had his subject been born a hundred years later much more about his childhood would have been known, if only because Pope himself would have thought it 'a stage of his life worth memorializing'. Noting how keen nineteenth-century writers became to recall this aspect of their experience, 'even to the extent of several hundred pages', he quotes De Quincey's warning in the preface to his *Autobiographic Sketches* that he will never be more likely to rise into a 'higher key' than when there is 'nothing on the stage but a solitary infant, and its solitary combat with grief – a mighty darkness, and a sorrow without a voice'. For Halbwachs this is precisely the stage which it would be impossible for the subject to remember, but Mack's objection to De Quincey is different. 'Today', he writes, such language seems better suited to the anguish of a King Lear than to the oral and anal preoccupations of one who, as Shakespeare with his never-failing sanity reminds us, spends much of this phase "meuling and puking in the nurse's arms".[8]

The appeal to Shakespeare's 'never-failing sanity' seems out of place here, but more unfortunate is 'oral and anal' which hints faintly at Freudian readings of childhood and puts Mack in the position of someone who, having appeared to regret not knowing more about Pope's early childhood, has gone on to claim, both defiantly and defensively, that the absence of knowledge does not matter anyway. This means that he might be taken to have *fallen back* on his excellent opening account of what it meant to be a Catholic at the time of Pope's birth whereas that information would have been highly relevant even if we knew far more than we do about his early days. Mack's aggression towards those who attribute great significance to early childhood experience, his partisan espousal of the eighteenth-century view that:

> the goal, especially for boys, was to attain as fast as possible the grown-up condition, the full socialized state that was required before one could make one's contribution to society, and the years prior to this effort were granted little intrinsic value of their own,[9]

threaten to make it seem that his more sociological emphasis is a *pis aller* when the importance of Pope's Catholicism is obviously crucial for any understanding of his character and career. It is not so much, however, the Catholic affiliations themselves which Mack stresses, but the exclusion from other, more privileged groups which they brought. To this disadvantage was added, in Pope's case, an illness at the age of twelve which left him stunted and semi-crippled for life. Mack explains the effect of both in the traditional way noting that

> if . . . among the impulses that drove Pope in his student days elements of sheer testiness and pugnacity were mixed in, we need not be surprised. Cripple and Roman Catholic he might be, but he *would* beat a path into his society's high places and bask in its applause.[10]

Equally traditional here is 'mixed in', a biographer's idiom which implicitly recognises the reversibility of *verstehen* psychology and acknowledges that there must have been plenty of people in Pope's time whose illnesses and Roman Catholic affiliations convincingly explained their failure in life rather than their success.

A more thoroughgoing sociological approach to literary biography than Mack's comes from a surprising source: Henry James in his life of Hawthorne in the 'English Men of Letters' series. At the beginning of this short book, James says that it will be necessary to give it the form of a critical essay rather than a biography, but later on he makes an implicit reference to himself as Hawthorne's biographer and his approach to his subject is chronological in the conventional 'life and works' manner. The initial disclaimer is motivated by consciousness of relying almost entirely for his biographical information on Hawthorne's own writings (in particular the volumes of the various Notebooks then in print), and George Lathrop's biographical *Study of Hawthorne*, which had been published in 1876, two years before his own book appeared. Yet rather than lamenting how relatively few details this one secondary source provided, James sometimes seems to regret that it gives so many. 'Of [Hawthorne's] childish years', he writes,

> there appears to be nothing very definite to relate, though his biographer devotes a good many graceful pages to them. There is a considerable sameness in the behaviour of small boys, and it is probable that if we were acquainted with the details of the author's career we should find it to be made up of the same pleasures and pains as that of many ingenuous lads for whom fame has had nothing in keeping.[11]

When Mack disputes the significance of childhood experience, he is aware of the intellectual capital Freud had been able to derive from Romantic thinking. But James is writing in 1878, and the English Romantic poets do not in any case appear to have bulked large for him. Given what was later to be made of his own boyhood years by Leon Edel, his remarks have an innocence which can seem in retrospect distinctly poignant.

Uninterested in Hawthorne's childhood, or in an event to which subsequent biographers were to pay much attention: the disappearance of his father at sea when he was only four, James does take some note of his ancestry, as he could hardly not do when it so preoccupied the subject himself. But descent from prominent early settlers meant for James no more than the inherited burden of a Puritan conscience which Hawthorne was able to lift by the transformation of its concerns into art:

> The old Puritan moral sense ... had been lodged in the mind of a man of Fancy, whose fancy had straightway begun to take liberties and play tricks with [its concerns] – to judge them ... from the poetic and aesthetic point of view, the point of view of entertainment and irony.

It is not so much how or why Hawhorne's Puritan stock could have produced 'a man of fancy' that concerns James, but how that man managed to become a writer in the New England of his time. The now famous premise of his essentially sociological case is that 'the flower of art blooms only where the soil is deep, that it takes a great deal of history to produce a little literature, that it needs a complex social machinery to set a writer in motion'. In James's view, and in comparison with what one could find in Europe, early nineteenth-century America offered little history, and its 'social machinery' was of the simplest kind: 'Poor Hawthorne', he says of that writer's time at what is now the highly expensive and exclusive college of Bowdoin, 'was indeed thousands of miles away from Oxford and Cambridge'. The 'lightness of the diet to which his observation was condemned' explains for James why Hawthorne so often turned to the past for his subjects, his fondness for 'romance' rather than the social realism of a Balzac or Thackeray, and the relative paucity of his literary output.[12]

More detailed knowledge of Hawthorne's life and circumstances may well have led James to more qualified conclusions, but even in its own necessarily restricted terms his argument can often seem shaky. In one of the more convincing demonstrations offered of why it was such a disadvantage for a writer to have been born in early nineteenth-century New England, he points to the lack of an appropriately discriminating reading public in 'a community in which the interest in literature was as yet of the smallest'. A little later, however, he describes the almost immediate success of *The Scarlet Letter* and the fame as well as comparative financial security this first novel of Hawthorne's maturity brought. Associated in James's mind with the absence of a reading public is that Hawthorne would have had no one suitable to whom he could talk about what he was trying to do:

> fifty years ago, greatly more than now, the literary man must have lacked the comfort and inspiration of belonging to a class. The best things come, as a general thing, from the talents that are members of a group; every man works better when he has companions working in the same line, and yielding the stimulus of suggestion, comparison, emulation.[13]

This is the authentically sociological emphasis in biography, the insistence on how bound up our behaviour must always be with the various groups to which we inevitably belong. In adopting it as he does in relation to Hawthorne's so-called 'solitary years' in Salem, when he had returned to his family home after graduating, James may be justified; and he may not have known how much Hawthorne saw of Melville when he was living in Lennox in the early 1850s. But in his account of the time the Hawthornes spent in Concord in the early 1840s he certainly recognises the opportunity that gave his subject of frequenting Thoreau and Emerson, as well as several other, less important writers. Completely deprived of communication with writers of his own distinction during the whole of the early part of his life in America Hawthorne was certainly not, so that the relative isolation which James imagines for him could just as easily have been a matter of temperament as social necessity.

The logical weaknesses of James's case can be taken as a sign of the vested interest he had in presenting it. Hawthorne was a very important figure for him and, as several critics have since pointed out, one with moral preoccupations very like those which would pervade his own, later work. But in 1878 James was ambitious to rival the great European writers and, rightly or wrongly, had concluded that there were not enough 'manners' in his own country – manners of the right kind – from which great novels could be made. By that date he had already decided he would live in Europe so that his life of Hawthorne became a way of justifying that momentous decision. Unless he could show the disadvantages for a gifted writer of living in America, the way it narrowed and distorted what he wrote and obliged him to make a virtue of necessity, the main purpose of his own acceptance of expatriation would disappear. More than most biographies, James's life of Hawthorne illustrates the truism that to some extent biography is always also autobiography. The depth of engagement which any serious life of another requires necessarily leads to a certain amount of *self*-definition, if not on occasions self-betrayal.

*

My two examples of a sociological emphasis in the writing of literary lives will have suggested how far from sociology proper is the usual practice of biographers. The question is not therefore whether they make adequate use of the procedures and methods of a discipline so different from their own, but to what extent they could be said to display a sociological imagination in the most general, least specialised sense of that term. To a very considerable extent might be the first impression. Top of Ferrarotti's list of primary groups is the family and not many biographers could now be accused of ignoring *its* determining effect on the subject. After or beyond the family the picture is less clear; but few biographers of Orwell (for example) would be likely to neglect the importance of his having gone to Eton as a scholarship boy, and since Graves himself indicates in *Goodbye to All That* how critical it was that, at the beginning of World War I, he should have joined the Royal Welch Fusiliers (rather than some other regiment) the formative effect of that decision is unlikely to be ignored either. Biographers of middle- and upper-class figures habitually stress the significance of the groups with which their subjects became associated at university, or the coteries and groupings which mattered to them in their professional lives. When the different social worlds the male or female subject inhabits are well-documented, reviewers are inclined to praise the biographer for providing a dense social context. Yet from the point of view of the concerns in this chapter, the question of how determining or influential that context is conceived as being might still remain, and it might still be asked whether or not its function in the narrative is primarily no more than 'background'. (The issue is similar to the one which divides the old from the new historicism in Shakespeare criticism.) What tends to relegate much of the documentation in biographies to 'background' is the reliance of their authors on the letters or diaries of their subjects. Very few people writing a letter or a diary entry are inclined to believe that they are not directly responsible for their own thought and feelings but that these have somehow been imposed on them from outside. They most usually and naturally think of themselves as the principal actors in a drama where other people form the supporting cast. Taking their lead from private documents of this kind, biographers can often appear to be neglecting what any individual owes to society: how largely what he or she has become can be attributed – by any commentator so inclined – to social factors.

That neglect is likely to be more evident in literary biographers for whom letters, diaries and the like tend to be not only more abundant but also better written, and therefore more powerful in effect. Compounding this difference is the fact that, since the Romantic period, many writers have quite deliberately and self-consciously chosen not to think of themselves as belonging to any social group. In an essay chiefly concerned with the problems of authorised biography, Edward Mendelson has suggested that 'most modern writers have made themselves exiles in one way or another, and so their biographers can suppress . . . their subjects' position in their economy, their history, their reading public and so forth', implying by 'so forth' that typical modern writers or artists repudiate their status as ordinary social beings. The example he cites is Joyce who left Ireland in his early twenties and lived the rest of his life abroad. 'To understand Joyce the man in a way that he himself wanted to be understood', Mendelson writes, 'one need focus only on the tiny circle of his family and friends; Joyce was in exile from everything else'.[14]

The context of Mendelson's remarks is an attack on Ellmann for speculating too much about Joyce's inner life and thereby confusing biography with the psychological novel. What he says is at least a reminder that someone like Joyce could only live as he did because writing is not a profession in the more orthodox sense, and not therefore so easily amenable to such fruitful sociological concepts as Goffman's 'moral career'. As Harré explains it, a moral career is an individual's social history seen in terms of 'the attitudes of respect and contempt that others have to him and of his understanding of those attitudes'. Like an obstacle course, it is punctuated by various 'hazards', or social events in which 'a person can gain respect by risking contempt'. Simple examples of these hazards would be an examination, or an application for promotion. To be unsuccessful in either of these might mean acquiring what Goffman termed 'stigmata', and the burden of either having to hide these from others in the future or find ways of presenting oneself in company so that they no longer matter.[15]

In his remarks on 'the social self' in the tenth chapter of his *Principles of Psychology*, William James noted that the power of attitudes of respect or contempt to determine behaviour had already been described by Locke (although the terms he had favoured were 'commendation and disgrace').[16] No one who has seen how the issue of promotion, for example, can dominate the whole of a person's life, so that no action in the public or indeed private sphere seems unrelated to it, will be inclined to think that power underestimated; but the effects of Goffman's 'hazards' are perhaps easier to study when people are regularly brought together in a common workplace. It is then that situations arise which social scientists can observe, or the essentials of which they can later simulate in laboratory conditions. Even when they are not exiles in the literal sense, writers characteristically work in isolation and, although they are in many ways 'professionals' in the same sense as doctors or lawyers, they have a much less obvious career structure. They can undergo

the 'hazard' of being nominated for a literary prize and take exec-
utive positions in their professional organisations; they can be
invited to give lectures or find themselves the object of academic
literary study; but in general the criteria for determining their relative standing, their success or failure in their chosen field, are not
always clear. In England, there is not even the equivalent of an
Académie Française to which a writer anxious to increase his status
can refuse to belong.

Reviews might be reasonably adduced as the expression of a
literary community's attitude towards a particular writer; but as
these are so largely ephemeral, a safer criterion for establishing the
status of writers would seem to be how many people read their
books, and by extension therefore how much money they are able
to earn. A painter's rise in his profession might be similarly estimated by the increasing prices he is able to charge for his pictures.
These methods of judging will seem crude to many but in a period
when the 'educated' public was smaller, more homogeneous and
easier to identify than it is in ours, Dr Johnson would not have
quarrelled with them. That at least is what one gathers from the
justly famous passages in his life of Richard Savage where he analyses
his subject's attitude to the reception of his work. The sale of his
poem 'The Bastard', Johnson points out, was always referred to by
Savage as an 'incontestable proof of a general acknowledgment of
his abilities', even though it was the only work of his which could
'justly boast a general reception'; and he goes on,

> But though he did not lose the opportunity which success gave him of
> setting a high rate on his abilities, but paid due deference to the
> suffrages of mankind when they were given in his favour, he did not
> suffer his esteem of himself to depend upon others, nor found anything
> sacred in the voice of the people when they were inclined to censure
> him; he then readily showed the folly of expecting that the public
> should judge right, observed how slowly poetical merit had often forced
> its way into the world; he contented himself with the applause of men
> of judgement, and was somewhat disposed to exclude all those from
> the character of men of judgement who did not applaud him.

There were other times, Johnson adds, when Savage would attribute a particular work's lack of success to the period when it was
published, or the failure of the publisher to advertise it properly,
so that 'the blame was laid rather on any person than the author'.
For two uncharacteristic paragraphs Johnson then flirts with the
idea that self-delusions of this kind might have something to

recommend them in a world in which no man's desires are properly satisfied; but he finally dismisses that possibility as a 'pleasing intoxication'. 'By imputing none of his miseries to himself' Savage was never made wiser by his sufferings and 'willingly turned his eyes from the light of reason, when it would have discovered the illusion, and shown him, what he never wished to see, his real state'.[17] The 'real state' around which this remarkably developed and virtuoso section of the 'Life of Savage' circles, concerns a writer who is conclusively proved to be much less important than he hopes or believes by the contemporary reception of his works. As Johnson makes clear elsewhere in his biography, a further way Savage had of evading recognition of his real state was by refusing to consider himself a writer at all: adopting the prejudice of his putative aristocratic origins that, although it was permissible to dabble in literature, no gentleman would demean himself so far as to consider himself a member of a literary *profession*. As one of the professionals of literature who did most to make writing respectable in the eighteenth century, it is not surprising to find Johnson treating this pretention with the same irony with which he describes all of Savage's other efforts to rationalise his failures. As the outside recorder of Savage's moral career, he sternly sets his own sense of matters against his subject's.

Being a professional writer in the eighteenth century meant escaping from aristocratic patronage and relying on the 'general public'. As that public became larger and more diversified, wide readership and the money which goes with it became an increasingly ambiguous sign of a writer's standing. Everyone who writes needs to be read by someone but not all writing is suitable for a mass audience. Stendhal recalled that his book on love (*De l'Amour*) sold only seventeen copies and that the bookseller in charge of the sale described it as a relic which customers regarded as too holy to handle (*'On peut dire qu'il est sacré; personne n'y touche'*). He began his posthumously published *Souvenirs d'Egotisme* with the confession that he would not have the courage to write without imagining that one day he would be read by 'the kind of person I'm fond of, by someone like Mme Roland or M. Gros, the geometrician'.[18] He needed, that is, to fantasise an ideal audience and he was fond of saying that only in 1880 would his work be properly appreciated. In Johnson's account, Savage's reminder to himself that 'poetical merit' often forces its way into the world slowly was futile, and its futility has in fact been confirmed by subsequent events since very few people now read Savage's poetry. But Stendhal's prediction proved uncannily accurate and no one would now suggest that the relative lack of success he enjoyed in his lifetime was an accurate indicator of his true standing. Since his death, popularity has become an increasingly unreliable measure as a quick glance at only the 'A's of our current literary world would confirm. Whether or not Martin Amis is now the leading English novelist cannot be settled by his decision some time ago to break with his former agent and negotiate through another a spectacularly lucrative contract when his *confrère* Jeffrey Archer could double even his sales and still not be sure of acquiring the critical esteem within the writing profession which he so clearly lacks.

When the criteria which determine status within a particular group are ambiguous, its social pressure is likely to decrease, and individuals should therefore find it easier to be independent of it. Savage may often have behaved as if the judgement of the educated public was of no importance but the contortions Johnson describes could be taken as proof of how much it did in fact matter to him. The ever-growing complexity in the composition of that public after his death ought to mean that it mattered less, and would seem at first to increase the difficulty of thinking of later writers in Goffmanesque terms. The esteem or contempt of the groups with which writers are associated becomes less important when they can realistically imagine themselves, as events proved Stendhal could, risking the 'hazard' of posterity. That option helps to explain the tactic of withdrawal which became so frequent among writers in the nineteenth century: the retreat into a sometimes defiant isolation, or their choice of exile in the fullest sense. Yet when Edward Mendelson suggests that the exile of many modern writers dispenses biographers from considering them in relation to the societies in which they had grown up, he forgets – either genuinely or for his own polemical purpose – that a man like Joyce was already a fully developed social being before he went abroad. Sitting in the cafés of Trieste or Paris did not make him any the less an Irishman of a very particular cast: in many ways it only increased his awareness of being such an Irishman. His position in the economy and history of his country (as Mendelson puts it) does not suddenly cease to have significance for the biographer merely because he became an expatriate.

Being able to live abroad, and carry on with their work, is what distinguishes writers and painters from doctors and lawyers.

Yet that Joyce was in fact a writer is what ensured that he would have a continuing interaction with his native community (the 'isolation' of those who periodically address members of their own language group is a contradiction in terms). This would be true even if he had not maintained a voluminous correspondence with the literary fraternity at home and, through reading work by his contemporaries and reviews of his own, remained acutely aware of his comparative standing. Social interaction may be most *conveniently* studied when members of the same groups are regularly brought together in a workplace; but, as Proust points out in his analysis of the 'unsociable isolation' in which his famous painter Elstir had chosen to live, it can also occur within the mind of one person:

> no doubt at first he had thought with pleasure, even in his solitude, that, thanks to his work, he was addressing from a distance, was imbuing with a loftier idea of himself, those who had misunderstood or offended him. Perhaps, in those days, he lived alone not from indifference but from love of his fellows, and, just as I had renounced Gilberte in order to appear to her again one day in more attractive colours, dedicated his work to certain people as a sort of new approach to them whereby, without actually seeing him, they would be brought to love him, admire him, talk about him;...[19]

This is striking confirmation of Halbwachs's claim that, even when they are alone, individuals are enclosed within a social group, and determined in their behaviour by the nature of their social being. It suggests that when biographers of recent writers or painters do neglect the social aspect, fail to exert their sociological imagination, it is likely to be because they take too seriously their subjects' own declarations of independence from the societies in which they live or grew up. And yet the passage above does not endorse the sociological approach entirely since Proust's narrator casts his analysis in a speculative form and, with his usual subtlety, later points out that, after a while, the 'practice of solitude' gave Elstir an entirely disinterested love for it.

*

Not all literary or artistic withdrawals can be explained in terms of the motives which Proust initially attributes to Elstir: when Rimbaud abandoned the world of letters he seems to have done so for good. But there are many that can, including – to switch to a real painter rather than an imaginary one – Cézanne's in the account which D. W. Harding once gave of him in a book entitled *Social Psychology and Individual Values*. Since this book was published as long ago as 1953 it may seem strange to cite it, but that Harding was a distinguished critic of literature who became a social scientist gives it a rare and possibly unique value. This move from 'the Humanities' to disciplines which, as the beginning of this chapter attempts to show, are in many ways so completely different has become more difficult in recent times as both fields have become more specialised. The gap is now so huge that a genuinely sociological, or social psychological approach to literary biography is hard to imagine; but Harding demonstrates that this was not always so.

He begins his account by referring to the 'infantile arrogance' with which Cézanne responded to the rejection of his pictures for the *Salon* of 1866 and comments,

> This demand for approbation exclusively on one's own terms suggests the immature attitude which wants the social world to be simply a mirror reflecting and intensifying the glory one already sees in oneself. It is not by any means self-sufficiency, for the desire to have one's excellence mirrored remains very strong in such a man and (as will appear) Cézanne had a deep craving for recognition and esteem.

The failure to be recognised and granted esteem fairly immediately led to withdrawal: like Coriolanus, Cézanne rejected the rejecting group. But he did not then (Harding notes) join a 'militant innovating' sub-group of which he could have become 'just one more respected member'. Instead he withdrew into solitude and 'set about with incredible persistence the endless study and development of his individual line of work in painting'. He speculates that the origin of Cézanne's rebellious individuality is to be found in the difficulties he experienced with his father and, since the early work gives so little clue of what would come later, suggests that 'it looks as if dissatisfaction and rebellion came first long before a convincing alternative to orthodoxy had been glimpsed'. Although he admits – like Proust in his analysis of Elstir, but rather confusingly for the case he is arguing – that 'during the most important part of his life (Cézanne) seems to have achieved unselfconscious absorption in his task and to have been very little distracted or divided by concern for its social effect', he nevertheless presents him as someone whose 'inordinate and insatiable appetite' for social esteem meant that, in withdrawing or isolating himself from the group, Cézanne remained heavily dependant upon it.[20]

Harding's account of Cézanne occurs in his chapter on 'Innovators', the other two cases studied being Manet and the Quaker, George Fox. One of his concerns is that the tactic of withdrawal it exemplifies is, like Stendhal's reliance on posterity, open to anyone ('much eccentricity is worthless'). As a consequence, he comments, the ethical implications it illustrates are,

> the uncertain borderline where rather morbid self-centeredness shades into single-minded devotion to one's own proper functioning and loyalty to the development of one's unique talent. Socially the fascinating problem is how to distinguish between a valuable persistence in individual development and the stubbornness of worthless self-conceit.[21]

What clearly makes the difference in both cases, one is tempted to say, is precisely what we can now recognise in Cézanne as the 'unique talent'; but that is something not really provided for in the social science categories Harding is choosing to employ. His suggestion that dissatisfaction and rebellion preceded Cézanne's remarkably original way of both seeing and representing the phenomenal world tends to imply that one produced the other when, of all the millions of young males who have experienced difficulty with their fathers, there has been only one who revolutionised modern art. Cézanne's exceptional gifts are both crucial to our understanding of the social psychological profile Harding offers and, at the same time, an element in it which seems fortuitous, adventitious. Logically speaking, they play much the same role in the analysis as the *deus ex machina* in classical drama.

This problem is related to another, at once more general as well as a more prominent one in discussions of a sociological or social-psychological cast. Given the power the group has to determine individual behaviour, how is it that innovation is ever able to take place? 'What an individual is, or could be', writes Goffman, repeating a commonplace of his discipline, 'derives from the place of his kind in the social structure'; and more pertinently, on the next page, 'the nature of an individual, as he himself and we impute it to him, is generated by the nature of his group affiliations'.[22] But when all the formative influences are directed from social groups on to the individual, how is it that he or she can sometimes succeed in radically altering the character of those groups? There are of course social psychologists who have been interested in this issue, although in their case the focus is on dissenting *minorities*.[23] When Harding was attempting its clarification, it was being made more difficult by the now classic experiments of Soloman Asch. In the simplest form of these, an experimental group would consist of eight people, seven of whom were Asch's confederates. Asked for a judgement, these seven would falsely pronounce one line displayed on a screen longer than another and thereby persuade the one genuine volunteer in the group to agree that it was indeed longer, against the patent evidence of his senses.[24]

Asch's experiments, which were of course more complicated and technical than my brief allusion suggests, would have interested D. H. Lawrence. Trying to explain why people were so outraged by Cézanne's paintings, when all they represented were a few apples or a jug, he suggested that the majority in a society is always so conditioned or coerced into perceiving the outside world in a conventional way that its members are deeply disturbed when artists come along who insist on looking for themselves.[25] Asch's work did not show that everyone could be coerced by social pressure and, interestingly enough for the issue of withdrawal, he demonstrated that the pressure was less effective when the genuine volunteer communicated with the experimenter's confederates without being in their presence. But he did not make it any easier for social scientists to account for change, or what Harding calls innovation. When resisting social conformity is so difficult how is it that certain individuals have been able to convince the majority that it should conform to *their* view? A shadow of a justification begins to emerge here for the largely subject-centred accounts of literary biographers. The accusation that they tend to neglect what in their subjects is representative, directly explicable in social terms (and what, after all, could *not* be explained by Lawrence having been born into a family which was working class or Woolf into one so intellectually distinguished?) may well be just; but almost by definition their subjects are exceptional individuals and to concentrate on what makes them so is only to tackle the problem of innovation from what, in the context of the social sciences, is the unfashionable end.

Invaluable as a social science point of view is as a corrective, there are complications in the relations between individuals and social groups which would impose immensely heavy burdens on biographers who were prepared to adopt it wholeheartedly. It is not always entirely clear in the first place how groups are to be defined: the number of members they need to have, for example, before they descend into what Goffman calls a 'focussed gathering'.[26] But however they are construed, it is evident that a writer (for example) is likely to belong to a multiplicity of them, quite apart from those comprised by putative readers and the literary fraternity; and that within the so-called fraternity itself, there is considerable fragmentation so that the esteem of one person can easily outweigh the contempt of ten others. This in itself will suggest the difficulties of the last phrase in Harré's description of the moral career: a person's social history seen in terms of 'the attitudes of respect and contempt that others have of him *and his understanding of those attitudes*'. Leaving aside the difficulty of our ever knowing what people really think of us or the ravages of what is popularly known as paranoia, Johnson's account of Savage demonstrates how ingenious individuals can be in avoiding what others would regard as the reality of their social situation. Partly at issue here is what in short-hand terms might be called temperament. As William James shrewdly observes in his reflections on the social self,

> there is a certain average tone of self-feeling which each one of us carries about with him, and which is independent of the objective reasons we may have for satisfaction or discontent. That is, a very meanly-conditioned man may abound in unfaltering conceit, and one whose success in life is secure and who is esteemed by all may remain diffident of his powers to the end.

Of course, it is always open to the social scientist to regard temperament in this sense, the individual's 'average tone of self-feeling', as the consequence of previous social relations, but (as James notes) that is not how it usually *feels*:

> we ourselves know how the barometer of our self-esteem and confidence rises and falls from one day to another through causes that seem to be visceral and organic rather than rational, and which certainly answer to no corresponding variations in the esteem in which we are held by our friends.[27]

There are immense complications in trying to think more sociologically about biographical subjects in either their development or their day-to-day dealings, but perhaps the crucial point, applicable to not merely literary biography but to biography in all its forms, is that in none of the social groups with which individuals are likely to be associated are they merely passive. In their anxiety to destroy the illusion that we make our own lives, social scientists frequently give the impression that the traffic between an individual and a social group is all one way. Franco Ferrarotti knows better, even if he expresses his knowledge in a prose which one suspects must have read more comfortably in its original foreign language:

The primary group thus reveals itself as the fundamental mediation between the social and the individual. It defines itself as the social field in which the totalization of its social context and the totalization which individual members make of this totalization coexist indissolubly. It presents itself as a sutured zone where there is a reciprocal articulation and mutual merging of the public and the private, of social structures and the self, of the social and the psychological, of the universal and the singular ... [28]

But if the relationship between individuals and society is so fundamentally dialectical (as at least the third sentence in this tortured passage would appear to suggest), what right has Ferrarotti, in the claim I quoted at the beginning of this chapter, to insist that effective lives of the former must dance attendance on biographies of primary groups? The individual may well be the sophisticated product of the social rather than its founder but, if it is indeed possible to conceive of a moment when there was no interaction, something we might call individuals are 'produced' relatively early and from then on have the potential to transform the primary and indeed other social groups, even as those groups are engaged with the task of transforming them. What gives individuals that potential is more likely to be revealed by the closeness which results from a biographer's immersion in a subject's diaries and letters than by an appeal to the methods and vocabulary of the social sciences.

7

History, Chance and Self-determination

Death will necessarily come, from ordinary causes. It is inevitable, and one's whole life is a preparation for it, an event as natural as the fall of raindrops. I cannot resign myself to that thought. Why not seek death of one's own free will, asserting one's right to choose, giving it some significance? Instead of passively letting it happen? Why not?

(Cesare Pavese, *This Business of Living*, trans. A. E. Murch (1961), p. 47)

When C. Wright Mills called for the exercise of a 'sociological imag-ination', it was with contemporary society chiefly in mind. Yet since most biographies deal with subjects who are dead, and in some cases long dead, the imagination required must clearly be histor-ical also. This not only means that biographers might be called upon to consider past group affiliations which could be significant for an understanding of their subjects, but also all those various circumstances that made life in the past so different from what it is now. To say this is of course to do no more than repeat the old truism that biographers must also be historians. Testing James's implied suggestion that Hawthorne was deprived of the kind of social contact and audience that would have allowed a greater flow-ering of his talent, means having the necessary historical knowledge and insight to evoke the social conditions in the New England of almost two hundred years ago.

When the social context of which the subject necessarily forms a part has been significantly influenced by major historical events it is unlikely to be ignored. In the past at least, biographers of Jane

117

Austen ambitious to chart her inner life could justify paying little attention to the Napoleonic wars because both their psychological and practical impact on her daily existence appeared to have been so minimal. No biographer of Graves, Proust, Lawrence, or Woolf, on the other hand, has ever been able to ignore the effect on these writers, and on most of their contemporaries, of World War I since almost nothing these four felt or thought after 1914 can be explained without some direct or implied reference to it. Such a dramatic illustration of the way lives are influenced by prevailing historical circumstances is not difficult to identify. Harder to take into account is the effect of those everyday habits and assumptions which change subtly over time and make the past a much less comfortably familiar place than we are always tempted to believe it was. Those dismayed by Mozart's fondness for scatological obscenities might well decide that he was suffering from a neurological impairment, or that depth psychology is required to account for what otherwise seems incomprehensible. But before following either of those paths it would be as well to establish whether the phenomenon might not equally well be explained under the rubric *autres temps, autres moeurs*. What one would like to know is how shocked or surprised a representative sample of Mozart's contemporaries would have been by his preoccupation with bowel movements. This is a question which arises naturally. Less obvious is that raised by one of Mozart's biographers when he is describing the begging letters his subject was in the habit of writing, especially to his Masonic 'lodge brother' Michael Puchberg. There were periods when these two met daily but, if Puchberg did decide to send Mozart money, it would be by a messenger. 'We don't know', Wolfgang Hildesheimer writes, 'whether he did so because his sense of tact forbade the tainting of a well-attended musical gathering with a show of material assistance'; and he goes on, 'We don't know how "tact" was valued at that time and in those circles'.[1]

The further back in time one goes, the more relevant these questions of cultural change become although, on occasions, it may be that moving out of the present century only makes them more *self-evidently* relevant. One of the more striking characteristics of the avant-garde writers and artists who were active during and then after World War I was how freely they spoke and wrote to each other about sex. In the letters of the Bloomsbury group especially, that freedom can often appear self-consciously daring and unpleasantly forced. 'When it comes to a creature with a cunt', wrote Lytton

Strachey to his brother James in 1916 (about Dora Carrington), 'one seems immediately désorienté. Perhaps it's because cunts don't immediately appeal to one'.[2] In theory, we know that language of this kind is at least partly to be attributed to a reaction against late Victorian prudery. Our conception of that prudery may have been irreversibly altered by Foucault but, however much the Victorians were preoccupied with sex, and however much they were inclined to express their preoccupation rather than repress it, the general tone of what they wrote and said could hardly be more different from Strachey's. We know these things but it is still a surprise to be made to realise by Ray Monk's long and detailed account of Bertrand Russell's courtship of his first wife, Alys Pearsall Smith, what this might mean for well-educated, progressive people of the 1890s. The evident but rather fearful disdain for sexual intercourse as a betrayal of spiritual aspirations in her letters, and the desperate attempts to somehow spiritualise sexual frustration in his, signal a yawning gap between our age and theirs.[3] Russell's contributions are hard to believe given his later career, although at the same time they help to explain it. Very similar feelings are raised by the courtship of Jessie Chambers by D. H. Lawrence which took place only a few years later, at the opposite end of the social scale. Both these cases suggest that the freedom of Bloomsbury only sounds forced because we are its present-day inheritors (or beneficiaries?), and that to place it in a fully realised historical context would be to respond – to hear it – quite differently.

The problem here is that Russell and Lawrence constitute only two examples, hardly enough for genuine historians among whom the nomothetists are even more dominant than they are in sociology: as the prosecuting counsel in a recent debate in *Contemporary British History* on the usefulness of political biography puts it, 'we must recognise that historians are educated to deal with group rather than personal behaviour'.[4] If the question is, 'how did young people in the period shortly before World War I think and talk about sex?', any systematic approach to an answer would have to begin with a division into groups and then develop methods for registering the variation not only between but also within those groups. Because their earlier responses can be compared with their later, the biographer who relies on the evidence of Russell and Lawrence is saved from absurdity: here are at least two individuals whose attitudes were transformed over time, and the tone or character of whose later responses are easier to estimate fairly in a chronological context. But the degree to which they are representative, so that their cases throw light on the *general* phenomenon of Bloomsbury frankness, is largely a hunch. To call for context in biography, in any but the most elementary sense, is usually to ask for something which most biographers are not in a position to provide. Letters and diaries are their favourite hunting ground whereas, although those historians interested in *mentalités* (a term always found among them in the plural) do also rely on documents of that kind, they are inclined to be more concerned with records from the law courts or public offices. What after all is the significance of a single individual's experience for the life of the group as a whole?

The greater reliance of the *mentalités* school of historians on public rather than private records is partly ideological, but partly also a consequence of their interest in periods when letters and diaries were much less available than they have been in the last two or three centuries. For no very obvious reason, its members have mostly been medievalists or historians of the early modern period.[5] It is harder to discover what individuals thought and felt when their more private records of experience either never existed or have been lost. As Schoenbaum has shown so well, a biography of Shakespeare in the modern sense – one that offered to chart his thoughts and feelings, and bring them into some kind of association with his works – is made impossible by the absence of appropriate evidence.[6] The simplest kind of association with those works would be the certain knowledge that he wrote them all but even that is not always attainable, as admirers of Marlowe have sometimes been the first to insist.

Putative atheist, homosexual and spy, Marlowe has always attracted acute biographical interest, in particular because of the dramatic circumstances of his early death. In his eminently readable as well as scholarly investigation of that event (*The Reckoning*), Charles Nicholl can offer considerable information about the three men who were with Marlowe in the room in Deptford when he was murdered, but very little about Marlowe himself. We might conclude from the company he was keeping at the time of his death (as well as from a number of other, earlier indications) that he had spied for the government, and deduce from the always unreliable reports of paid informers, as well as a certain reading of the plays, that he was a homosexual and an atheist; but there is nothing which would allow us to be certain of any one of those assumptions. Particularly serious for true knowledge of his sexual preferences or religious beliefs is the complete absence of any direct, first-person utterances. The present situation as regards Marlowe is exemplified by the Corpus Christi portrait, now firmly associated in the public mind with his name and the object, in Nicholl's book, of detailed psychological analysis.[7] In 1953, the painting of a richly dressed young man was discovered in the rubble left by workmen who were making repairs to the Master's Lodge at Corpus. The only genuine reasons for believing it represents Marlowe are that Corpus Christi was his Cambridge college and that, with its inscribed dating: '*Anno Dni* 1585, *Aetatis suae* 21', it attributes to its subject an age that would have been his.[8] In times of plenty people eat three meals a day but when there is famine they are obliged to make do with scraps.

The difficulties which literary biographers of figures from the earlier period face are strikingly illustrated by Derek Pearsall who begins his excellent *Life of Geoffrey Chaucer* with, 'The evidence for Chaucer's existence is very sound'. It would never occur to biographers of a more modern figure that they were obliged to show their subject once existed. What Pearsall partly means is that we have more information about Chaucer than about Shakespeare. Four hundred and ninety-three documentary records survive but not one of these is what Pearsall calls 'intimate'.[9] As a result, we know that Chaucer was captured and then ransomed while fighting in France but nothing about the particular circumstances in which either of these events took place. More importantly, given that fighting and being ransomed was a relatively common experience in the fourteenth century, we know that on 1 May 1380 he was released by one Cecily Champain from any legal action relating to her rape; yet why he needed to be released remains a mystery as do the circumstances which lie behind what Pearsall speculates was an out-of-court settlement. The documentary record testifies to certain events without explaining how the biographical subject was involved in them. Sometimes it does not do even that. In 1360 Chaucer was attached to the household of the second surviving son of Edward III; but by 1367 he was in the service of the king himself. 'These', Pearsall comments,

> are the lost years in the Chaucer biographical record . . . and it is impossible to know precisely what Chaucer was doing during this period, though it is likely to have been some service in a royal household, in England or Aquitaine. It is important, however, to try to convey some impression of the general nature of his experience during these years,

as a young man in the service of a royal household, and it is a task that can be reliably undertaken.[10]

Biographers of a modern figure have so much 'intimate' material to contend with that they are often in danger of ignoring the social context. For those who want to write the life of someone from an earlier period, social context may sometimes be all they have. This was largely the problem, for example, for Peter Ackroyd when he set out to record the early life of Thomas More. Once More had become involved in public affairs the documents are plentiful, but for his time at school, in the household of the Archbishop of Canterbury, at Oxford and one of the inns of Chancery, direct evidence is sparse. Ackroyd compensated for this lack with unusually impressive evocations of what is likely to have been the experience of any young person taken into Archbishop Morton's household or attending these institutions; like Pearsall in dealing with Chaucer's lost years, he conveys impressions of a 'general nature' the unavoidable difficulty then being of knowing how far these impressions or experiences accorded with the subject's own.[11]

*

The longer the subject has been dead, the more likely it is that their 'life' will be what, from the point of view of much modern biographical practice, is *Hamlet* without the Prince: a series of episodes organised in relation to an absent centre, a missing individual consciousness. This means that how we are able to think about other human beings from the past is dependent on the kinds of documents which happen to have survived. To a very considerable extent biographers do not choose a particular approach but have it thrust upon them. No one can read Ian Hamilton's *Keepers of the Flame*, with its tales of literary estates accidently discovered or destroyed, without recognising how much survival is a matter of chance: good or bad luck. What is hard for biographers to remember is that the element of chance, in the number and kind of documents on which they base a life, is always present, even in those cases, characteristic of more modern times, where papers have been conscientiously preserved and deposited in the libraries of universities. Research into the most copiously documented existence will always reveal gaps for which the biographer can then make allowances but, from time to time, an item of evidence will suddenly appear which disrupts a phase in the narrative that had previously seemed quite unproblematic. It would be foolish to imagine that the possibility of such disruption could ever be eliminated entirely, or to believe, therefore, that accidents of survival or availability do not continue to influence how we think of even those biographical subjects whose papers fill countless boxes in Texas, or elsewhere.

Chance is not only an important element in how we recall the lives of others but also an easily overlooked factor in those lives themselves. The role it plays seems at first easiest to define in relation to major historical events, especially when the effect of those events is dramatised by accidents of chronology. Wilfred Owen's death in the last week of World War I inevitably makes one wonder how things might have been had the Armistice come a few days sooner. A similar psychological impression derives from considering certain aspects of the history of tuberculosis. There seems no point in speculating how different Keats's life would have been had he been born, not before but after the discovery of streptomycin. For the world in which Keats lived to have been one in which the drugs for dealing with tuberculosis were finally developed, so many other of its features would have had to be different that it becomes quite literally inconceivable. There does not seem much more point in speculating in the same way about Katherine Mansfield; but George Orwell's case, as both Bernard Crick and Michael Sheldon movingly describe it, is different. Orwell lived long enough for one of his doctors to send to America for streptomycin but, in those very earlier stages of its use, it was not clear what other drugs it needed to be combined with if its side-effects were to be moderated. These in fact proved so severe that Orwell's treatment had to be discontinued so that the drug which, in the next few years, would play a major role in the virtual elimination of tuberculosis, proved in the end to be of no use to him.

Like Owen's, Orwell's case is one we think of as 'bad luck' even if, technically speaking, he was no more unlucky than Mansfield or Keats. (Only with great reluctance do we really believe that a miss is as good as a mile.) When it is not forced on them by chronology, as it is in these two cases, luck in this sense is a factor in lives which biographers do not find it easy to convey. The more unobtrusive the vast array of contingent facts which send lives in one direction rather than another, the harder it is to do justice to them. If one were to accept that the major historical circumstances which help determine the existence of individuals are inevitable, on the perhaps sensible grounds that World War I was not going to stop a week early for Owen's sole benefit or the development of a cure for tuberculosis accelerate for Orwell's, there would still remain a host of minor ones whose relation to the subject seems in no way pre-ordained. The difference might be between which treatments were available in Orwell's time (a question quite clearly beyond his personal control), and which doctor he happened to see. The more local the context becomes, the more details there are in a subject's life which can be made to seem arbitrary. In 1912, after being advised by his doctor to give up elementary school teaching unless he wanted to run the risk of developing tuberculosis, D. H. Lawrence was thinking of applying for a job as a language assistant in a German university. He therefore went to seek the advice of Ernest Weekley, the professor who had taught modern languages when Lawrence was studying for his teaching certificate at Nottingham University. When he arrived at Weekley's home, he was entertained by his German wife Frieda. The effect Frieda Weekley was to have on Lawrence's life and art is remarkable and it is just not the case that, had he not happened to visit the Weekley home on that particular day, he would have met her anyway.[12]

There is a sense in which the story of any life comes to the prospective biographer already told. Many of its salient features (education, choice of profession, marriage) are common knowledge and, partly for that reason, it is difficult to imagine how they could ever have been otherwise, and how undetermined a particular possibility might have seemed to all concerned before it was realised. In *The Bostonians* Henry James writes of those 'hours of backward clearness [which] come to all men and women, . . . when they read the past in the light of the present, with the reasons of things, like unobserved finger posts, protruding where they never saw them before'.[13] This is a perception relevant to autobiography. When he applied it to biography, it worried James that the image of his friend James Russell Lowell had been 'strangely simplified and summarized' by his death.

> The hand of death, in passing over it, has smoothed the folds, made it more typical and general. The figure retained by the memory is compressed and intensified; accidents have dropped away from it and shades have ceased to count; it stands, sharply, for a few estimated and cherished things, rather than nebulously, for a swarm of possibilities.[14]

To Lowell also, life must have seemed while he was living it 'a swarm of possibilities' or at least, when he found himself in situations with several different possible outcomes, he must have felt that he had a choice. 'Around the narrow confines of what has really come to pass', writes Jaspers, 'lie the rejected, missed and vanished possibilities'.[15] Whether they already had it before they began their work, or have acquired it through research, biographers' knowledge of what a particular outcome actually was can often lead them to write in a way which ignores these possibilities and deprives their subjects of choice. Their knowledge gives them a superiority which betrays itself most commonly in familiar references to, for example, the first meeting with a future partner, or the last visit to a certain town, when neither 'first' nor 'last' are aspects of experience of which the subject could, at the time, have been aware. The chief usefulness of these rhetorical devices is that they impart additional narrative significance to episodes which might otherwise have seemed unimportant, but the danger they always run is of seeming too odiously 'knowing'. That danger is increased of course if biographers, in making clear that they know what the result of certain actions will be (and how could they not know?), also suggest that they have a better sense than the subject of the motives which led to them.

With their access to private diaries or letters, and their decoding of literary texts or paintings in biographical terms, biographers of relatively recent figures are often concerned to convey to readers the day-to-day reality or texture of their subjects' experience. For that to be entirely successful, it would have to involve some attempt to share the subject's own ignorance of the future: a wilful suspension of biographical hindsight. One direction in which that effort naturally leads is towards a consideration of what is known, in technical terms, as the counter-factual: speculation as to what might have happened if the subject had gone to university, married X rather than Y, broken a leg. One potent objection to counter-factual thinking has already been suggested. When a man (for example) looks back over the course of his life and wonders what it would have been like had he gone to university, or not married his present wife, he is tempted to imagine that the alteration of one major aspect could have left the rest intact whereas it would necessarily have brought in its train so many others that trying to imagine the different person he might then have been becomes futile. A second objection is that, even when it is a question of a human life still being lived, we have no means of testing counter-factuals. A man moves towards the check-out counters in a supermarket (in this case there is perhaps no harm in being gender-specific). Joining the shorter of two roughly equal queues, he soon realises that, because of a slower cashier or more complicated transactions, the last person to join the other queue will be out of the shop long before he is. He can say with some confidence therefore that he would have saved a good deal of time had he joined the other queue. In the much more complicated matters of education and marriage, however, and because there are no mechanisms for going back to a fork in life's path and trying another direction, there are no comparable ways of testing outcomes. Why bother asking 'What if?' when, in considering a life, there are no reliable ways of ever formulating a satisfactory reply.

In his recent long and detailed introduction to *Virtual History*, a collection of essays in which historians consider such questions as what might have happened if the South had won the American Civil War, or the Germans had succeeded in invading Britain in 1940, Niall Ferguson protests against the prejudices which counter-factual thinking normally encounters among his colleagues. Arguing that, if speculation about alternatives is limited to only those which were available to the participants in any historical situation, it can help moderate the excessive determinism of much historical writing, he associates that determinism with the triumphalism of nineteenth-century science. But developments since then, and quantum mechanics in particular, have reintroduced into science a principle of indeterminacy. The new model he therefore proposes for historical narrative is derived from chaos theory whose proponents (according to Ferguson) fully accept that the world we live in is dominated by scientific determinism but point out that, since it is beyond our present capacity to understand precisely how many events which take place in it are determined, then these might just as well be regarded as chance or accident.[16]

'To the extent that they have anything to say about causes, and are not mere annalists', Antony Flew has written, '[historians and social scientists] cannot but say things which carry implications about what might have been but was not', and he supports his claim with a reference to Max Weber on 'The Logic of Historical Explanation'.[17] If that is true then, insofar as biographers are indeed historians, there are perhaps more among them who are what Flew calls annalists (and I have termed chroniclers) than was previously thought. Weber was concerned with political decision-making and

126

with battles, and he argued that it was impossible to talk about the significance of either without imagining what would have happened if another decision had been taken, or a certain battle had been lost rather than won. But the significance of events in the lives of individuals who are not politicians can rarely be discussed in a similar way because the context in which they occur is not sufficiently well documented and there is no comparable public record of their consequences. However much biographers may want to convey that 'swarm of possibilities' which Henry James says the subject once represented, by the time they come to offer their accounts the possibilities are hard to recapture. The chief narrative model for their labours, moreover, is the nineteenth-century realist novel where, as Birkin tells Ursula in *Women in Love* (referring not of course to novels but to 'life'), 'it all hangs together in the deepest sense'.[18] They could perhaps take a self-conscious decision to go back to the picturesque, in imitation of Boswell or even Aubrey, although it would be hard for them then to distinguish themselves from colleagues who are naturally addicted to shapelessness, and one damned thing after another. For those colleagues, on the other hand, such a move on any large scale would be a triumphant demonstration that they had been speaking prose all their lives.

More reasonably, the effort to restore an element of contingency to a life history might require the elaboration of new narrative forms, analogous to those once associated with the 'new novel' and its successors, even if it is precisely Biography's refusal to abandon the conventions of nineteenth-century realist narrative which (in the opinion of many) has made it so popular. In the meantime the fullness with which some biographers are willing to record their subjects' lives, and the lightness with which they insist on the causal links essential to any 'story', can give readers that room for manoeuvre which allows them to imagine other possible outcomes to the ones described. The claim that the materials of a life are simply being presented to readers so that they can form their own judgements is always more or less disingenuous because presentation must imply both selection and arrangement and the establishment therefore of parameters. But some parameters are narrower than others and one can imagine biographies where there is certainly a shape, but also enough detail and flexibility to allow speculation as to what other shapes there might have been.

*

127

Taking full account of good or bad luck, and all the contingent facts that obtain before a life is nudged in one direction rather than another, may not be possible. If it were, a life might seem less pre-determined but not for that reason any more in the subject's control: the impression of choice he or she had any the less illusory. Little would have been done to counter the fact that, down all the various avenues of explanation: psychological, sociological or organicist, the subject tends to figure as a more or less passive figure. Twenty years after his death, Sartre is still the biographer who, with his notion of existential choice, has most explicitly and self-consciously met the determinist challenge in these approaches derived from social or medical science. The philosophical route by which he was able to defy them is highly complicated and technical; but it became clear enough to a lay public in his biographical essay on Baudelaire. The crucial moment in Baudelaire's life, all the commentators agree, was the re-marriage of his widowed mother when he was seven. In conventional psychoanalytic terms, this would be a trauma from which he was never to recover. For Sartre, on the other hand, it was the moment when Baudelaire chose to be the person he eventually became ('*Nous touchons ici au choix originel que Baulelaire a fait de lui-même*'); and when, instead of passively suffering the solitude into which he was plunged by what he felt was his mother's defection, he embraced it eagerly so that he could at least feel it was his own doing ('*pour qu'elle vienne au moins de lui-même*').[19]

As these last words suggest, what is involved here is not choice in its fullest, most commonly understood sense but rather reaction to circumstances Baudelaire could do nothing about. Relatively soon after having described them, Sartre became dissatisfied with his Baudelaire essay and in particular his failure to provide an adequate context for his subject's behaviour and actions. One consequence of his determination to ensure that his lives of Genet and then Flaubert did not suffer from that same weakness is that the notion of choice, although not abandoned, becomes even more complex and circumscribed. The role of Flaubert's mother in his miseries as a child, Sartre speculates, although not so obvious as that of Baudelaire's, was just as vital. Deducing from the details of her background that she would have loved her husband more than her children, he assumes that the birth of her second son, Gustave, was not the joyful occasion it might have been because by this time she wanted a girl, and because the death of two previous babies at an early age had in any case made her chary of becoming too attached to her new born son. The consequence, Sartre again assumes, is that, although she would have provided competent maternal care (she was after all a doctor's wife), Gustave did not receive in the first months that warm, loving attention which endows children with feelings of self-worth for the rest of their lives. The importance of this was not immediate because of the attention Flaubert received from his father (Achille-Cléophas), but his happy days were over for ever once the process began of training him to serve the family ambition.

A contradiction Sartre makes much of is that between the spectacular success in his profession of Flaubert *père* (the son of a country vet), so characteristic of an age of bourgeois individualism, and the old-fashioned, essentially feudal structures within the Flaubert family, both of whose principals had rural backgrounds. This not only meant that the relation of Gustave to his father was like that of a vassal to his feudal lord, but that the contemporary society's call for everyone to 'get on' was interpreted as applicable to Gustave's family as an integrated, hierarchically organised whole, rather than to its individual members. The discovery that he had difficulty reading therefore, and the failure of his father's efforts to remedy the situation, were interpreted as a collective rather than personal misfortune. It was at this point that Gustave became, especially in comparison with his academically successful elder brother, 'the family idiot'.

The miseries of this position Sartre finds reflected in Flaubert's later writing and correspondence, but particularly in his juvenilia which he reads as scarcely disguised autobiography. It is from the stories Flaubert wrote when he was in his early teens that Sartre deduces his subject must have occasionally contemplated suicide as a solution to his unhappiness. However,

> voluntary death was impossible for this submissive son because it was *forbidden*. Achille-Cléophas brought a younger son into the world, one of the damned, it is true; the father's inflexible rejection condemned this son to death. But to a *slow death*. The child could not ignore the almost exaggerated attentions with which he was surrounded, evidently intended to prolong his life as long as possible. Here we rediscover the contradiction with which we began: suicide is seductive because it co-opts the Other's condemnation and affirms by destroying; but it is also *disobedience*, and Gustave, the passive victim of an abusive father, was so

constituted that he could not disobey. He dreamed of *realising* the
autonomy of his spontaneity through a sovereign act. But the possibility of acting is refused him if he does not act *as if he were another
person.*[20]

Any attempt to give the flavour of Sartre's biography of Flaubert
is likely to remind its admirers of the Greek who would recommend his house to friends by displaying one of its bricks which he
carried in his pocket. Passages that make reasonable sense in isolation are nearly always too long for convenient quotation; the
terminology, which only becomes fully intelligible in context, is
idiosyncratic; and the manner not only abstract in a familiar French
fashion, but decidedly periphrastic. Yet there is perhaps enough
here to indicate how the very intricacy of the analysis, as dense in
its socio-historical sections as it is in the largely psychological one
from which this passage comes, seems to reduce the subject's power
of choice. In these sentences I have quoted of course, choice has
not merely been reduced but disposed of altogether. Gustave might
have wanted to act spontaneously and perform a 'sovereign act',
but he is 'so constituted' (*ainsi fait*) that, although he might dream
of suicide, he could never go through with it.

*

As I have said before, suicide raises the issue of self-determination
in an acute form because we are inclined to think of it as such a
private, personal act, an assertion of 'one's right to choose' as Pavese
puts it. The authors of two biographies of Virginia Woolf published
in 1996, Hermione Lee and Panthea Reid, describe the prelude to
her death very well. A key to understanding in Reid's book as a
whole is sibling rivalry and she therefore places special emphasis
on the last letter Woolf received from her sister, Vanessa. Partly by
challenging the usually accepted chronology of Woolf's three
suicide notes, Reid offers this letter as 'a major provocation for
Virginia's suicide'.[21] This makes the relationship with Vanessa
crucially influential on Woolf from her cradle to her grave, but it
does not mean that Reid ignores other important 'provocations':
the war, her lack of satisfaction with the recently completed *Between
the Acts*, and above all her fear of once more going mad.

On the effect of the war especially, Lee, who is not inclined to
give the letter from Vanessa any special prominence, is admirably
detailed and evocative. A sign of how deeply her work is imagined

is the vividness with which she is able to convey the Woolfs' apprehension as they looked up from their Sussex garden to watch stray episodes from the Battle of Britain, aware that they would be in one or other of the groups targeted for arrest should the Germans succeed in invading. Throughout her book she chronicles carefully the extent to which Woolf's self-esteem was dependent on her writing, the devastating effect of hostile criticism as it resonated with her own insecurities, and the danger of the period just after she had finished a book – especially when she was dissatisfied with what she had just done but not yet in the right frame of mind for beginning to write again. Unlike Reid, Lee has sentences which suggest that Woolf's husband may also have helped to provoke her death by 'no longer paying very close attention to her state of mind';[22] but in general her emphasis does not fall on the blame which can be attached to this or that person. What she stresses instead is Woolf's courage in deciding to kill herself as she felt the approach of another breakdown. Some people who have in the past lived through psychotic interludes learn to recognise the warning signs and are capable of checking themselves into a hospital before it is too late. Justifiably lacking confidence in the available treatments, beginning once again to hear strange voices, and feeling at fifty-nine no longer resilient enough to withstand another attack, Woolf claimed in her suicide notes that killing herself was the best way out: not only for herself but also for her family. The consequence is that for Lee, as indeed for Reid, this seems to have been suicide not, as the coroner put it, while the balance of the mind was disturbed, but in the rational expectation that it would shortly be so.

In neither biography is this interpretation argued for explicitly: a number of possible determinants are advanced and it is more through rhetorical emphasis than reasoning that readers become aware of the ones to which they are expected to attach most importance. The method is traditional and can perhaps be illustrated in miniature by a passage from Johnson in which he is describing the yearly visits Swift would pay to his mother in Leicester, while he was living with Temple.

> He travelled on foot, unless some violence of weather drove him into a waggon, and at night he would go to a penny lodging, where he purchased clean sheets for sixpence. This practice Lord Orrery imputes to his innate love of grossness and vulgarity: some may ascribe it to his desire of surveying human life through all its varieties; and others,

perhaps with equal probability, to a passion which seems to have been deep fixed in his heart – the love of a shilling.[23]

All three explanations for Swift's conduct are described by Johnson as being equally probable, but the rhythm of his sentences, the positioning of his clauses, and the place this passage occupies in the context of the life as a whole, leave the reader in little doubt as to which he prefers. In a similar way, although on a far larger scale, Lee and Reid set out the various factors which may have driven Woolf to suicide; but the immediate one they both end by privileging is her fear of encroaching madness and the trouble that would bring to those she cared about most. In doing this, they are both confirming the subject's ability to be authoritative about her own state, and granting her the power of choice.

The general effect of these two biographers' treatment of Woolf becomes clearer when compared with the way Kenneth Lynn deals with the suicide of Ernest Hemingway. From almost his first page to his last, Lynn depicts his subject as the prisoner of his family background. When he moved to Key West in 1930 with his wealthy second wife, Hemingway's circumstances altered dramatically but, 'Change . . . was no guarantee of growth. He remained unable to transcend the past and forgive his mother'; 'in regard to his father', we are told on the next page, 'he was likewise caught in a web of unworked-out emotion'.[24] It is the continuing tightening of this web which, in Lynn's account, leads inexorably to suicide, and there is nothing in his description of his subject before the act, or of the act itself, which is suggestive of either rational choice or heroism. In comparison with the sympathy Lee and Reid extend to Woolf, Lynn's narrative is hostile. He notes how Hemingway came to feel that his father, who shot himself in 1928, had been cowardly in allowing himself to be driven to suicide by his wife; but since for Lynn unresolved conflict with that wife in her role as mother is the key to his subject's character, Hemingway's own death, more than thirty years later, becomes by implication an act of cowardice also. (Even those biographers who spend most of their time on the attack, can find themselves inadvertently in thrall to their subjects' own terms of reference.) That his father killed himself is not taken by Lynn as a sign of any genetic predisposition towards suicide in Hemingway; and no special role is accorded the electroconvulsive therapy (ECT) he was given in his last months. He confirms energetically his subject's own anguished sense in his last years that his creative powers were on the wane, attributing the phenomenal success of *The Old*

132

Man and the Sea to extra-literary factors; but he does not suggest that this could ever be a compelling reason for killing oneself, even in such a dedicated writer. His account of his subject's death reinforces the chief purpose of his biography which is to demonstrate that the tough guy image Hemingway himself projected, and the public enthusiastically took up, was a sham. Even if there had been a suicide note in which Hemingway gave apparently rational explanations for his action, it is unlikely that it would have made a difference when all his other statements about himself are treated by Lynn with scepticism, and the whole drive of the narrative is to show a man dying in the same self-ignorance in which he lived.

For Reid and Lee the survival of the suicide notes is crucial in a way it could never have been for Lynn. Although both these biographers of Woolf may suggest qualifications as to the authority of their subject, neither is willing to deny it by ignoring or contradicting what Woolf herself had to say about her death. The reasons she gave in those notes for killing herself are the reasons they largely accept. It was not any final notes which determined how Ann Sexton's biographer would think about her subject's suicide but the tapes of sessions with her psychiatrist. For Daine Wood Middlebrook these offered far more than mere information, 'they provided intimacy', and as a result, 'I came to see [Sexton's] self-inflicted death as an act that protected her from worse to come; I came even, to see it as timely – an action taken with care and performed with dignity'.[25] Because Middlebrook had heard her subject talking about her own mental sufferings, she felt obliged to accept as deliberate and rational the means she took to end them.

When in 1953 Sylvia Plath tried to kill herself, she left no note; but she later described her reasons for the attempt in terms much like Woolf's. There had seemed no point in living on, she wrote in a letter, when all the future held was 'an eternity of hell . . . in a mental hospital'; and to kill herself would in any case be 'more merciful and inexpensive to my family'. This was why she had decided to make use of her 'last ounce of free choice'.[26] Yet it is hardly 'free choice' one is made aware of when, in her excellent biography of Plath, Anne Stevenson treats her subject's final and successful suicide attempt ten years later. This can be associated with the absence of any explicit testimony from the subject herself as to why she had *chosen* self-destruction, especially as Stevenson's book happens to provide a good, general illustration of the extent to which the form of any biography is determined by the documents available. For the first half, she is able to draw on Plath's remarkably detailed and intimate diaries, but those which might have helped her in the composition of the second have been either lost or destroyed. The consequence is that, in the description of Plath's earlier life, we are made acutely aware of the depth of her mental anguish and the impressive degree of her self-understanding. We sympathise with her suffering and admire the clarity with which she could often analyse its causes. With letters and poems on which to rely but *without the diaries*, Stevenson's account of Plath's later years is by comparison necessarily more 'external': we listen to witness after witness describing how impossibly rude and difficult she could be in social situations but are rarely if ever able either to hear her own explanations of why she acted as she did, or know if she understood how offensive her behaviour could sometimes be to others. The overriding impression is therefore of someone out of control, unable to see herself as others saw her or decide her own destiny in matters either large or small.

In the later part of Stevenson's biography, Plath appears as Hemingway does in Lynn's account of him: someone driven inexorably towards self-destruction by the severity of inner conflicts. The key to these in Plath's case is presented to us as the death of her father when she was eight. It is this which explains her overdependence on her mother, her tendency to look for father substitutes among the men to whom she became attached, and her acute anxiety they would abandon her just as she felt her father had. In a passage from her journals, written when she was undergoing psychotherapy in Boston in 1958, Plath herself commented on her tendency to identify her husband with her father, and explained her rage at any hint that Ted Hughes might be interested in other women with a reference to the way her father had, by dying, 'deserted [her] forever'. 'It was beginning to bear in on Sylvia', Stevenson comments, 'how closely a Freudian explanation fitted the enigma of her strangeness'.[27] Whether or not 'Freudian' is the appropriate word here, 'fitted' (rather than solved) is an excellent one; but the scepticism it suggests does not prevent Stevenson from adopting more or less completely the explanation for her miseries which, with the help of her analyst, Plath herself evolved. Although there can be no certainty that this explanation is valid, it is hard to see how Stevenson could have done anything else when it was expressed in so many memorable poems. To a considerable extent, Plath dictates to Stevenson through those poems the terms in which her life story should be told; and yet this does not mean that her biographer grants her the power, accorded to Woolf by both Lee and Reid, of having been able to step to one side of her difficulties and decide in a recognisably rational way that enough was enough: the exercise of what Plath called, in relation to her first suicide attempt, 'that last ounce of free choice'. The terms in which her death is described leave it open to the reader to sympathise with her misfortunes, but not to celebrate the clear-eyed courage of her final act as both Lee and Reid celebrate Woolf's.

The general tendency of Stevenson's account of Plath's death is towards psychological determinism, but she is sometimes willing to entertain other possible explanations. Some of these are organicist, although not in the sense of an appeal to any inherited, biochemical disposition towards suicide. The electroconvulsive therapy to which Plath had been subjected in 1953 may, Stevenson suggests, have 'substantially contributed to her cool, logically-arrived-at decision' to attempt suicide in that year; and it may also be that 'she never really recovered from it, that it changed her personality permanently'. Just before her later, successful attempt, Plath's doctor prescribed a course of antidepressants. As he admitted, these could sometimes have an unintended effect, or more precisely (to use his words): 'There may be a point at which the antidepressant begins to make a depressed person a little more active, though still desolate, hence capable of carrying out a determined, desperate action'.[28]

Luck is certainly recognised as having possibly played its part. It was unfortunate, we are told, that the telephone of the London flat into which Plath moved took such a long time to be connected (so that on the night of her death she could not call for help); and also that it was so cold: 'Had the weather been easier, Sylvia might not have felt quite so desperate'.[29] Yet as in the first two reasons Johnson gives for Swift's meanness, it is neither luck nor biochemistry which receive the emphasis. This is reserved for the problems which had dogged her since her childhood or, to put it more crudely and more generally, for the fact that, since Plath had always been unstable, her death could come as no surprise. To see matters in that light might be entirely justifiable, and remain so even if a lengthy suicide note, offering explanations analogous to those she associated with her earlier attempt, were now discovered.

Each case is different and has to be judged on its own terms, although there are conventions of thinking in every culture – intellectual frameworks within which we habitually contemplate self-destruction – which may complicate that task. It might seem strange to some, for example, that Sartre should investigate in such detail how a very young boy contemplated suicide when we are instinctively inclined to restrict the power of doing that satisfactorily to adults. At thirty Plath was certainly old enough to know how she thought and felt, but in her case age can play a different role. In the perhaps wholly irrelevant rationalist attitude sometimes adopted towards suicide, one of the questions the dead person is imagined as having asked is, 'What after all do I still have to live for?' A negative answer to that question can seem less 'reasonable' for a woman only thirty than for one who, like Woolf, was fifty nine when she died. That in her suicide note Woolf mentions her age as one reason for not wanting to go on, strongly reinforces the impression that hers was an act of free will. The young Flaubert was incapable of committing suicide, one might say, because he could never disobey his lord and father; Plath's life-long psychological difficulties eventually drove her over the edge; but Woolf reviewed her situation with relative calm and concluded that another bout of insanity was more than either she, or her husband, should be asked to bear.

It may be age was one of factors which inclined Lee and Reid to take a view of Woolf's situation that makes it an example of self-determination; but the inapplicability of general rules in this context is shown by how little age matters to Lynn. By the time of his death in 1961, Hemingway was sixty two and afflicted with a variety of painful and debilitating illnesses or disorders. In 1982, his much younger brother Leicester became, at sixty seven, the third member of the Hemingway family to shoot himself after being told by his doctor that he would have to have both his legs amputated.[30] Even taking into account the power of example, this action could well be interpreted as an instance of rational choice. But in Lynn's account of Hemingway (which might of course be as justifiable as any other) neither age nor illness has a bearing that makes suicide the reasonable option Lee and Reid finally make us feel it was for Woolf. Rather than rescuing his subject from determinism, his description of the final act only confirms its hold.

8

Compatibility, Sartre and Long Biographies

How can one deny that biography is of outstanding significance for the understanding of the great context of the historical world? After all, it is the interaction between the depths of human nature and the universal context of broad historical life which has an effect at every point of history and this is the most fundamental connection between life itself and history.

Our problem becomes all the more urgent: is biography possible?

(Wilhelm Dilthey, *Meaning in History*, ed. H. P. Rickman (1962), p. 90)

One of the chapters in W. M. Runyan's *Life Histories and Psychobiography* is devoted to the question of why Van Gogh should have cut off the lower half of his left ear, and then gone to the local brothel in order to entrust it to a prostitute he knew. Runyan lists thirteen possible explanations for this bizarre event, most of them taken from A. J. Lubin's *Stranger on the Earth: A Psychological Biography of Vincent Van Gogh.* Not surprisingly, in none of these does Van Gogh figure as someone who, having taken a rational view of his situation, decided that self-mutilation was the sensible option. Several of the thirteen explanations are compatible in that they relate to different aspects of the episode: to the mood which determined Van Gogh's attack on himself, for instance, or to its particular object. Thus some interpret his action as an attempt to redirect back towards himself the attention of his brother Theo, who had recently become engaged, while the choice of the ear can be explained by visits to the bullfight at Arles where he had seen the matador cut off the dead bull's ear and present it to a woman in

the crowd. Yet although some of the explanations might be recon-
ciled in this way, and all of them fall roughly into the same area of
psychodynamics, there are several which do not sit very comfortably
alongside each other. There seems to be a lurking contradiction,
for example, between the idea that this was an episode of symbolic
castration, resulting from homosexual impulses aroused by the presence of Gauguin; and the notion that, during the psychotic attacks
to which Van Gogh was subject, he would hear strange voices which
he hoped to silence by the amputation of his ear.[1]

Biographers are not of course obliged to reconcile incompatible
determinants: they can simply allow a number of different opinions
to be heard. Anne Stevenson's approach is overwhelmingly psychological but she very reasonably shows no discomfort in repeating
without comment a view of Plath's suicide expressed by her doctor:

> I believe ... she was liable to large swings of mood, but so excessive
> that a doctor inevitably thinks in terms of brain chemistry. This does
> not reduce the concurrent importance of marriage break-up or of
> exhaustion after a period of unusual artistic activity or from recent
> infectious illness or from the difficulties of being a responsible, prac-
> tical mother. The full explanation has to take all these factors into
> account and more. But the irrational compulsion to end it makes me
> think that the body was governing the mind.[2]

Precisely how the stress which resulted from the break-up of Plath's
marriage is 'concurrent' with the question of her brain chemistry
is the doctor's problem not Stevenson's; she is merely recording
his opinion and leaving the reader to deduce how much it conflicts
with her own. Real difficulty is raised, however, when Panthea Reid
not only repeats but also adopts Thomas Caramagno's diagnosis of
Virginia Woolf as 'manic-depressive', even though she spends most
of her own energy in her biography on illustrating the causal effects
of Woolf's rivalry with her sister. Carmagno's insistence on his diagnosis was in polemical opposition to various 'psychobiographies'
which had recently appeared, and he was keen to establish that
many of the features of Woolf's behaviour which had been attributed to childhood trauma were in fact a consequence of
biochemical imbalance. In an appendix on manic depression where
Reid acknowledges her debt to Caramagno, she describes him as
arguing that the cause of Woolf's 'mood disorder was an inherited
syndrome which could be triggered by physical and mental circumstances';[3] but that the word 'trigger' satisfactorily reconciles her
approach with his is not an impression borne out by his book.

138

In attacking the reliance of many of Woolf's biographers on psychoanalysis, Caramagno sees how inevitably it often conflicts with what at one moment he calls 'neurobiography'. Shrewdly noting that a Freudian paradigm will be popular with the authors of lives because it allows them to 'explain mentality through events, which are, of course, the staple of life histories', he attacks Shirley Panken's ingenious psychoanalytic interpretation of Woolf's hallucinations on the grounds that 'neurotics, who might be supposed to make such associations, rarely hallucinate, and manics, who often do, are driven by biochemistry, not by mental trauma'. When he comes to deal directly with why Woolf might have committed suicide, he points out that, since manic-depressive relapses increase with age, she may have died 'for nothing more meaningful than the fact that the biochemistry of aging bodies changes and intensifies depression'. In a surprising excursus into Durkheim territory he suggests that the season may have been influential and reproduces a chart to show a 'striking peak incidence of suicide in May, a rise that begins in March' (the month at the end of which Woolf drowned herself). Coming back to his own ground, Caramagno then reports the frequency with which manic-depressives turn to alcohol, a short-term remedy which always worsens their condition. If, as he speculates, Woolf had become an alcoholic then 'the resulting neurochemical changes could have contributed to the severity of her last depression and increased the risk of suicide'. He knows that there could never be one simple solution to the problem of Woolf's death but is anxious to insist that 'we cannot hope fully to explain Woolf's suicide by means of traumatic events in her life'.[4]

Without denying that psychological and physical events can work in concert, Caramagno is always keen to assert the primacy of the latter, and he has a view of 'triggering' which is in marked contrast to the simplicity of Reid's:

> An event can activate a genetically determined, pre-existing affective vulnerability, usually in the first few episodes, but once the disorder has been established, life events usually play little or no role in new breakdowns. . . . Biology, not psychodymanics, is the primary mechanism of predisposition; life events can trigger but not cause madness, and many breakdowns are initiated by purely biological changes. It is also possible that traumatic life events only appear to precede affective episodes, that breakdowns begin biochemically and subtly, skewing the patient's perception of and reaction to a subsequent event, causing him or her to misinterpret and magnify its causative power.[5]

This is not exactly a picture of psychological and organicist approaches to the explanation of human behaviour working harmoniously together, and Caramagno is too knowledgeable to be unaware of the conflict there often is between them. A forceful champion of the biochemical, he points out that, 'Biology lifts from Woolf's shoulders the derogatory weight of responsibility for her illness'.[6] This is true but then the same could be said of certain forms of appeal to the Freudian unconscious, and the consequence of both approaches is that they will also tend to diminish, if not entirely discredit, the courage or heroism of Woolf's final act.

So antagonist are certain methods of explanation that one solution is to regard them as simply belonging to quite disparate fields of knowledge, or to different 'language strata', '*régime de discours*', as some commentators would prefer to say. In that case, the responsibility of enquirers is not to synthesise, but rather to make sure that they are absolutely clear about the kind of question they want to ask. The lifting of an arm can be explained in terms of the neuro-physical mechanisms which allow that action to take place, or the intention of its owner to call a taxi. This is thorny philosophical territory whose general climate Anthony Flew has attempted to lighten for the lay reader by reference to an Andy Capp cartoon. 'There was twelve light ales in the pantry this morning', says Mrs Capp, four-square and Northern, 'now there's only ONE! 'ow d'yer explain THAT!'. 'It was dark there', replies Andy, 'I didn't see it'.[7] To properly understand and make clear the questions one is asking may be conceived as the only real responsibility the biographer has.

In fact, of course, rigour in these matters is not only beyond the expertise of most biographers, it is also, and perhaps very properly, against their instinct. Like Panken or Caramagno, some of them do approach the problem of other lives from a single, clearly defined point of view; but most are content to lay out as many determinants of a particular action as seem to them probable, privileging those they prefer with Johnsonian emphasis. On occasions however, they also tend to seek refuge in 'overdetermination', a fashionable notion which seems to have made its way into the non-specialist world of biography largely through the agency of Freud. Its appeal is that it sounds technical although since, on examination, it often turns out to amount to no more than the truism that a single effect can have multiple causes, its further weakness is that it conveys the impression of solving a problem while doing no more than rephrasing it. In certain circumstances a weakness of that kind can of course be an advantage, but 'overdetermination' does not help when the determinants alleged appear incompatible, and the way Freud himself sometimes finds refuge in it ought surely to make a biographer pause. In 'The Wolf Man', for example, Freud reminds his readers that his patient's preference for sexual intercourse *a tergo* had been traced back to the primal scene, when he saw his parents copulating. What makes it a 'case of overdetermination' however is that, 'The person who was the subject of his observation of this posture during intercourse was, after all, his father in the flesh, and it may also have been from him that he had inherited this constitutional predilection'. Although wearing both a belt and braces certainly diminishes the likelihood of trousers falling down, adding one reason to another does not make an intellectual case any stronger if both are dubious; and if one of them could be established satisfactorily (the case for inheritance, for example), it is hard to see why there would be any need for the other. The same worries arise a little later when Freud is trying to deal more directly with his critics' scepticism about the primal scene. Whether or not its content was a fantasy or a reality, he writes (surprisingly), is 'not a matter of very great importance'. This is because, 'These scenes of observing parental intercourse, of being seduced in childhood, and of being threatened with castration are unquestionably an inherited endowment, a phylogenetic heritage, but they may just as easily be acquired by personal experience'.[8] The use of 'unquestionable' here is staggering; but if it is a fact that we all inherit a disposition to see our parents copulating, even though we never have an opportunity for doing so; if, that is, the primal scene is a common fantasy, why has Freud spent so much time attempting to establish its historicity and the details of the Wolf Man's background? The truth is that 'overdetermination' is often used by Freud as an alternative he can fall back on when the case he is arguing comes under attack so that, insofar as biographers do borrow from him, it is a dangerous concept, always liable to obscure the issue and promise more than it can perform. Certainly Plath's doctor could have appealed to it all he liked without the effect of his remarks becoming any clearer.

*

What still makes Jean-Paul Sartre so important and interesting for the main topic of this book is that he is the biographer who was most preoccupied with the problem of how the various items in an explanation could be brought together and *hierarchisés* (to use his own term).[9] This is the issue he can be found struggling with in the diaries he wrote when he was briefly a soldier during what is known in English as the 'phoney war'. Reading Emil Ludwig's popular biography of Kaiser Wilhem II had reminded him of conversations with Simone de Beauvoir before being called up in which they had agreed that, in the explanation of any historical event, there are 'layers of signification' which remain parallel so that 'it's not possible to move from one to another'. 'A common error of historians', he writes in his diary,

> is to put these explanations on the same level, linking them by an 'and' – as if their juxtaposition ought to give rise to an organised totality, with ordered structures, which would be the phenomenon itself unfolding its causes and various processes.

But in fact, Sartre concludes, 'the significations remain separate'. Using Ludwig's information, Sartre attempts in a number of entries to show how such a personal detail as the Kaiser's withered left arm, torn from its shoulder socket at birth, could be integrated with other features of his life 'in order to determine to what extent William II is the *cause* of the '14 war'.[10] The key element in this integration is the Sartrean notion of the 'project', which involves external events not acting upon a passive individual but that individual 'projecting himself as a totality through them'. 'Human reality', Sartre would say in *Being and Nothingness*, 'announces and defines itself by the ends it pursues';[11] but those ends are the consequence of certain crucial choices. For Sartre, this is demonstrated by the career of William II who, although he was so different from most other people in being born to rule, was not positively obliged to embrace that destiny in a way which forced him continually to disguise his withered arm. 'We mustn't say, like Ludwig', Sartre writes,

> *'Feeling* himself a weakling, he sought to emphasise his strength'. For by making himself master in the intellectual realm, and by cynically displaying his disability, he could have *really been* strong. Instead – understanding himself as a soldier-emperor by divine right, who had to surpass and deny his disability as a scandal through perpetual struggle – he *chose* that his strength should be weakness. He *chose* the hidden flaw. He *'made himself'* a weakling. In other words, he chose himself to be defective.[12]

It is not hard to see how these words could be considered a dry run for the way in which Baudelaire's life-choices (and his syphilis) would be described.

Through the fact that William II had an English mother who supposedly despised him because of his disability, Sartre associates the withered arm with the Kaiser's anglophobia and therefore with his foreign policy. This is hardly a complete solution to all those causal questions raised by World War I which he had begun by asking himself, but he would continue to work at their more general biographical aspects as long as he lived. Chapter ii of the Fourth Part of *Being and Nothingness* opens with an attack on all previous biographical accounts of Flaubert for offering only the illusion of explanation and understanding. Paul Bourget, for example, had derived Flaubert's literary temperament or vocation from the 'two-fold feeling of his grandiose ambition and his invincible power', experienced during adolescence. That for Sartre was clearly not sufficiently specific: it did not offer the causal links which would explain why Flaubert became a writer rather than an adventurer, debauchee, mystic, painter or actor.

> The *transitions*, the becomings, the transformations, have been care-fully veiled from us, and we have been limited to putting order into the succession by invoking empirically established but literally unin-telligible sequences (the need to act preceding in the adolescent the need to write). Yet this is what is called psychology. Open any biog-raphy at random, and this is the kind of description you will find more or less interspersed with accounts of external events and allusions to the great explanatory idols of our epoch – heredity, education, envi-ronment, physiological constitution.[13]

The 'hero' of Sartre's pre-war novel *Nausea* is writing a biography of an eighteenth-century courtier, the Marquis de Rollebon, but abandons the enterprise because he feels that all the hypotheses come from his side with not a glimmer of illumination from his subject's: that instead of offering insight into the past, they do no more than provide a convenient form for what he happens to know.[14] In contrast to Roquentin, Sartre developed after the war an extraordinary confidence in his ability to enjoy complete knowl-edge of historical figures and to do much better therefore than the biographers he is castigating here. Originally written as an intro-duction to an edition of the *Ecrits Intimes*, his account of Baudelaire is short; but his life of Jean Genet (*Saint Genet: Comédien et Martyr*) is a lengthy affair and, notoriously, the biography of Flaubert, which

Sartre spent his last years writing, is even lengthier. It is there above all that he would attempt to show how *all* the elements which might help us to understand a historical figure can be harmonised into a coherent life story.

Before beginning *The Family Idiot*, Sartre had laid the theoretical ground in *Search for a Method*, the introduction to his *Critique of Dialectical Reason*. It was the growing impact of Marxism on his thinking that obliged him to modify the optimistic notions about the extent to which individuals are free to choose the way they live, apparent in the Baudelaire essay. *Search for a Method* accepts the basic premises of Marx but, in an effort to 'reconquer man within Marxism', protests vigorously against a simple-minded economic determinism. Anyone, Sartre claims, seriously interested in understanding Robespierre's behaviour in 1793, or why Flaubert became a writer, cannot refer themselves directly to the underlying economic realities which give rise to class conflict, but needs to take into account a number of what he calls 'mediations'. One of these is 'psychoanalysis' in his own, non-Freudian interpretation of that term (one which, in addition to many other differences, takes away the centrality of sex while retaining the empasis on early familial relations). It is only through existential psychoanalysis that he feels the vital role played in a life by the family can be appreciated. The second 'mediation' is sociology, but with a historical dimension which Sartre accuses its immediate post-war American practitioners of neglecting and a realisation that sociological observers can never be separated from whatever they observe. These disciplines clearly involve different methods of analysis. In attempting to unify them Sartre is faithful to his notion of the project: 'Everything changes', he writes at one point in *Search for a Method*, 'if one considers that society is presented to each man as a *perspective of the future* and that this future penetrates to the heart of each one as a real motivation for his behaviour'.[15]

What is required in investigating the project, he argues, is a highly sophisticated and specifically 'dialectical' approach. The key to this is that it is not inhibited by chronology but both 'progressive and regressive': continually looking forwards and back; and that it involves also a constant coming and going (*un va-et-vient*) between the particular circumstances of the subject and the larger socio-economic context. It is this method, Sartre claims, that 'will progressively determine a biography by examining in depth the period, and the period by studying the biography'. The approach

144

he describes, with many more details and subtle qualifications than I can take account of here, gives in his view a 'totalising movement' (*un mouvement totalisateur*) to what otherwise is always likely to be an inert succession of data, and allows the biographer to discover the 'multidimensional *unity*' of human behaviour.[16] In 1971, after two volumes of the Flaubert biography had appeared, he was asked in an interview whether his ambitions as a biographer did not mean that he was attributing to himself powers of reading into the hearts of other human beings which only God could possess. Not at all, he replied,

> The underlying intention of the *Flaubert* is to show that in the end everything is communicable and that one can, without being God but just a man like any other, arrive at perfect understanding of a man, if one has all the necessary elements. I can anticipate (*prévoir*) Flaubert, I know him and that's my aim: to prove that every man is perfectly knowable as long as one uses the appropriate methods and has available the necessary documents.[17]

The obligation to give Sartre more extended attention than any other biographer in this study arises because, neither during nor since his time, has anyone with a similar grasp of the problems of explanation (and similarly impressive literary powers) made such large claims for the form and been so sanguine about our ability to understand other human beings.

*

Flaubert was a figure who had fascinated Sartre all his life, and there is nothing skimped or half-hearted about the biography which he eventually undertook after so many years of preparatory thinking. In his Preface he describes *The Family Idiot* as the continuation of *Search for a Method* and claims that he has set out to discover what, in our day, can be learned about a man. He says he will reply to this question by 'totalising' all that is known about Flaubert. Alluding once more to the issues which had preoccupied him in relation to Kaiser Wilhelm, he wonders (rhetorically) whether this will not mean ending up with 'layers of heterogeneous and irreducible meanings'. His book will attempt to prove, he goes on, that the 'irreducibility is only apparent'.[18]

In the context of a principal concern in this chapter (the conflict Caramagno points to between psychological and organicist explanations), there is at least one way in which this attempt is a failure.

A crucial event in Flaubert's life took place when he was twenty two and driving in his carriage with his brother, near to the town of Pont-L'Evêque. Without warning, he collapsed into a cataleptic state and was subject to such sudden attacks for a good deal of his future life (because they were often accompanied by convulsions, epilepsy was the favoured diagnosis of the time). Chiefly as a result of this event, Flaubert gave up his law studies in Paris and 'retired' to a life of letters in his home town. For many commentators this determining episode was a fateful *accident* – one of them ascribes it to 'some earlier brain damage'[19] – but not for a moment does Sartre entertain the idea that it might have had a physical cause. In his long analysis in volume ii of his biography, he describes the episode at one point as '*l'option névrotique*',[20] and he conceives it as the 'choice' Flaubert made which simultaneously confirmed him in his literary vocation and challenged (as well as punished) his father, who had wanted him to take up a more orthodox career. Heredity, in the organicist sense, and physiological constitution – two of those 'great explanatory idols' of biography to which Sartre had referred in *Being and Nothingness* – are not here integrated into a 'total' narrative, but polemically combatted and denied, and that is true throughout his book.

In his account of how Flaubert's elder brother was destined to succeed his father as the leading doctor in Rouen, for example, Sartre tells his reader not to ask what would have happened if the brother had been stupid. To do that would be to make the history of the Flaubert family a matter of red corpuscles and grey matter, and to adopt the same middle-class materialism dear to Flaubert's father. The confidence which that father continually manifested in his elder son was (Sartre insists) not a result of the latter's exceptional intelligence; rather, the intelligence itself was a consequence of the irrevocable decision, made at his conception or perhaps before, that as the first born male he would be the family's crown prince. Writing later of Flaubert's very early ambitions to be an actor, Sartre comments that these resulted from need and not ability: 'As an actor, Gustave was not *gifted*'. A footnote attached to the italicised word (*doué*) reads: 'No-one is'.[21] This is a position which might well be adopted by anyone anxious to defend the way D. W. Harding implicitly derives Cézanne's originality from troubles with *his* father. 'Gifts', 'talent', 'genius' – all these terms are, in the logic of Sartre's approach, different ways biographers have of hiding from themselves (and their readers) ignorance of what they are talking about.

Sartre's battle against notions of the innate, his determination to attribute as much as possible to nurture (in the widest sense), and as little as possible to nature, is one of the reasons he probes so far back into Flaubert's childhood. Not even he wants to deny that, when a baby is born, there is a certain physical 'given'; but it is how that baby is treated on its first arrival which, in his view, will determine what he calls its 'constitution'. Temperament, or in William James's words 'that certain average tone of self-feeling', is not for Sartre a question of genes, but largely a consequence of the relationship with the mother in the earliest days. It is not a series of biochemical accidents which made Flaubert passive, melancholy, and inclined to boredom (*ennui*), but rather what Sartre frequently describes as his subject's protohistory and his prehistoric times.

For historians to investigate the *pre*historic is a contradiction in terms: how can they begin to discover the true state of affairs when there is so little surviving evidence? Sartre is acutely aware of this problem as it relates to the life history of individuals, but a bold speculator nonetheless. To establish why Flaubert's mother should have been the type of woman more attached to her husband than her children (a reason for her not being especially overjoyed at the birth of Gustave ancillary to the several major ones he presents), he feels that he needs to investigate *her* earliest days also. But that is hard when there is so little evidence as to the manner in which she experienced them.

> Caroline Flaubert, daughter of Dr Fleuriot and of Anne-Charlotte-Justine née Cambremer de Croixmare, had the saddest of childhoods. Her parents were married on 27 November, 1792; people said it was like a novel and even spoke of an elopement. In any event, they loved each other passionately. On 7 September 1793, the young wife died in childbirth. The infant girl had to be put out to nurse. It often happens that the widower resents the child who has killed his wife; above all, the criminal offspring is very soon conscious of its guilt. We won't swear that this was true of poor Caroline: but in any case the doctor did not love her enough to want to live on: *he suffered his grief bodily*, as one ought, declined in health, and in 1803 passed away. His daughter was then 10 years old. It seems that she had spent most of these years in an empty house, at Pont-Audemer, in the company of an inconsolable father, gloomy as all widowers are. Double frustration: motherless, she adored her father; inattentive, perhaps morose, he at least was there, living with her. When this flickering flame was blown out, the little girl was alone. She lost the love of Dr Fleuriot – who was scarcely extravagant with it – and above all, the joy of loving.

> Orphans obscurely feel that they have been disavowed: in dying, their disgusted parents have denied and abandoned them. Did Caroline, already convinced she was at fault, see her father's precipitous departure as a condemnation? We don't know. What we do know on the other hand is that from then on her future needs were engraved on her heart: she would marry only her father.[22]

Bernard Crick's objection to many contemporary biographers was that they purported to know what was going on inside other people's minds and were therefore writing bad novels rather than good lives. Certainly, that *The Family Idiot* is really a novel is a familiar claim, or charge. Yet speculation as to how others think and feel is an essential aspect of social life so that there would be a case for arguing, not that biography borrows the habit from novels, but that it has an origin common to both literary forms in the way people interact with one another. The difference in social life, of course, is that the speculation concerns living people and can therefore often be established as wrong or right. For biographers (rather than novelists) the frequent impossibility of ever being sure whether it is one or the other means that they ought always to be committed to indicating to their readers that what they offer is in fact speculation, however probable and well-informed it might appear.

The conventional way to signal speculation is through words like 'perhaps', 'seems' and use of the conditional (features of style which copy editors then do their best to remove). In this passage, Sartre signals it more via a certain degree of quiet humour and a tone which tells us that he no more expects us to believe that *all* widowers are gloomy ('*tous les veufs sont sinistres*') than Lehar would have expected his listeners to think all widows were merry. A major difference from a novel is that the dates and names are accurate, or at least freely offer themselves for verification in historical records. Sartre's method for drawing conclusions from this data is the same as Dr Johnson's when, in the sentences I quoted in my first chapter, he is trying to fathom Harley's motives for responding so indecisively to the demands of the October Club. A certain number of general psychological principles are proposed from which inferences as to the particular case being examined are then drawn. In this passage, one of these principles is that a child whose birth led to the death of her mother might later feel guilt on that account; another, that children can experience the death of a parent as desertion (as Sylvia Plath certainly appears to have done). Yet crucial to the effect, and very different to what is usually found in fiction, are the disclaimers which accompany the inferences. Sartre cannot swear that Caroline felt guilt because of her mother's death and he does not know precisely how she responded to her father's. These signals ought to be enough to ensure that when readers come to the final assertion they take it, not as a statement of absolute fact, but a hypothesis to be tested when it is placed alongside all the other details aiming to show that Caroline Flaubert was an unusually dependent, grateful and obedient wife.

Assertive, confident, persuasive, Sartre can often make his reader feel that he goes too far, but this is not because he is writing a novel (the passage I have quoted above is as 'novelistic' as he ever gets), but rather a biography with unusual ambitions. A more well-founded objection to his procedures was voiced by two admirers who published books on his work in the early 1980s. In *Sartre as Biographer*, Douglas Collins is writing of *Saint Genet* rather than the *The Family Idiot* when he claims that, 'Sartre often seems to operate on the basis of a coherence rather than correspondence theory of truth. Propositions are considered true to the extent that they agree, not with empirically verifiable data, but with other propositions in the series'; yet the general context makes clear that he would be willing to apply these remarks to both books. Michael Scriven makes a similar point specifically in relation to the account of infancy in the Flaubert life: 'It is not necessarily what actually happened, merely what Sartre believes must have happened in order to lead to the next stage in the dialectical process'.[23] These charges are particularly serious because, in *Search for a Method*, Sartre had been so sarcastically withering about what he calls there a priori thinking, describing how the granite on which Budapest is built came to be considered unhelpfully 'counter-revolutionary' by a leader of the Hungarian Communist Party who had decided, a priori, that his capital ought to be provided with an underground system.[24] The 'totalising' biography he is attempting to write may be a sufficiently inspiring ideal to make his readers forget that he avoids the always potentially difficult clash between psychological and organic explanations by completely discounting the latter; but when they feel evidence is being ignored or fabricated, for the benefit of a theory or scheme, they may well develop a fondness for loose ends and decide that the greater or lesser extent of inconclusiveness and disorder found in most other biographies is no bad thing.

Ignoring the evidence, being led by theory rather than ascertainable facts, might sometimes account for the boldness with which

Sartre reconstructs Flaubert's patterns of thought and feeling, or interprets his motives. Yet on the whole – and his book is so long and complex that any generalisations about it are dangerous – he not only interpolates at crucial moments warnings as to the limits of his information, but is also very attentive to the items of evidence that can be found. In the 1971 interview, although he makes perfect knowledge of a man dependent, not only on an appropriate method, but also the availability of the necessary documents, what he seems to be thinking of are lives where there is *not* that relative abundance of material associated with Flaubert. Evidence may be lacking to confirm Sartre's hypotheses regarding the background and earliest times of his subject, but there are nonetheless a good number of memoirs, a correspondence which begins in childhood (the first surviving letter was written when Flaubert was ten), the many published and unpublished writings of his maturity, and above all an extensive juvenilia. The use he makes of this early writing is considerable. Almost as difficult for him as discovering how his subject was treated as a baby, for example, is establishing the degree of trauma associated with Flaubert's early failure to read. He has no very obvious evidence the father was crucially involved but assumes that it must have been so:

> he himself, Achille-Cléophas, professor of general medicine and of surgery, would teach his second son to read. Guided by a person of iron will and exceptional intelligence, the child would make up for lost time in a few months. He began the task and made a complete mess of it. Humiliated by his son, he would humiliate that son for the rest of his life.

People will ask, Sartre goes on, how he knows all this. His answer is simply, 'I've read Flaubert' (*J'ai lu Flaubert*), and he then embarks on the biographical interpretation of a story his subject wrote when he was fifteen.[25]

The impression *The Family Idiot* often makes of going far beyond what can reasonably be known about its subject may occasionally be a result of its author's novelistic powers seizing control; it can sometimes be attributed to the need to work out a particular theoretical position, even when the evidence for carrying that position forward in a legitimate manner is missing; but more often than not it is a consequence of a particular kind of reading of the 'creative' works. The boldness of Sartre's speculation derives more than anything from his strong feeling of inwardness with Flaubert's work as a whole (*J'ai lu Flaubert*). His interviewers in 1971 gave a hint of things to come when they reminded him that much contemporary criticism had abandoned the notion of a literary work's paternity and was no longer interested in the author but the text, 'in the sense in which contemporary semioticians give to that word'. 'I am completely opposed to this idea of the text', Sartre promptly replied, like Canute telling the sea to go back, 'and that's precisely why I chose Flaubert whose abundant correspondence and juvenilia offer us the equivalent of a "psychoanalytic discourse."'[26] In his use of the juvenilia he is completely uninhibited, clearly feeling that it offered privileged insight into how his subject thought and felt. Now the post-structuralist dust has settled,[27] the objection might be, not that his procedures were in essence illegitimate, but that he takes insufficient account of the difference between (for example) a story and a letter. Of course, Sartre implicitly responds to this challenge on several occasions, Flaubert's early writing is stuffed with literary conventions, but why then this particular convention, this or that aspect of it?[28]

*

Apart from the more intellectual objections which might be levelled against it, most of which are associated with its daring (or foolhardy) speculation, the most immediately striking characteristic of *The Family Idiot* is its stupendous length. According to Sartre, Flaubert's early ambitions to be an actor gave him a fondness for the spoken over the written word and he was therefore always keen to read out his compositions to his friends, even though he realised how tiring a business this might be. Inviting the Goncourts to hear *Salammbô* declaimed, he wrote that the performance would take place 'between 4 and 7 and then after coffee until the listeners croak'. 'One could say', Sartre comments,

> that although he is aware of doing everything to ensure failure he can't help himself: he knows very well that he will make his listeners 'croak' (*crever*). Not of course from cardiac arrest but from boredom, having demanded from them an almost intolerable effort of attention which will end, sooner or later, in a sort of tetanus of the mind.[29]

This last phrase is a strange one, but it conveys reasonably well what can happen to readers as they make their way through the almost 3,000 closely printed, and closely argued, pages of *The Family Idiot*. No novel could be such hard work because no novel was ever so predominantly analytical. The length can seem surprising in retrospect because, in the first two volumes, the focus is almost always on the inner life. There are interpolated philosophical disquisitions but, as Hazel Barnes has said, 'the fairly lengthy phenomenological descriptions of the actor and his function, of the laugh, and of the comic . . . are too thoroughly interwoven with the development of Flaubert's personalization for them to be considered as pure digressions' ('personalization' being one of Sartre's key terms, and not Barnes's fault).[30] When political events are described, it is always for their bearing on the Flaubert family. In Sartre's approach to biography, Douglas Collins has written, there are,

> no words wasted on undecisive events, no anecdotes told for their own sake, no attempt to reproduce the formless flux of life, no effort to recreate the sensual world of the subject, no painterly touches – in short, no untendentious curiosity.[31]

This is largely true and sounds very much like a formula for brevity. *The Family Idiot* provides startling proof that it is not.

The idea of an undecisive event is antagonistic to Sartre's aim of 'totalising' all that can be known about Flaubert; because of that aim, he never tells an anecdote for its own sake; and for him the flux of life is never formless, but shaped by crucial episodes and – limited though the scope for them might be – decisive personal choices. He is at the extreme, Johnsonian end of that spectrum of biographical practice which has Aubrey pottering happily away at the other. Everything in Sartre contributes to the same analytic end. That there are in his work *no* recreations of a sensual world and *no* painterly touches is doubtful: his subject's life is too vividly imagined for that to be the case; but it is certainly not these recreations or touches which account for his biography's tremendous length.

Long biographies are not of course exclusive to the French and it would hardly be seemly for an English-speaking person to complain too much about them. Edel, Painter, Holroyd . . . these writers established a tradition within which a more obvious contributor to length than any of the non-Sartrean features Douglas Collins lists, is the sheer plethora of evidence with which their authors have to deal. There are occasions also when a biography is required to double as a work of reference, in the sense that everything the subject wrote in a certain period needs to receive some kind of mention. With a writer such as D. H. Lawrence, for example, so prolific in so many different genres, this not only poses a problem of organisation but makes it impossible to be brief. There is more than one way to skin a cat, and more than one reason or method for telling readers rather more about a biographical subject than some of them may care to know.

The Family Idiot purports to be an attempt at perfect understanding of Flaubert through the meaningful organisation of all that can be known about him. Yet its length is not in fact a consequence of parading all the available information (that would *really* have made it long). It comes rather from the intensity of the analysis to which a rigorously selected number of items are subjected. In the first two volumes, the result is probably the most complete, psychological portrait of a writer ever attempted (in the third and shortest volume the approach becomes more exclusively historical or sociological). Sartre's confidence that the understanding which the portrait represents is perfect can be invigorating in the present intellectual climate where relativity is the name of the game, and indeterminacy something of a fetish. There is far less embarrassment today in admitting you don't know than in giving the impression that you don't know you don't know. Something of this atmosphere may be evident in my previous chapters where I have been anxious to make clear the limits of our likely knowledge of a biographical subject's childhood and physical state, or stress the difficulty of assessing the influence of social relations. Sartre has a keen understanding of limits, but optimistic notions as to their comparative importance. He is not a timid writer and never hides behind a plaintive, 'What after all can we ever know for certain?'

The ambition to achieve perfect understanding is coincident in Sartre with the belief that the various methods for reaching it are, as he says in the Preface to *The Family Idiot,* 'profoundly homogeneous'. Yet the work which follows is not of course the harmonisation of *all* possible approaches, and never could have been. In what is as much a matter of exclusion as integration, two of these are privileged at the necessary expense of others. 'Psychoanalysis' is the name Sartre gives to one form of his investigations and as I have said, in his conception of it, organicist considerations become irrelevant. The second form is an approach to the subject's inner life through history. Not many commentators have felt that, in his third volume, Sartre was able to show convincingly how Flaubert's collapse in the carriage near Pont-L'Evêque was an individual resolution of his personal problems and *at the same time* (the italics are his own) a way of responding to the social conflicts which determined the position of the French writer or artist in the nineteenth century.[32] Yet in the first two of them, he often emerges as one of the few literary biographers to have succeeded in making history more than a background; to have shown the continual rather than merely occasional effect of social and historical circumstances on the subject's ways of thinking and feeling.

That is a more complicated task than it might seem. Roy Foster is himself a distinguished historian of Ireland and in the opening of his Yeats biography there are various ways in which he suggests that this will make an important difference. The visit of Yeats's father to his friend George Pollexfen, and his meeting therefore with his future wife, led (Foster writes) 'to the union of two original and distinctive families, which together embrace the ethos of mid-Victorian Protestant Ireland'; and a short while later he claims that, 'The Irish Protestant sense of displacement, their loss of social and psychological integration, was particularly acute in the Yeates' case: the family experience had anticipated the decline of the whole subculture'.[33] These are clearly attempts by Foster to make his subject's family origins not merely typical or representative but, as Sartre might have said, a 'totalisation' of late nineteenth-century Irish Protestant experience. The question then is how all this mattered to his subject. When he comes to deal with Yeats himself, and immerse himself as he must in a mass of documents of a private nature, Foster's narrative in fact becomes as subject-centred as most other literary lives by biographers who are not historians. His historical expertise is invaluable in describing various historical developments with which Yeats had to deal, but the dominant impression he conveys is of someone responding to events from a position outside their formative influence. As his notion of various of Yeats' forbears 'embracing' the ethos of Irish Protestantism or 'anticipating' its decline might suggest, there is little sense of reciprocity, *inter*penetration. History is a process which goes on outside and around the subject, but not within.

In Chapter 3, I mentioned how Sartre finds the major contradictions of early nineteenth-century French society in the power relations within the Flaubert family, that 'irreducible micro organism which cannot evade the historical conjunction but both suffers and totalises it in its own way'.[34] For him, the consequence is that these relations become the very constituents of a sensibility which Flaubert then struggles to express in his writings. The conflict between bourgeois liberalism and the old feudal values, or between Catholicism and Voltarian scepticism, are not merely the *background* to Flaubert's life and career but integral to them. According to Sartre, they help to explain not only what Flaubert wrote (the content of his writing) but how and why he wrote: the internal dynamism of his writing career. His aim is to make 'history' count in crucially intimate rather than merely external or ancillary ways, and to respond on at least one level therefore to the intractable problem of the relation between the gifted individual and the group: the one to which he had alluded in *Search for a Method* by pointing out that, although Valéry was a petit bourgeois intellectual, not all petit bourgeois intellectuals were Valéry (a well-known phrase proleptically parodied by Yeats' compatriot Wilde when he said that one should not regret that poets were drunkards but rather that all drunkards were not poets).[35] In Foster's account of Yeats, the writing is by comparison much more of an accidental given: a tool not forged by the social and historical circumstances of his time but one that happened to be at his disposal when he was responding to them.

Impressive though Sartre's treatment of history and the Flaubert family often is, it has been suggested that his analysis is fatally weakened by his mistaken assumption that Gustave's mother was a Christian, and not a sceptic like his father.[36] Whether or not that is true, the important point to make here about his approach to these issues is not that it excludes a rival in the same way that his psychoanalysis excludes organicism, but that it is inspired by Marxism. Because 'history' will always matter to individuals, even when they are far removed from public life, no respectable biographer could ever ignore it; but, as Foster might very reasonably object, there are very different, competing methods for describing *how* it matters. In his 1971 interview Sartre said that he wanted to show that one could reach perfect understanding of another person by being, not God, but a man like any other. Yet Sartre was not a man like any other (how many of those others are so interested in Marx?), but someone with very particular attitudes and opinions. As a consequence, his understanding of Flaubert was always destined to be partial rather than perfect.

The God with whom he was invited to contrast himself has the advantage of omniscience, but there is no reason why this attribute should be accompanied by impartiality. The judgements in which He is traditionally involved are necessarily made according to certain criteria. Despite the advantage of being all-knowing, there-fore, even God is not in the position to write that definitive biography implied by Sartre's reference to 'perfect understanding', but would have to approach the biographical subject from a specific point of view and (as Milton's *Paradise Lost* shows) leave the way open for alternative approaches. *The Family Idiot*, that is, was doomed from the start to partiality and incompleteness, hard as it is to imagine anyone else trying harder than Sartre to understand Flaubert. His criticism of other biographers was that they gave an illusion of understanding, presenting a certain number of facts or episodes in sequence without there being any but the most super-ficial explanation of why one thing followed another. In trying to remedy this weakness, he also sought to show that the reasons why certain people wake up in the morning feeling gloomy, think them-selves older than they are, or always expect the worst, are not necessarily matters which have to be attributed to such conveniently vague notions as nature, temperament, or constitution (in its usual, non-Sartrean sense). These are terms he clearly regarded in the same light as gifts, talents or genius. In a BBC programme on Wagner, George Steiner was asked what he thought of the composer's anti-Semitism and replied that it was not for him to attempt to understand the thought-processes of such an over-whelming genius.[37] This is the attitude towards which Sartre's practice is most fiercely hostile. His determination to explain what is usually considered beyond explanation is remarkable; yet the present-day biographer inspired by his example would be faced with the painful paradox that the work in which new, more rigorous standards of intelligibility seem to be set is also impracticably long and complex and therefore, for all but the most dedicated students, unreadable.

9

'Dignity and Uses of Biography'

And let me ask by the way: Is it a fact that a thing has been misunderstood and unrecognised when it has only been touched upon in passing, glanced at, flashed at?
(Friedrich Nietzsche, 'The Question of Intelligibility', in *Joyful Wisdom*, trans. Thomas Common (New York, 1960), p. 349)

THERE IS A ROBUST conservatism among biographers. When, after Sartre's death, the proponents of Theory were busy not only severing the links between authors and their works but also deconstructing that 'self' which biographies purport to describe, it was more or less business as usual. That the Theoreticians seemed to consider biography an activity unworthy of grown-ups did not prevent lives being written in the usual way. There was indeed a possible sense of relief in the idea that, since their form had sunk beneath the eye-line of academic attention, there was no growing corpus of work that biographers might not like, but to which they might one day feel obliged to respond.

Although by the time he had done with *The Family Idiot* Sartre was well on the way to becoming a conservative figure himself, he is often regarded with suspicion by English biographers for whom the virtual unreadability of his book was, and still is, a grim warning of what happens to those who meddle with philosophy. The cake can be over-cooked. 'We never do anything well', writes Hazlitt, 'until we cease to think about the manner of doing it'.[1] In this view, the way Ray Monk has triumphantly combined being a philosopher with writing lives provides an exception to the rule. He falls in any case (the argument would go) into a special category since

157

he writes the lives of philosophers themselves, using his expertise to provide lucid expositions of his subjects' views rather than attempting to reconceive the whole biographical enterprise, as Sartre did.

Although complaints about Sartre's over-elaboration are certainly not without foundation, it would be easy to exaggerate the extent to which he is in fact philosophical (in the narrower sense). However much he might claim in *The Family Idiot* that he is appealing to his own, philosophically defined version of psycho-analysis, his investigations of his subject's inner life could often be equally well categorised under the unjustifiably derogatory heading of vernacular psychology. A thinker with the ability to manipulate abstract notions of a highly complex kind, Sartre is also what used to be called a man of letters. His commentaries on Flaubert's thoughts and feelings owe just as much to a specifically literary tradition which stretches from Montaigne to Proust than to philos-ophy, (or indeed to that much shorter, more scientific line of enquiry running between Janet – to whom he at one moment refers – and Lacan – by whom he was widely believed to have been influenced). Not everyone would take this view, but that the 'vernacular' in which he happens to write has a literary tradition so rich in psychological insight can hardly have been a disadvantage. With a switch of nationalities, this is a very similar tradition to the one which, in his remarks on Harley, Dr Johnson both exemplifies and, as one of the 'fathers' of British biography, helps to found.

The degree of pleasure an alerted reader of *The Family Idiot* would be able to trace to specifically literary sources is considerable; but it is the consequence of elements in the book which are by no means overwhelmingly important. That is true even if one were often to detect this form of pleasure in extracts which otherwise go by the name of Sartrean phenomenology. Making his book seem even longer than it is for lay readers, are numerous passages of a highly abstract, often technical nature in which they are unlikely to find any pleasure at all. Only in exceptional circumstances would it be a suitable Christmas present for that aunt of whose literary taste one was uncertain. *The Family Idiot* is not an easy read, and to an extent that makes its difficulty a legitimate cause for criticism. Part of what Johnson refers to as the use of biography, in the title of his well-known *Rambler* essay, is its popular appeal; and there is always a danger of that use disappearing when biographers stand too firmly on their intellectual dignity, or when (others might say) they complicate their labours by giving to explanation an importance it does not deserve.

Sartre offers plenty of reasons why explanation is essential but opposition to it is more often demonstrated in the practice of biographers than in their theoretical pronouncements. P. N. Furbank is unusual in trying to make clear the grounds for his dislike. In a recent review of Mitchell Leaska's *Granite and Rainbow: The Hidden Life of Virginia Woolf*, for example, he refers to the 'fatal theory that knowledge of the life will help one to respond to the works'; and he illustrates his point by reference to Leaska's treatment of a moment in *To the Lighthouse* when, after Mr Ramsey has observed that he does not like to see his wife looking sad, and she has replied that she was only 'woolgathering', both parties are described as feeling 'uncomfortable'. According to Leaska this reaction is incomprehensible until one remembers that, as Woolf herself so often made clear, the Ramseys are portraits of her parents. In Leaska's view what explains the discomfort is that Mrs Ramsey/Stephen must have been 'daydreaming about her first husband'. But then, Furbank retorts, 'as far as we know, Mrs Ramsey, unlike Woolf's mother, did not have a first husband!'

This is an effective put-down rather than a reasoned reply – Leaska is presumably aware that Mrs Ramsey is not presented to us in *To the Lighthouse* as having been married before – but Furbank immediately goes on to make his case clear:

> What we are encountering here is a causal theory, a matter of explaining, by biographical causes, how a given work of art came to take the shape it did; and I am with Wittgenstein in thinking that causal explanations have no rightful place in aesthetics. One can indeed extend this objection and say that biographers (like historians) might do well to eschew causal explanations in general, for – the events they are studying being non-repeatable – such explanations can only ever be pure guesswork. They might be better left to the reader.[2]

The first complaint here is one that has been heard several times before in this study. Yet if the New Critics, T. S. Eliot, and many Structuralists as well as Post-Structuralists all thought that biographical information was irrelevant to the consideration of works of art, it was for reasons rather different from those of Wittgenstein. It is true that on occasions he can suggest that in aesthetic matters causal issues are conceptually inappropriate; but what one retains most from his reflections is the rather different view that we habitually misunderstand our own needs in assuming that, when faced with an aesthetic challenge or perplexity, we want more information, especially information about the origins of works of art. What we are in fact, or should be, looking for, he suggests, is clarification of our own feelings.[3]

From the familiar protest against the misuse of biographical data in artistic matters, Furbank wants to 'extend' his objection to the habit of asking causal questions about individuals, and indeed the past in general. That would however be difficult when the objection is not in fact the same. It is in principle (Wittgensteinian or otherwise) that causal questions are being considered here as having no rightful place in aesthetics. The objection to asking them where individuals are concerned is not that they are out of place but impossible to answer; or rather that the accuracy of the answers cannot be tested because the events in a life are not repeatable. What Furbank's claim seems to amount to in the second half of my quotation is that there is no experimental method for making them any more than speculation. The proof that he does not nevertheless regard such questions as illegitimate, in the same way that (in his view) causal enquiries in aesthetics are for Wittgenstein, can be found in the last sentence. It is not that biographers have no right to offer causal explanations but that 'they might be better left to the reader'.

The usefulness of Furbank's remarks is that they state forcefully the anti-Sartrean position. In John Richardson's *Picasso*, two explanatory claims are found in close proximity which could well be taken as inadvertently offering powerful support for what he has to say. In one of these, Richardson describes how Picasso's maternal aunts were at one point 'reduced to making gold braid for the caps of railway workers'. Early in his childhood, these two women joined the Picasso household with the result that they 'deserve recognition for having beguiled their nephew's inquisitive eye with the minutiae of their ornate craft':

> The artist's ironical use of embroidery-like arabesques and foliate patterns, which are a recurrent feature of 'rococo' cubist still lifes and decorative passages in prints and drawings as late as the sixties, can be traced back to the encrustations of gold braid with which the aunts adorned the caps of provincial station-masters.

According to Richardson, these embroidering aunts adored Picasso whose upbringing was otherwise in the hands of an equally doting mother and grandmother. This predominance of the female made it 'typically Andalusian' and 'in keeping with [Picasso's] subsequent alternations of misogyny and tenderness towards women: his insatiable need for their love and attention on the one hand, his affectionate though sometimes heartless manipulation of them on the other'. Often in later life, Richardson elaborates, when setting out on a journey,

> the great man would time and time again turn back into a fractious child and oblige his wife or mistress to indulge his infantile rituals and tantrums . . . just as the infant Picasso obliged the women of the Plaza de la Merced [where he was born] to submit to his will.[4]

After having offered a precise link between a detail in Picasso's background and his works of art, Richardson has thus gone on here to make a more general explanatory claim about why his subject behaved as he did towards women in later life. For Furbank, the first of his suggestions would presumably be illegitimate, and the second pointless because it is so hard to prove.

The causal relation between Picasso's taste for arabesques and the decoration his aunts embroidered on stationmasters' caps could have been made more convincing by Richardson through detailed illustration. With examples to show his readers, it would have been easier for him to clarify quite in what sense Picasso's use of these motifs was 'ironical': whom the irony was directed against. Yet if by means of this kind he had been able to make the connection between the arabesques and the caps entirely unequivocal, eliminating or at least seriously diminishing the possibility that Picasso's fondness might also have derived from other people's painting, the result would still not have satisfied Furbank (or Wittgenstein). For them, the idea that whatever puzzlement or interest the arabesques might cause a viewer of Picasso's art could be answered or satisfied by knowledge of their origins is simply a mistake. Whether or not it is, the huge variety of works of art, and the even greater variety in those who engage with them, suggest that to extract from particular examples any rule about the irrelevance of *all* biographical data might well be a mistake also. Certainly there would seem to be cases where it would be foolish to ignore it, even if its function is often only negative. Someone who claimed, for example, that the effect of a particular passage in Wordsworth's poetry partly depended on the way it echoed certain lines in a predecessor, could hardly regard as completely irrelevant the biographical information that Wordsworth had never read that predecessor.

Clear-cut illustrations of this kind are hard to come by: the terms in which the debate has to be conducted are characteristically looser. Many teachers of English literature will know how enthusiastically students often respond to Wilfred Owen's 'Dulce et Decorum Est'. This is a powerful poem but one way of demonstrating its occasional stylistic infelicities is to compare it with the magnificent lines on World War I in Pound's *Hugh Selwyn Mauberley*, especially of course those that begin, ' . . . Died some, pro patria, / non "dulce" non "et decor"'. In his biography of Pound, Humphrey Carpenter calls these 'fine stuff', but then goes on to say that 'one cannot help remembering that Ezra spent the war at his typewriter in Kensington and Stone Cottage'.[5] If this is for many a remark completely irrelevant to a reading of *Hugh Selwyn Mauberley*, are the biographical circumstances which lie behind Owen's 'Dulce et Decorum Est' equally so? Would any reader of the poem which precedes Primo Levi's *If This is a Man* be comfortable with considering it on exclusively stylistic grounds? Our engagement with literature and art is a messy business. We come to books and pictures already full of information – biographical and otherwise – information which, as Carpenter rightly says, we cannot help remembering. As a result our responses are inevitably composite, impure. If Furbank could convince a suitably qualified body of experts that in nine out of ten cases the use of biographical information had been misguided, the tenth would still show how equally misguided it is to offer general rules in this area. Causal explanation may occupy too large a place in aesthetics but, as I have argued before, both the nature of literature and art, and of our responses to them, seem too heterogeneous for it to have no place at all.

More obviously supportive of Furbank's position than Richardson's remarks on arabesques are his general reflections on Picasso's upbringing; but it seems to me that is more because of the quality of those reflections than the category of remark into which they happen to fall. The connections he suggests between a predominantly female household and Picasso's behaviour towards women in later life assume a degree of intimate biographical knowledge for which no evidence is offered. Were all the women in the Picasso home so simple-minded as to be always 'doting', and did they always submit to the young boy's will? If they sometimes frustrated it, why would not those occasions have had as much influence on his adult behaviour (seeking to enjoy what had previously been denied) than their total acquiescence? Richardson clearly has in mind stereo-types of how Spaniards in Andalusia bring up their children, but the fact that he thinks his subject's upbringing 'typically Andalusian' can hardly mean that all Andalusians behave as he did when they are going on a journey. His claim that Picasso's upbringing was 'in keeping' with his 'later alternations of tenderness and misogyny' is an example of those 'unintelligible sequences' Sartre complains of in *Being and Nothingness,* and really no more than a variation on the popular 'I blame his mother'. As such it has about the same value as George Miller's thoughts on the effect of swaddling on Pavlov:

> The Russian peasant custom of swaddling their babies for long periods, alternating with joyous episodes of play and affection, has been blamed for generating personalities that alternate between stolid, patient, self-restraint and explosive, emotional release. Whether or not swaddling has anything to do with these extreme fluctuations is debatable, but certainly Pavlov's behaviour often fell into this pattern. He would flare up at trivialities. If his surgery went badly, he might blame his assis-tant, waving his arms and swearing profusely.[6]

When the connection between swaddling and adult behaviour is 'debatable', it is hard to see why Miller should rely on it? The reason appears to be that to a biographer, or someone writing in the biographical mode, links between childhood experience and adult behaviour are often irresistible, if only because without them the narrative of a life threatens to fall apart. Yet those links are not always as unconvincingly established as they are here, or in Richardson. Most of the claims which have already been cited for the influence of childhood experience on later life in my previous chapters are a considerable improvement on both, even if none of them could ever be described as certain. Furbank's suggested response to the almost inevitable absence of certainty in this area of biographical explanation is to leave it to the reader. But that is an anomalous solution when readers can only speculate with the material which biographers have both selected and arranged.

It was after he had finished his biography of E. M. Forster that Furbank's hard line on explanation must have developed. In Chapter 2, I referred to the reasons he is quite happy to offer for the peculiarities of Forster's publishing career. In describing his subject's 'first sex encounter', far from avoiding explanation, he makes both of the moves he warns against in his review of Leaska. During his second term at prep school, he tells us, the young Forster was walking alone in the country when he came across a middle-aged man 'urinating in full view'. After he had finished, the boy found himself invited to play with this man's penis. Obeying the call, he was startled by its 'inflamed tip' and 'further astonished when he saw some white drops trickling out'. In Furbank's view this unpleasant incident had 'some significance . . . for [Forster's] later development'. More particularly he claims that, although the episode 'taught him nothing he could understand' and 'soon sank out of his daily thoughts',

> as a pattern of panic and cross-purposes it evidently left a lasting impression on him. One senses that he returned to the incident, and his own reactions during it, when writing *A Passage to India*, and that it became a model for Adela's vengeful and confused behaviour after she imagines herself molested by Aziz.[7]

The journey between the feelings aroused in Forster by the middle-aged man and Adela is at least as long and tortuous as that between Woolf's memories of her parents and certain episodes in *To the Lighthouse*, or between the embroidery of Picasso's aunts and his arabesques. In taking it, Furbank was merely following the conventions which tend to govern a literary life. Although it seems he would now repudiate them, the result was one of the best literary biographies in recent times.

Furbank's biography is good in many different respects yet what makes it exceptional is that, in its final sections, he was able to draw on his memories of meeting Forster in his last years as a fellow of King's College, Cambridge. These give a flavour to the narrative which biographers who were never in the presence of their subjects can only admire and envy, although the effect is one which they can occasionally have some success in simulating. In his biography of W. H. Auden, for example, Humphrey Carpenter was able to collect enough information to convey a vivid impression of what it was like to have his subject as a house guest. Rising virtually at dawn, Carpenter says, Auden talked so loudly once he was up that 'he could not be ignored'. He demanded and drank 'an endless succession of cups of tea', 'would scatter tobacco ash over [the sitting room] and burn the furniture with cigarettes', and 'could quell a meal into silence by his taciturnity and by the frown which was his usual expression'.

> He was sometimes discovered in the middle of the night raiding the larder for cold potatoes ('I just wanted to see if the beef was still there', he explained on one such occasion). He invariably piled a huge weight

of bedclothes on his bed: blankets, eiderdowns, bedspreads, anything that would make it heavy. If there were not enough of these he would appropriate anything else he could find. At the Fishers' he put the bedroom carpet on his bed. Staying with another family, he took down the bedroom curtains and used these as extra blankets. Another time it was the stair-carpet. Once he was discovered in the morning sleeping beneath (among other things) a large framed picture.[8]

In an essay in which he has argued that there ought to be room for 'unmediated matter' in biographies, and that there is no reason why they should not have 'some of the qualities of a scrapbook', Ian MacKillop has tried to give passages such as this a formal status by calling them 'vignettes'.[9] Noting the difference there often is between what we think we are going to say to certain people as we travel to meet them and what we do in fact say in their physical presence, he values the vignette for the way it inhibits too easy a slide towards summary and explanation. People are no longer so easy to encapsulate when the biographer brings them back to life in all their angularity and awkwardness. Combined with Furbank's strictures, and still bearing in mind how hard *The Family Idiot* is to read, his remarks provide at least the beginnings of a rationale for the Aubrey school of life-writing.

*

Impracticably probing and intricate the questions Sartre asks may often be, yet there are nevertheless many readers who would feel that this is better than asking none at all. The counter case to Furbank's was well put by Elizabeth Hardwick in a review of a biography of Hemingway in the *New York Review of Books*, soon after that writer's death (whether her remarks were fair and accurate criticism is not the issue). Hemingway's widow had 'authorized' this biography so that its author, Carlos Baker, was the first to see many new documents. The consequence in Hardwick's view was 'only an accumulation, a heap', and she felt faced with a book 'written by the materials' where 'nothing is weighed or judged or considered. A catalogue', she rather cruelly added, 'does not gossip about its entries'. Hardwick felt that this absence of gossip, or of analytical curiosity, extended to the whole of Baker's biography but she particularly regretted it in relation to Hemingway's suicide:

Would it be facile to connect it with his father's, when it came upon him so much later and accompanied by so many other physical torments? Perhaps it came not from his youth but from his skull fractures, those injuries he, or the life he led, was prone to. Why did he drink so much? No one could give an answer to all this. What one wants is to feel the questions somewhere in the shadows.[10]

That certain questions are unanswerable would be a good enough reason for many people to regard them as not worth asking but, although there may be no possibility of a reliable response to 'all this', some of it may be capable of clarification and those who, like Hardwick, think it worth a try must be at least as numerous as those who do not.

Unanswerability may well be associated with the fact that life-events are non-repeatable, but it could also be a consequence of the lack of that condition often referred to with the oxymoron 'full documentation'. It has been estimated that within the last two centuries more than 60,000 biographies of Jesus have appeared even though, as W. M. Runyan puts it, 'the established facts of his life occupy no more than a few paragraphs'.[11] Like Shakespeare, Jesus is a special case and it is easy to see what there is in both figures which would prompt people to undertake lives where lack of evidence makes it hopeless to think one could ever answer satisfactorily many of those Hardwick-like questions it still seems reasonable to pose in relation to more modern, better-documented figures. Yet even with these latter there is always, as Reggie Turner said of his friend the Botticelli biographer, a shirt missing. Any attempt to give a definitive answer to the question of why Hemingway drank would almost certainly be foiled by the absence, here and there, of crucial information. What would foil it also, of course, is the likelihood of biographers, at the end of their investigations, being faced by two competing explanations: the biochemical and the psychological, which were not easy to reconcile. That is to say that unanswerability is not inevitably a result of inadequate documentation but can also lie in the very nature of the questions being posed.

Even tougher than the conflict between psychology and biochemistry, for example, and often prominent in discussions of suicide (as I have tried to show), is the old conundrum of determinism and free will. In a recent review of the issues involved, Galen Strawson has lucidly explained why it is that philosophical discussion is deadlocked and 'no radically new options are likely to emerge after millennia of debate'. 'Pessimists' is the name he gives to those who believe that, since we are determined by our antecedents, nothing we ever do can be accurately described as choice; and he explains how the 'Compatibilists', who challenge this view, admit that our characters may be determined but do not think this necessarily means all our actions are. The Compatibilist position is developed in order to deal with the paradox that, although it is very hard to find rational grounds for refuting determinism, most individuals will have a strong sense of being endowed with the power of choice when (to use Strawson's example) they have ten pounds in their pocket and need to decide whether they should buy a cake or put the money in an Oxfam tin:

> Standing there, you may believe determinism is true: you may believe that in five minutes time you will be able to look back on the situation you are now in and say, of what you will by then have done, 'It was determined that I should do that'. But even if you do wholeheartedly believe this, it does not seem to touch your current sense of the absoluteness of your freedom and moral responsibility.[12]

It is not hard to see the relevance of these remarks to the biography of a modern figure. Immersion in diaries and letters gives biographers a strong sense of subjects in control of their own destinies. Private documents are redolent with the feeling we almost all have of making choices and exercising our free will in ways that shape our lives. The problem is that, because no one is in fact self-originating, the impression these create must be balanced by a consideration of all the determining factors of background, health and social relations which suggest that the subject is not, and never has been, free at all. That biographers often seem to make the result of this balancing act an untidy compromise is not surprising when the problem to which it relates is one over which philosophers can only wring their hands.

Dealing with private documents requires more skill from the biographer than I have yet had the opportunity to suggest. This is partly because the difference between private and public is not as clear-cut as it might seem. Widely recognised but not always remembered is the truism that the tone and content of letters is largely dependant on the addressee; but private diaries are also rarely written without a listener or reader in mind, even if that imagined listener is posterity or a supernatural power. This means that the very idiom in which a subject's 'free will' expresses itself is also socially or culturally constrained, and that those statements habitually quoted in biographies as expressive of direct, uncontaminated thought or feeling can therefore be as conditioned by their context as a public address. Yet even assuming that a biographer is appropriately sceptical and subtle in handling these matters, and fully alert to the impossibility of a totally private language, there is always the danger of enclosure within the subject's point of view, and a corresponding need to set off the impression that will make on readers against the determining conditions of the life which is being described.

There are at least two ways in which my attempt to categorise these conditions has obviously not been exhaustive. In the first place, each item in my list has been explored only briefly. Biography's relations with psychology, medicine and the social sciences are clearly topics on which a great deal more could be said. If the intention had been to achieve comprehensiveness rather than be suggestive, then with more and different kinds of examples, the treatment of each topic could itself have formed the basis for a book. The second way in which comprehensiveness may have been avoided is in the components of the list itself. With the help of Borges, Foucault once wittily demonstrated, in his preface to *Words and Things*, that listing is an activity very much governed by convention. But it may also be governed by ignorance. If there had been categories of whose strong case for inclusion I was aware, I would of course have included them. The fact is that many of the more interesting possibilities seemed on closer inspection not to be radically new categories, but sub-sections of the existing ones.

Many lives are shaped or distorted by commonly held expectations associated with the careers which their owners take up: by ideas, for example, of what it really means to be a soldier, doctor, priest or teacher. That at certain times it has been assumed there is some natural association between creativity and drinking may help to explain why a number of people who became writers also became drunks. The career does not have to be one which is officially recognised since a reading of the more romantically inclined crime novels makes it easy to imagine a burglar whose life would have been completely different without his subscription to the precept that there is honour among thieves. Much more broadly, it is reasonable to contemplate how many lives in the United States have been governed, influenced or determined by what is loosely known as 'the American dream'. Success is of course defined differently in different countries, and among different groups, so that *not* to succeed will rarely have entirely the same meaning, even within the same culture. According to Ivan Morris, the meaning is not at all the same in Japan because of the existence and influence there of a cult of heroic failure. It is the fact that those who fail after an initial peak of success are accorded greater prestige than those who remain successful which, in this rather broad view, explains the suicide of Yukio Mishima or the behaviour of the kamikaze pilots.[13] Even more broadly, and rapidly retreating back to the safety of our own culture, it is evident that lives are and always have been determined by what it means to be a man in the West and, perhaps more significantly in our time, what it means and has meant to be a woman.

In lives of women by women, Jenny Uglow on Elizabeth Gaskell, for example, or Claire Harmon on Sylvia Townsend Warner, the interpretative framework is often strengthened by the way we are invited to pause from time to time and consider how the subject's life corresponded to the common patterns of women's lives in her time. The focus is moved away from the inner life towards the degree of the subject's representativeness. This is always likely to be a tendency in what has been termed feminist biography, and explains why it should acquire that name. The individual is contextualised by an appeal to social or cultural stereotypes (in the non-pejorative sense of that word). This is a procedure which, like the appeal to cultural models generally, opens up endless possibilities of enquiry. My excuse for not having felt obliged to seize them is that they can all be considered as coming under a broadly sociological banner: that they all concern the degree to which our lives are thought of as determined by our status as social beings. We can only say, it used to be fashionable to insist, what the language allows us to say. In a similar way it has been argued that what we can *be* is strictly conditioned by the social models available.

With ingenuity, most biographical approaches can be found a place within the terms which I have offered; but intellectual life is too diverse for there not to be exceptions. If Freud has been referred to with relative frequency in this book, it is not because I am under the illusion nothing happened in psychoanalysis after he had made his impact. The reason is rather that it is on Freud, or at least on a popular Freudianism, biographers have most usually relied. Relatively rare are references to the rival systems of his former disciples and competitors the most prominent of whom was Jung. After his break with Freud, Jung went on to develop what is now known as archetypal psychology. The foremost American proponent of this therapy and doctrine is James Hillman who claims that it represents a third method of considering human behaviour, 'away from both social and personalistic explanations' (in these terms, organicism would presumably be a fourth method). 'Our lives follow mythical figures', he writes, 'Our psychological lives are mimetic to myths . . . The task of archetypal psychology, and its therapy, is to discover the archetypal pattern for forms of behaviour'.[14] This is a claim which can genuinely be taken to indicate a quite different category of enquiry and explanation from any I have yet proposed.

So too can the idea that the character of subjects may be explained by the astrological sign under which they were born. This possibility was once investigated in a totally serious fashion by the well-known psychologist H. J. Eysenck. With the assistance of various charts and tables, he concluded in 'Biography in the Service of Science: A Look at Astrology' that, 'biographical study added to statistical analysis of planetary positions, has enabled us to make an important discovery, namely that there is a relationship between personality and planetary position at birth', although he went on to note that further research would be required to establish 'how the particular relationship came about'.[15] Here also is an additional explanatory category, yet as in the case of the Jungian archetypes, it is not *only* a lack of adequate qualifications which has made me doubt that serious investigation of it, and 'further research' along the lines Eysenck suggests, would be an attractive proposition.

*

A lot more could have been written but it would seem wrong to raise the issue of the excessive length of many biographies in a format which was not itself relatively short, and when my chief concern has been to point out new directions, map out new territory: to find a legitimate way of talking about the method of biography *in general.* As I said at the end of my first chapter, this has seemed worthwhile not only for its possible bearing on the reading and writing of biographies, but also for its relevance to all the other contexts (casual or institutionalised) in which we gossip about other human beings. The near-unavoidability of that way of expressing the matter is evident in Elizabeth Hardwick's use of 'gossip' in one of the sentences from her review which I have already quoted. She falls back on it again when complaining that Baker's methods put his readers in the position of Hemingway's valet, laying out his clothes, ordering his wine, accepting his hangovers, and travelling with him here and there. All this while, she writes, 'somebody else, somewhere, gets the real joy of the man, his charm, his uniqueness, his deeply puzzling inner life. Someone else gossips about him, turns over his traits, ponders the mystery of his talent'.[16]

It is on the whole an unfortunate word, but there are all kinds of gossip just as there are all kinds of biographers. Aubrey is himself a gossip in a sense that takes away from the description the implication it almost always carries of malice. Yet where there is malice, or what seems like it, there is almost always also some kind of effort of analysis, interpretation. What my enquiry has attempted to suggest is that it is the quality of that effort which matters. In her memoir of D. H. Lawrence, Brigit Patmore describes an episode when she was invited with some other friends to the Lawrences' flat:

> During tea Dorothy Richardson asked for news of a friend of ours she had met recently. There had been much gossip about this woman and her husband and Dorothy repeated one of the many stories – an untrue one. Before I could speak Lorenzo banged his hand on the table and cried:
> 'That's a lie. I can't let that pass'.
> Then he told the real story, truthfully and kindly – for I knew it well, as fully as an outsider can know the ultimate truth between a man and a woman. One could see that our friend gained more by this pure statement of the truth than by advocacy or an attempt to justify. Dorothy Richardson was given a deeper understanding of a woman who had suffered and liked her the better for it.[17]

Patmore was a warm admirer of Lawrence and one can hear faint echoes in her account of his own insistence that what other people require from us is justice rather than extenuation, and how wrong it would therefore be to insult them by providing excuses for their living.[18] It would be easy to suspect that her admiration led her to give Lawrence more credit than he deserved, or to be sceptical about the possibility of a 'pure statement of truth' (as – to give Patmore her due – she herself partly is). The anecdote is nonetheless useful because it provides a paradigmatic instance of the difference between varieties of gossip, and also suggests, by extension, important reasons why some biographies may on occasions be so much better than others. The implication in Patmore is that Lawrence's superiority was a question of attitude, but although both that and correct information certainly matter a great deal, what also counts is method. Wanting to be fair or just to what Lawrence elsewhere calls 'the struggling, battered thing any human soul is'[19] does not mean that one necessarily has the means to be so.

One of the reasons that in his *Rambler* essay Dr Johnson thought no other species of writing 'more delightful and more useful' than biography, more able to 'enchain the heart by irresistible interest', was that it was easy for readers to identify with its subjects. This was because biographers directed attention towards 'domestic privacies', the 'minute details of daily life': that they opened to posterity 'the private and familiar character' of fellow human beings.[20] It was precisely this emphasis which, a century or so later, made many people feel that biography had added – in that memorable phrase – 'a new terror to death'.[21] For at least the last hundred years, biography has been feared by many as a monstrous invasion of privacy, a manifestation of gossip in its worst sense. In a poem on this topic, D. J. Enright addresses the kind of writer who is likely to be a victim of biographical intrusion and complains on his behalf of other people's supposed knowledge of those 'Velleities that even you / Would hardly know you felt / But all biographers do'. 'What of your views on women's shoes', he goes on,

> If you collected orange peel
> What *did* you do with the juice?
> Much easier than your works
> To sell your quirks
> So burn your letters, hers and his –
> Better no Life at all than this.[22]

A high moment in the old literary 'canon' occurs in *Middlemarch* when Bulstrode has been exposed as a pious fraud and his wife signals both her forgiveness for his past actions, and her willingness to resume life on a lower level of expectation, with the memorable, 'Look up, Nicholas'.[23] The drama of this may be more or less intense according to how keenly individual readers are themselves inclined to feel shame, and shame itself is closely associated with the concept of privacy. No cultural change has been more significant in the last hundred years than the erosion of privacy, a process more advanced in some Western countries than others. Not yet in Europe are we likely to see sitting together in the same television studio, and answering the enquiries of their interrogator with relative calm, a father and the child he has sexually abused, or a brother and sister whose relations are incestuous. Here are potential victims of the American ideology of 'openness' who have so successfully interiorised its principles that it can no longer do them

172

much harm. For them, that loss of privacy to which biographical writings of all kinds have so powerfully contributed, is no disaster because with its disappearance has also disappeared (or seemed to disappear) feelings of shame. What, after all, was Nicholas Bulstrode making so much fuss about?

In recent times, men and women sufficiently prominent to feel that they might one day be the subject of biographies have not always been so comfortable with openness. However sure some of them might have been that there was nothing of which they should ever feel ashamed, their confidence in the interpretative skills of future biographers allowing them to see it that way has not always been high. They have therefore wanted to protect their privacy, not only during their lives but after they were dead, and have adopted various stratagems for doing so. Of these the one that has in many ways been the least successful is writing an autobiography. Sending a privately printed copy of his *Education* to Henry James, Henry Adams explained, 'The volume is a mere shield of protection in the grave'; and he went on, 'I advise you to take your own life in the same way, in order to prevent biographers taking it in theirs'.[24] The shield Adams hoped his autobiography would provide proved predictably flimsy and, since his time, writing the whole or merely aspects of one's life story has more frequently stimulated biographical enquiry than inhibited it. In Chapter 4 I pointed out that, in the treatment of childhood experiences especially, the autobiographer has genuine advantages (what Johnson called 'the knowledge of truth'); but in a culture sceptical of the ability of individuals to describe themselves truly, these often go unrecognised.

An extreme example of the futility of the attempt to make an autobiographical statement, not only more authoritative than any other could ever be, but also one that closed the account: said all that could ever be said, can be found in the long suicide note left by Ralph Barton, a cartoonist for the *New Yorker*, who shot himself in May 1931, three months before his forty-fourth birthday. Although the Stock Exchange crash had affected him as badly as it had so many other people, Barton wanted to insist that the reasons for suicide are 'invariably psycho-pathological' and have nothing to do with the ordinary difficulties of existence. His own life, he wrote, had been glamorous, with more than its fair share of 'affection and appreciation'; but since his childhood he had suffered from melancholia which in the last few years had 'begun to show definite signs of manic-depressive insanity'. This had prevented him from enjoying 'the simple pleasures of life' and made him run 'from wife to wife'. For the act he had committed,

> No one thing is responsible and no one person – except myself. If the gossips insist on something more definite and thrilling as a reason, let them choose my pending appointment with the dentist or the fact that I happened to be painfully short of cash at the moment . . . After all, one has to choose a moment; and the air is always full of reasons at any given moment. I did it because I am fed up with inventing devices for getting through twenty-four hours a day and with bridging over a few months periodically with some beautiful interest, such as a new gal who annoyed me to the point where I forgot my own troubles.[25]

One of the reasons Woolf's suicide note had a chance of being taken at face-value was that its tone suggested single-minded concentration on the task in hand. By turning his attention outwards and aggressively challenging the gossips to accept his own explanation of events, Barton virtually guaranteed further biographical speculation. Preoccupied with, but also baffled by the question of why he should be choosing one particular moment to kill himself rather than another, he wants to dissociate his act from money or his relations with women. Yet equating his painful shortness of cash with a visit to the dentist, or attributing the interest of a new girl friend to the annoyance she brings, are awkward, would-be humorous gestures that have the opposite of their intended effect. They attract attention to matters Barton wants to claim do not deserve it.

As in the cases of Woolf or Plath, the credit which being able to write so lucidly about manic-depressive insanity brings could easily be destroyed by anyone inclined to interpret the writer's lucidity as a symptom of the insanity itself. Like Adams in his more general account, Barton's attempt to forestall discussion of one highly significant moment in his life does not offer to the outside world a surface so smooth that it would be impossible to get a grip but, instead, far more incitements to biographical reassessment than if he had said nothing at all. One proof of this is that the general reader is now most likely to come across Barton's note in the chapter devoted to him in John Updike's *Just Looking: Essays in Art.* Updike points out in this chapter that, in part of his note, Barton had paid a strangely fervid tribute to the third of his four wives ('my beautiful lost angel, Carlota, the only woman I ever loved'); and he suggests also that 'the failure of his career to develop a significant literary side' was one of the 'non-chemical reasons' for his unhappiness.[26]

Aware perhaps that autobiographical statement would not keep the jackals at bay, and with what may have been a shrewd insight into the shape of things to come, Thomas Hardy wrote down the things he felt mattered about his own early life so that after his death they could be passed off as the work of his wife.[27] As several short stories by Henry James indicate, destroying private documents offered another solution, and a third consisted in instructing your executors to 'authorise' a biography in the hope of thereby exerting a measure of control. In what must, to some extent at least, have been an exercise in future damage limitation, Graham Greene took the comparatively unusual step of choosing his own biographer before he died. With moves like these, the potential victims of biography have struggled to defend themselves, and instructively ineffective they have always been. Hardy's disguised autobiography has proved a stimulus for further 'lives' rather than a deterrent, and the same has been true of Sherry's biography of Greene. Documents that have been destroyed encourage people to believe there was something to hide, and spur them to fashion a life from other sources (it is easy to burn all the letters one has received but harder to ensure the same fate for all those one ever sent). Such is the climate now that reputable writers are unlikely to accept a commission for an authorised biography without insisting on *carte blanche*. Trying to prevent a posthumous invasion of all one's private doings, when the only real protection is a life wholly dull and uninteresting, is like putting a finger in the dike. Sooner or later the insatiable public appetite for gossip bursts through.

Since nothing is likely to stop biographies being written, the only legitimate hope both its likely subjects and the rest of us can have is that they should get better. In one of Woody Allen's less successful works (*Stardust Memories*), he plays a director of comic films tormented by his success and convinced he ought to be concerned with more serious matters. At one point he encounters a group of super-intelligent aliens – on the earthly scale, they inform him, their IQ is 1,600 – and profits from the occasion in order to ask them the meaning of life. To his anguished enquiry as to how he should conduct himself in future, they reply, 'Tell funnier jokes'. The lesson is presumably that although he is condemned to doing more or less the same things, he ought to do them better. Because there is no prospect of fewer biographies being published in the immediate future, it may be a waste of energy to deplore their popularity rather than pondering their characteristics and the

175

reasons for their varying quality. The writing of better biographies is of course largely dependent on many factors which seem haphazard. In spite of what Sartre has to say about 'gifts', it appears indisputable that some people will always tell a story better than others, display more human understanding, or show more dogged-ness and ingenuity in research. But putting aside that man's art or this woman's scope, it would surely help if there were more consensus among reviewers and critics as to what is involved in telling lives, especially when biographers set out to understand their subjects in the way Elizabeth Hardwick would have liked to have understood Hemingway. 'Improve the quality of your gossip', the aliens might have said, their super-sensitive hearing having detected that it was going on, not only in biographies, but all round.

Notes

Unless otherwise indicated, place of publication is London and translations from French texts are my own.

Chapter 1: Lives without Theory

1. Oliver Lawson Dick (ed.), *Aubrey's Brief Lives* (1972), p. 66; Samuel Beckett, *'Molloy', 'Malone Dies', 'The Unnamable'* (1959), p. 26.
2. Samuel Johnson, *The Lives of the Poets* (Everyman edition, 1925), vol. ii, p. 252.
3. James Boswell, *The Life of Johnson* (1927), ii, p. 260.
4. See W. Jackson Bate, *Samuel Johnson* (1978), pp. 529–30.
5. *Lives of the Poets*, vol. 2, p. 245. What are now known as *The Lives of the Poets* were originally called – far more appropriately – *Prefaces, Biographical and Critical, to the Works of the English Poets.*
6. *Life of Johnson*, p. 4 (advertisement to the first edition).
7. See the section on 'Victorian Lives' in Christopher Ricks, *Essays in Appreciation* (1996).
8. Howard Mills (ed.), *Wordsworth's Literary Criticism* (Bristol, 1980), p. 92.
9. *Letters of D. H. Lawrence*, vol. vi, eds James T. Boulton and Margaret H. Boulton, with Gerald M. Lacy (Cambridge, 1991), p. 231 (5 December 1927).
10. W. J. Bate, John M. Bullitt and L. F. Powell (eds), *'The Idler' and 'The Adventurer'* (New Haven, 1963), p. 263.
11. R. F. Foster, *W. B. Yeats: A Life. 1. The Apprentice Mage. 1865–1914* (1997), pp. xxv, 59.
12. *Correspondence of Thomas Gray*, ed. Paget Toybee and Leonard Whibley, with corrections and additions by H. W. Starr (Oxford, 1935), p. 587 (6 September 1758).

13. Ray Monk, *Betrand Russell: The Spirit of Solitude* (1996), p. 360.
14. Leon Edel, *Writing Lives: Principia Biographica* (1987), pp. 27, 28–9. Compare also 'the biographer's quest is . . . to discover the lies and delusions by which all men and women defend themselves against the indignities of life' from the 'Manifesto' in the first number of *Biography: an Interdisciplinary Quarterly* (University of Hawaii). For over twenty years this periodical has published interesting material on life-writing, but nearly half of it is on autobiography and the rest is predominantly concerned with ilustrations of biographical practice.
15. Peter Ackroyd, *Dickens* (1990), p. 18.
16. See Ernest Jones, *The Life and Work of Sigmund Freud* (New York, 1953), vol. i, pp. 7–8 and *The Complete Letters of Sigmund Freud and Wilhelm Fliess. 1887–1904*, ed. and trans. by Jeffrey Moussaieff Masson (Cambridge: Mass., 1985), p. 268 (3 October 1897).
17. 'The mind of the poet is the shred of platinum. It may partly or exclusively operate upon the experience of the man himself; but, the more perfect the artist, the more completely separate in him will be the man who suffers and the mind which creates; . . .'
    T. S. Eliot, 'Tradition and the Individual Talent' in *Selected Essays* (1932), p. 18.
18. Bernard Crick, *George Orwell: A Life* (1992), pp. 29–30.
19. Aristotle, *Ethica Nichomachea*, trans. W. D. Ross (Oxford, 1915), 1094a–1094b.
20. Ira Bruce Nadal, *Biography: Fiction, Fact, Form* (New York, 1984), pp. 9, 154, 157.
21. David Coward, *Times Literary Supplement*, 5 October 1984.
22. These contrasting feelings can be most conveniently followed through the index of *A Writer's Diary: Being Extracts from the Diary of Virginia Woolf*, ed. Leonard Woolf (1972), but see also Panthea Reed, *Art and Affection: A Life of Virginia Woolf* (1996), pp. 392, 399, 416.
23. Jenny Uglow, *Elizabeth Gaskell: A Habit of Stories* (1993), p. 397.
24. Ray Monk, *Bertrand Russell*, p. xviii. Monk is here relying on a similar claim made by Richard Holmes in 'Biography: Inventing the Truth', the valuably suggestive opening essay in *The Art of Literary Biography*, ed. J. Batchelor (1995), pp. 15–25.
25. Alan Shelston, *Biography* (Critical Idiom Series, 1977), p. 13.

Chapter 2: Biography and Explanation

1. One of several accounts of Chaplin's divorce from Lita Grey can be found in Charles L. Maland, *Chaplin and American Culture: The Evolution of a Star Image* (New Jersey, 1989), pp. 94–105.
2. For one resolution of the enigma, see George D. Painter, *Marcel Proust* (1959), vol. ii, pp. 268–9.

3. P. N. Furbank, *E. M. Forster: A Life* (1977), vol. i, pp. 131–3; Mark Holloway, *Norman Douglas* (1976).
4. Izaak Walton, *The Lives of Dr John Donne, Sir Henry Wotton, Mr Richard Hooker, Mr George Herbert and Dr Robert Sanderson* (Oxford, 1924), p. 217. For useful remarks on Walton as a biographer see Alan Shelston, *Biography*, pp. 28–30.
5. Edwin Harland Miller, *Salem is My Dwelling Place: A Life of Nathaniel Hawthorne* (1991), p. 210.
6. Jean-Paul Sartre, *L'Idiot de la famille: Gustave Flaubert de 1821 à 1857* (Paris, 1988), tome i, p. 55.
7. Alexander and Juliette George, *Woodrow Wilson and Colonel House: a Personality Study*, (New York, 1964), p. 3.
8. *Guardian*, 16 February 1993.
9. Thomas C. Caramagno, *The Flight of the Mind: Virginia Woolf's Art and Manic-Depressve Illness* (1992), p. 62.
10. See below p. 113.
11. Emile Durkheim, *Les Règles de la Méthode Sociologique* (Paris: Flammarion, 1988), pp. 98–9.
12. Hermione Lee, *Virginia Woolf* (1997), p. 3.
13. 'Sketch of the Past' in *Moments of Being*, ed. Jeanne Schulkind (1995), p. 167.
14. Jean-Paul Sartre *L'Idiot de la famille*, tome i, p. 121.
15. Jean-Paul Sartre, *Baudelaire* (1948), p. 110.
16. Frederick A. Pottle, *James Boswell: The Earlier Years* (1966), p. 321.
17. William McKinley Runyon, *Life Histories and Pyschobiography: Explorations in Theory and Method* (Oxford, 1982), p. 58.
18. Osip Mandelstam, 'The End of the Novel' in *Selected Essays*, trans. Sidney Monas (1977), p. 87.
19. Dr Johnson *The Rambler (no. 60)*, (Everyman edn., 1953), pp. 134–5.
20. *Letters of D. H. Lawrence*, vol. v, eds. James T. Boulton and Lindeth Vasey (Cambridge, 1989), p. 585.
21. Stanley Weintraub, *Reggie: A Portrait of Reggie Turner* (New York, 1965), p. 139.
22. James Clifford, '"Hanging the Looking Glasses at Odd Corners": Ethnobiogrpahical Prospects' in *Studies in Biography*, ed. Daniel Aaron (1978), pp. 44–5.
23. *The Rambler no. 60*, p. 133.
24. *Aubrey's Brief Lives*, p. 155.
25. Boswell, *Life of Johnson*, ii, p. 478.
26. *Essays of Virginia Woolf*, ed. Andrew McNellie (1986), vol. i, p. 252.
27. Peter Ackroyd, *Dickens*, pp. 162–3.
28. *Aubrey's Brief Lives*, pp. 18, 138, 160.
29. Ibid,. p. 255.
30. Ibid., p. 126.

31. Norman Sherry, *The Life of Graham Greene. vol. 1: 1904–1939* (1989), p. 725.
32. Ibid., pp. 343–4, 398.
33. Ibid., p. 81.

Chapter 3: Ancestors

1. John Richardson, *A Life of Picasso. Vol. i: 1881–1906* (1991), p. 16.
2. Max Geisberg, *The German Single-Leaf Woodcut: 1500–1550* (1975).
3. Herbert Spencer, *Autobiography* (1904), vol. ii, pp. 437–45.
4. D. H. Lawrence, *Fantasia of the Unconscious* (1961 Phoenix ed.), p. 25.
5. George A. Miller, *Psychology: The Science of Life* (1964), pp. 136, 177.
6. Panthea Reid, *Art and Afffection: A Life of Viriginia Woolf,* (1996) p. 4.
7. Peter Ackroyd, *Dickens*, pp. 3–4.
8. Ibid., pp. 4–5.
9. Ibid., p. 8.
10. Edwin Haviland Miller, *Salem is My Dwelling Place*, p. xiii (and compare pp. 18, 22).
11. Robert Graves, *Goodbye to All That* (Revised edn., 1957), p. 5.
12. Miranda Seymour, *Ottoline Morrell: Life on the Grand Scale* (1992).
13. Jeremy Lewis, *Cyril Connolly: A Life* (1997), p. 535.
14. Ray Monk, *Bertrand Russell: The Spirit of Solitude* (1996), pp. 84, 561.
15. Edmund Wilson, 'Oscar Wilde: One Must Always Seek What Is Most Tragic' in *Classics and Commercials* (1957), p. 333.
16. Noel Annan, *Leslie Stephen: His Thought and Character in Relation to his Times* (1951), pp. 3–4. There is a good deal more in this vein in Annan's later *Leslie Stephen: The Godless Victorian* (1984).
17. Noel Annan, 'The Intellectual Aristocracy' in *Studies in Social History: A Tribute to G. M. Trevelyan*, ed. J. H. Plumb (1955), p. 243.
18. *Aubrey's Brief Lives*, p. 316; 'The Autobiography of Joseph Carey Merrick' in Ashley Montagu, *The Elephant Man: A Study in Human Dignity* (Lafayette, 1971), p. 109.
19. Jean-Paul Sartre, *Questions de Méthode* (Paris, 1960), pp. 86, 83.
20. Steve Jones, *The Language of the Genes: Biology, History and the Evolutionary Future* (1994), pp. 58, 59.
21. Ida Macalpine and Richard Hunter, *George III and the Mad-Business* (1969), p. 173.
22. *British Journal of Psychiatry*, vol. 117 (1970), pp. 106–7.
23. *The Language of the Genes*, p. 59.
24. Somerset Maugham, *A Writer's Notebook* (1951), p. 293.
25. Pascal, *Oeuvres Complètes* (Paris: Pléiade, 1962), p. 1133.
26. Boswell, *Life of Johnson*, ii, p. 496.

Chapter 4: Primal Scenes

1. Angela Richards (ed.), *Case Histories ii*, Pelican Freud Library, 9 (1979), p. 228.
2. Although the Wolf Man *began* by not remembering the primal scence there is some ambiguity in Freud as to whether, during the course of the analysis, he recalled various of its details. See pp. 284–5 for a negative view and p. 327 for a more positive one.
3. Compton Mackenzie, *My Life and Times: Octave One 1883–1891* (1963), pp. 191–4.
4. Marcel Proust, *Jean Santeuil* (Paris: Pléiade, 1971), pp. 202–11; *A la recherche du temps perdu* (Paris: Pléiade, 1954), tome i, pp. 27–48.
5. Andro Linklater, *Compton Mackenzie: A Life* (1992), pp. 25–7.
6. George D. Painter, *Marcel Proust*, vol. i, pp. 9–11.
7. Brenda Maddox, *The Married Man: A life of D. H. Lawrence* (1994), p. 31.
8. In his analysis of the one distinct memory of childhood which Freud could find in Leonardo da Vinci's notebooks, he assumed that the word *nibbio* meant a vulture (when in fact it means a kite) and via Mut, the vulture goddess of the Egyptians, and the myth that all vultures are females impregnated in flight by the wind, set out on a long and entirely false trail. He explained the youthfulness of Saint Anne by noting that when at an early age Leonardo – who was illegitimate – was taken away from his young mother and brought into his father's household, the stepmother he found there was also young. But as many commentators have since pointed out, depicting the Virgin's mother as youthful was an artistic convention of the period by no means exclusive to Leonardo. For other shortcomings in Freud's treatment of the very few details of Leonardo's life which are available, see the convenient summary in Brian Farrell's introduction to the Pelican edition of the text (1963), pp. 26–9. They have been dealt with recently by David E. Stannard in Frederick C. Crews (ed.), *Unauthorized Freud: Doubters Confront a Legend* (1998), pp. 200–11. For more sympathetic views of the essay see Bradley Collins, *Leornardo, Psychoanalysis and Art History* (1997).
9. Anthony West, *Principles and Persuasions* (1958). pp. 158, 159.
10. Michael Sheldon, *Orwell: The Authorized Biography* (1991), pp. 430–1.
11. Bernard Crick, *George Orwell* (1992), p. 64–5.
12. Ibid., p. 69.
13. George Orwell, 'Such, Such were the Joys', *Complete Works*, ed. Peter Davison. Assisted by Ian Angus and Sheila Davison (1998), vol. xix, p. 358.
14. Bernard Crick, *George Orwell*, p. 70.
15. 'Such, Such were the Joys', p. 359.

16. Bernard Crick, *George Orwell*, p. 71.
17. Ibid., pp. 78–9.
18. Ibid., p. 80.
19. Alan Judd, *Ford Maddox Ford* (1990), pp. i, 68, 97.
20. For useful thoughts on the relevance of this concept to work in the humanities see Richard Allen and Murray Smith (eds), *Film Theory and Philosophy* (1997). The topic is also dealt with from an even more specialist point of view in Susan Haack, *Evidence and Inquiry* (1993).
21. William H. Gass, *New York Review of Books* (10 July 1969).
22. See Michael Sheringham, 'Le tournant autobiographique: mort ou vif?' in *Le tournant d'une vie*, ed. Phillipe Lejeune and Claude Leroy (Paris, 1995).
23. Betrand Russell, *Autobiography* (1967), p. 146.
24. Ray Monk, *Bertrand Russell*, pp. 134–8.
25. Hans Binnevald, *From Shell Shock to Combat Stress: A Comparative History of Military Pyschiatry*, trans. John O'Kane (Amsterdam University Press, 1997), p. 118.
26. Hermione Lee, *Virginia Woolf*, pp. 126–7.
27. Ibid., p. 158.
28. Sigmund Freud, *Case Histories ii*, p. 292.
29. AE's poem is entitled 'Germinal'; the lyrics of the well-known song are by Johnny Mercer and Harry Warren who may well have written 'And' rather than "Cos' (but that doesn't make the point so well!).

Chapter 5: Body Matters

1. George Orwell, *Complete Works*, vol. xvi, p. 509 (the author of the biography was Edwin Morgan).
2. Richard Ellmann, *Oscar Wilde* (1987), p. 88.
3. Jean-Jacques Rousseau, *Les confessions* (Paris: Pléiade, 1959), pp. 227–8.
4. Catherine Carswell, *The Savage Pilgrimage: A Narrative of D. H. Lawrence* (Cambridge, 1981), p. 77.
5. *Letters of D. H. Lawrence, vol. ii*, eds George J. Zytaruk and James T. Boulton (Cambridge, 1991), pp. 72–3.
6. D. H. Lawrence, *Women in Love*, eds David Farmer, Lindeth Vasey and John Worthen (Cambridge, 1987), p. 128.
7. George Pickering, *Creative Malady: Illness in the Lives and Minds of Charles Darwin, Florence Nightingale, Mary Baker Eddy, Sigmund Freud, Marcel Proust and Elizabeth Barrett Browning* (1974), p. 80.
8. Florence Nightingale, *Cassandra and Other Selections from Suggestions for Thought* (1991), ed. Mary Poovey, p. 213.
9. James Le Fanu, 'Florence Nightingale deserves our apology', *The Times*, 18 January 1996.

10. George D. Painter, *Marcel Proust*, vol. i, p. 11.
11. Richard Ellmann, *Golden Codgers: Biographical Speculations* (1973), pp. 11–13.
12. Oliver Sacks, *The Man Who Mistook His Wife for a Hat* (1986), p. 16.
13. Erik H. Erikson, *Young Man Luther: A Study in Psychoanalysis and History* (1962), pp. 79, 248.
14. Arthur K. Shapiro, Elaine S. Shapiro, Ruth D. Bruun and Richard D. Sweet, *Gilles de la Tourette Syndrome* (New York, 1978), p. 5.
15. Sir James Watt, 'Medical Aspects and Consequences of Cook's Voyages' in *Captain Cook and His Times*, ed. Robin Fisher and Hugh Johnston (1979), p. 156.
16. Gananeth Obeyesekere, *The Apotheosis of Captain Cook* (New Jersey, 1992), p. 31.
17. See Ralph Colp, *To Be an Invalid: The Illness of Charles Darwin* (Chicago, 1977).
18. David Garnett, *Golden Echo* (1954), p. 254. Passages from my account of D. H. Lawrence and illness have previously appeared in 'Explaining the Abnormal: D. H. Lawrence and Tuberculosis' in *Writing the Lives of Writers*, ed. Warwick Gould and Thomas F. Stacey (1998), pp. 77–96.
19. See John Worthen, *D. H. Lawrence: The Early Years* (Cambridge, 1991), p. 323.
20. See Michael Howell and Peter Ford, *The Ghost Disease* (1986), pp. 281–305.
21. These phrases occur in an as yet unpublished paper by John Wiltshire, author of *Jane Austen and the Body* (Cambridge, 1992) and one of the three editors of the Australian journal *Hysteric: Body, Text, Medecine* (Melbourne).
22. Edmund Wilson, *Classics and Commercials* (1951), pp. 340–2.
23. Karl Jaspers, *Nietzsche: An Introduction to the Understanding of His Philosophical Activity*, trans. Charles F. Wallraff and Frederick J. Schnitz (Tuscon, 1965), pp. 88–115.
24. See Catherine Thompson, '"Dawn Poems in Blood": Sylvia Plath and PMS', *TriQuarterly 80* (1990–91), pp. 221–49 and John Newton, 'Reading Bleeding: Sylvia Plath and the Poetics of Clinical Reductivism', *Hysteric*, no. 1 (1995), pp. 3–19.
25. See the *Journal of Katherine Mansfield*, ed. J. Middleton Murry (1954), p. 146 and Paul Delany, *D. H. Lawrence's Nightmare: The Writer and his Circle in the Years of the Great War* (1979), p. 249.
26. The phrase, which is common, appears in Garnett's review of *Phoenix* in the London Mercury, vol. xxxv (December, 1936). See *D. H. Lawrence: Critical Assessments*, ed. David Ellis and Ornella De Zordo (1992), vol. i, p. 86.
27. Curtis Brown, *Contacts* (1935), p. 82.
28. W. B. Yeats, *Memoirs*, ed. Denis Donoghue (1972), p. 92.

29. Edmund Wilson, *Classics and Commercials*, pp. 340–1.
30. Charles Lamb, 'The Convalescent' in *Essays of Elia* (Scott Library edn.), pp. 284–5.
31. Ivo Geikie-Cobb, *The Glands of Destiny: A Study of Personality* (1947), pp. 238–9, 240.
32. Boswell, *Life of Johnson*, vol. i, pp. 44–5.
33. Karl Jaspers, *Nietzsche*, p. 101.
34. Ian Hamilton, 'The Frailties of Robert Burns' in *Keepers of the Flame: Literary Estates and the Rise of Biography* (1992), p. 100.
35. Jane Austen, *Minor Works*, ed. R. W. Chapman (Oxford, 1954), pp. 397–8.

Chapter 6: The Sociological Imagination

1. Mick Imlah, 'Captain cheerless', *Times Literary Supplement*, 6 December 1996.
2. Maurice Halbwachs, *La mémoire collective* (Paris, 1950), p. 15.
3. Stendhal, *Oeuvres Intimes* (Paris: Pléiade, 1966), p. 21.
4. Halbwachs, *La mémoire collective*, p. 17.
5. Franco Ferrarotti, 'On the Autonomy of the Biographical Method' in Daniel Bertaux (ed.), *Biography and Society: The Life History Approach in the Social Sciences* (1981), pp. 26–7.
6. Rom Harré, *Social Being: A Theory for Social Psychology* (1979), p. 323.
7. Ibid., pp. 324–6. A more detailed account can be found in J.-P. De Waele, *La méthode des Cas Programmés en Criminologie* (Brussels, 1971).
8. Maynard Mack, *Alexander Pope* (1985), p. 13.
9. Ibid.
10. Ibid., p. 80.
11. Henry James, *Hawthorne*, ed. Tony Tanner (1967), p. 34.
12. Ibid., pp. 69, 23, 37.
13. Ibid., p. 45.
14. Edward Mendelson, 'Authorized Biography and Its Discontents' in *Studies in Biography*, ed. Daniel Aaron (1978), pp. 21–2.
15. Harré, *Social Being*, pp. 312–13.
16. William James, *Principles of Psychology* (1908), vol. i, p. 295.
17. Samuel Johnson, *Lives of the Poets*, vol. ii, p. 102.
18. Stendhal, *De L'Amour* (Paris, 1963), p. 23 (*Troisième Préface*); *Oeuvres Intimes* (Paris: Pléiade, 1955), p. 1394.
19. Marcel Proust, *A la recherche du temps perdu*, tome 1, p. 828.
20. D. W. Harding, *Social Psychology and Individual Values* (1953), pp. 144–9.
21. Ibid., p. 145–6.
22. Erving Goffman, *Stigma* (1968), pp. 137, 138.
23. Compare for example Serge Moscovici, *Social Influence and Social Change* (1976) and see, for a comprehensive review of the relevant

material, Rupert Brown, *Group Processes: Dynamics within and between groups* (2nd edn, 1999), chapter iv.
24. For a simple account of Asch's experiments, see Steven Schwartz, *Pavlov's Heirs* (1987), pp. 108–11.
25. D. H. Lawrence, 'Art and Morality' in *'Study of Thomas Hardy' and Other Essays* (Cambridge, 1985), pp. 161–8.
26. Erving Goffman, *Encounters: Two Studies in the Sociology of Interaction* (New York, 1961), p. 8.
27. James, *Principles of Psychology*, vol. i, p. 306.
28. Ferrarotti, *Biography and Society*, p. 24.

Chapter 7: History, Chance and Self-determination

1. Wolfgang Hildesheimer, *Mozart*, trans. Marion Faber (1982), p. 21.
2. Michael Holroyd, *Lytton Strachey* (1968), p. 198.
3. See Ray Monk, *Bertrand Russell*, part 1, chapter 3.
4. Patrick O'Brien, 'Is Political Biography a Good Thing' in *Contemporary British History*, vol. x, no. 4 (Winter, 1996), p. 60.
5. See Peter Burke, *The French Historical Revolution: The Annales School: 1929–1989* (1990).
6. The first 34 pages of S. Schoenbaum's *Shakespeare's Lives* (Oxford, 1991) summarise the little that is known about Shakespeare and the following 534 describe the often bizarre attempts to make that little go farther than it can, or should.
7. Charles Nicholl, *The Reckoning: The Murder of Christopher Marlowe* (1992), pp. 5–6, 91, 100.
8. For full details of the discovery, see A. D. Wraight and Virginia F. Stern, *In Search of Christopher Marlowe: A Pictorial Biography* (1965), pp. 63–71.
9. Derek Pearsall, *The Life of Geoffrey Chaucer* (1992), pp. 1, 2.
10. Ibid., p. 47.
11. See Peter Ackroyd, *The Life of Thomas More* (1998).
12. For Lawrence's first meeting with Frieda Weekley see John Worthen, *D. H. Lawrence: The Early Years* (Cambridge, 1991), pp. 372, 380. For further examples of how lives can be affected by chance, see Jerome G. Manis, 'The Aleatory Element in Biography' in *Biography*, vol. xv, n. 4 (Fall, 1992), pp. 390–9.
13. Henry James, *The Bostonians* (The Chiltern Library, 1952), p. 351 (chap. xxxix).
14. See Edel, *The Life of Henry James*, vol. ii, pp. 28–9.
15. Karl Jaspers, 'Biographical Study (Biographik)' in *General Psychopathology*, trans. J. Hoenig and Marian W. Hamilton (Chicago, 1963), pp. 671–2.

Biography and the Search for Understanding

16. See Niall Ferguson, *Virtual History: Towards a 'Chaotic' Theory of the Past* (1997).
17. Antony Flew, *Thinking about Social Thinking: The Philosophy of the Social Sciences* (1985), p. 93.
18. D. H. Lawrence, *Woman in Love*, p. 26
19. Jean-Paul Sartre, *Baudelaire*, p. 21.
20. Jean-Paul Sartre, *L'Idiot de la Famille*, tome 1, pp. 405–6.
21. Panthea Reid, *Art and Affection*, p. 472.
22. Hermione Lee, *Virginia Woolf*, p. 751.
23. Samuel Johnson, *The Lives of the Poets*, vol. ii, p. 247.
24. Kenneth S. Lynn, *Hemingway* (1987), pp. 394–5.
25. Diane Wood Middlebrook, 'Spinning Straw into Gold' in *The Literary Biography: Problems and Solutions*, ed. Dale Salwak (1996), p. 89.
26. Anne Stevenson, *Bitter Fame: A Life of Sylvia Plath* (Penguin, 1989), p. 45.
27. Ibid., pp. 131–2.
28. Ibid., pp. 47, 297.
29. Ibid., pp. 279, 286.
30. Lynn, *Hemingway*, p. 379.

Chapter 8: Compatibility, Sartre and Long Biographies

1. W. M. Runyon, *Life Histories and Psychobiography* (Oxford, 1982), pp. 38–41.
2. Stevenson, *Bitter Fame*, p. 298.
3. Reid, *Art and Affection*, p. 463.
4. Thomas Caramagno, *The Flight of the Mind: Virginia Woolf's Art and Manic-Depressive Illness* (University of California Press, 1992), pp. 2, 9, 48, 61, 62.
5. Ibid., p. 98.
6. Ibid., p. 2.
7. Anthony Flew, *Thinking About Social Thinking*, p. 40.
8. Freud, *Case Histories ii*, pp. 291, 337.
9. Jean-Paul Sartre, *War Diaries: Notebooks from the Phoney War, November 1939 – March 1940*, transl. Quinton Hoare (1984), p. 318.
10. Sartre, *War Diaries*, pp. 294–5, 301.
11. Sartre, *L'être et le néant* (Paris, 1943), p. 645.
12. Sartre, *War Diaries*, p. 309.
13. Sartre, *L'être et le néant*, p. 645.
14. Sartre, *Oeuvres Romanesque* (Paris: Pléiade, 1981), p. 19.
15. Sartre, *Questions de Méthode*, (Paris, 1960), pp. 118, 135.
16. Ibid., pp. 188, 155.
17. Sartre, *Situations X: Politique et Autobiographie* (Paris, 1976), p. 106.
18. Sartre, *L'Idiot de la Famille*, tome i, pp. 7–8.

19. See Hazel E. Barnes, *Sartre and Flaubert* (1981), p. 184.
20. Sartre, *L'idiot de la Famille*, tome ii, p. 1811.
21. Ibid., tome i, pp. 114–15, 907.
22. Ibid., tome i, p. 81.
23. Douglas Collins, *Sartre as Biographer* (Cambridge, MA., 1980), pp. 107–8; Michael Scriven, *Sartre's Existential Biographies* (1984), p. 107.
24. Sartre, *Questions de Méthode*, p. 34.
25. Sartre, *L'Idiot de la Famille*, tome i, p. 366.
26. Sartre, *Situations X*, p. 106.
27. One sign that it was beginning to settle can be found in Stanley Fish's opening essay to a collection edited by William H. Epstein and entitled *Contesting the Subject: Essays in the Postmodern Theory and Practice of Biography and Biographical Criticism* (West Lafayette, IN, 1991). Fish argues in this essay that, since 'the act of construing meaning is ipso facto the act of assigning intention within a specific set of circumstances', it is impossible to read other than biographically (in the sense of 'some specification of what kind of person . . . is the source of the words you are reading'). He claims that the post-structuralist dissolution of the subject only relocates agency and that to read something as the product of some 'transcendental agency' is to 'endow that anonymity with an intention and a biography' (pp. 11–13). He does not however indicate what the biography of an anonymous transcendental agency would look like, and the other essays in this collection suggest that the fundamental conflicts between post-structuralist and post-modernist theory on the other hand, and traditional biographical practice on the other, will not be resolved by discussion but by the two parties deciding to go their own ways.
28. See Sartre, *L'Idiot de la Famille*, tome i, p. 225.
29. Ibid., tome i, pp. 887–8.
30. Barnes, *Sartre and Flaubert*, p. 103.
31. Collins, *Sartre As Biographer*, p. 21.
32. Sartre, *L'Idiot de la Famille*, tome iii, p. 39.
33. Roy Foster, *W. B. Yeats* (1997), pp. 5, 50.
34. Sartre, *L'Idiot de la Famille*, tome iii, p. 10.
35. Sartre, *Questions de Méthode*, p. 80; Richard Ellmann, *Oscar Wilde*, p. 509.
36. See Barnes, *Sartre and Flaubert*, pp. 51–2.
37. The programme was part of BBC2's 'Great Composers' series, available on video from Warner Vision.

Chapter 9: 'Dignity and Uses of Biography'

1. William Hazlitt, 'Prejudice' in *Complete Works*, ed. P. P. Howe, vol. xx, p. 326.

2. P. N. Furbank, 'Ferocious, Vital, Heroic', *Times Literary Supplement*, 11 December 1998.
3. See Ludwig Wittgenstein, *Lectures and Conversations on Aesthetics, Psychology and Religious Belief*, ed. Cyril Barnett (Oxford, 1970); the remarks on Frazer in 'Wittgenstein's Lectures in 1930–33', in G. E. Moore, *Philosophical Papers* (1959); and Frank Cioffi, *Wittgenstein on Freud and Frazer* (Cambridge, 1998), pp. 1–79.
4. John Richardson, *Picasso*, vol. i, pp. 20, 26–7.
5. Humphrey Carpenter, *A Serious Character: The Life of Ezra Pound* (1988), p. 366.
6. George A. Miller, *Psychology: The Science of Life*, p. 199.
7. P. N. Furbank, *E. M. Forster: A Life*, vol. i, p. 38.
8. Humphrey Carpenter, *W. H. Auden* (1981), p. 45.
9. Ian MacKillop, 'Vignettes: Leavis, Biography and the Body' in *Writing the Lives of Writers*, p. 294.
10. Elizabeth Hardwick, 'Dead Souls', *New York Review of Books*, 5 June 1060.
11. W. M. Runyan, *Life Histories and Psychobiography*, p. 23.
12. Galen Strawsen, 'Free Will' in the *Routledge Encyclopedia of Philosophy*, ed. Edward Craig (1998).
13. See Ivan Morris, *The Nobility of Failure* (1975).
14. James Hillman, 'Pothos: The Nostalgia for the *Puer Eternus*' in *Loose Ends: Primary Papers in Archetypal Psychology* (New York, 1975), p. 50.
15. See *Biography*, vol. ii, no. 1 (Winter, 1979), pp. 25–34.
16. Hardwick, op. cit.
17. *D. H. Lawrence: A Composite Biography*, ed. Edward Nehls (Wisconsin, 1959), vol. iii, p. 101.
18. See D. H. Lawrence, *Memoir of Maurice Magnus* (1924), p. 91.
19. D. H. Lawrence, *Lady Chatterley's Lover*, ed. Michael Squires (Cambridge, 1993), p. 101.
20. Samuel Johnson, *The Rambler* (no. 60), pp. 132–4.
21. See Edward Braithwaite Sugden (Baron St Leonards), *Misrepresentations in Campbell's Lives of Lyndhurst and Brougham* (1869), p. 3 (but the phrase was first used in the eighteenth century by John Arbuthnot).
22. D. J. Enright, *Collected Poems: 1948–1998* (Oxford, 1998), p. 263.
23. George Eliot, *Middlemarch* (1872), chapter 74.
24. See *The Biographer's Art: New Essays*, ed. Jeffrey Myers (1989), p. 2.
25. See John Updike, 'A Case of Melancholia' in *Just Looking: Essays on Art* (New York, 1989), p. 141.
26. Ibid., pp. 137, 149.
27. See Florence Emily Hardy, *The Early Life of Thomas Hardy: 1840–1891* (1928).

Index

189

Russell, Bertrand, 8–9 (and Helen
  Dudley), 10, 17, 46 (importance
  to him of his ancestry), 60, 71
  (seeing Evelyn Whitehead in
  pain), 119 (courtship of his first
  wife)
Russell, George ('AE'), 75

Sacks, Oliver, 83–4 (Dr P's painting)
Sackville-West, Vita, 15
Saint Augustine, 70
Sallust, 33
Sand, George, 59
Sartre, Jean-Paul, 24, 26–7 (on
  Flaubert's older brother), 50
  (effect of the family on Flaubert),
  128–30 (impossibilty of suicide for
  Flaubert), 136, 142–56 (*L'Idiot de
  la Famille*), 158, 159, 163, 165, 176
Savage, Richard, 108–9 (his self-
  deceptions), 110
Schoenbaum, S., 120
Scott, Walter, 31
Scriven, Michael, 149
Sexton, Ann, 133
Seymour, Miranda, 45
Shakespeare, William, 106, 120, 166
Sheldon, Michael, 63, 123
Shelston, Alan, 17
Sheringham, Michael, 70
Sherry, Norman, 35–8 (on the life
  of Graham Greene), 175
Sontag, Susan, 92
Spencer, Herbert, 40 (what he felt
  he owed to his grandfather), 41,
  45
Steiner, George, 156
Stendhal, 98 (his first memory), 109
  (his reliance on posterity), 110,
  113
Stephen, Leslie, 47–8 (his family
  connections)
Stevenson, Anne, 133–6 (on Plath's
  suicide), 138
Strachey, Lytton, 7, 8, 9, 118–19
  (frankness on sexual matters)
Strawson, Galen, 166 (on free will)
Suetonius, 4

Swift, Jonanthan, 5 (his place of
  birth), 14, 131–2 (habits when
  travelling), 135

Thackeray, William Makepeace, 104
Thoreau, Henry David, 105
Townsend Warner, Sylvia, 169
Turner, Reggie, 31, 166

Uglow, Jenny, 169
Updike, John, 174

Valery, Paul, 155
Van Gogh, Theo, 137
Van Gogh, Vincent, 20, 137
  (possible reasons for his self-
  mutilation)
Victoria, Queen, 51
Von Ranke, Heinrich, 45
Von Ranke, Leopold, 45
Voltaire, 31

Wagner, Richard, 156
Walton, Izaac, 4, 23 (reasons for
  Herbert's abandonment of his
  Courtly ambitions)
Watson, Dr, 21
Watt, Sir James, 85 (on vitamin B
  deficiency), 93
Weber, Max, 126
Weekley, Ernest, 124
West, Anthony, 63–4 (effect of
  Orwell's prep school education on
  1984), 67
White, Hayden, 13
Whitehead, Mrs Evelyn, 71–2 (attack
  of 'pseudo-angina')
Wilde, Lady Jane Francesca, 47
Wilde, Oscar, 77 (his possible
  syphilis), 88, 155
Wilhelm II, Kaiser, 142–3 (and his
  withered arm), 145
Wilson, Edmund, 47, 88 (on Wilde's
  syphilis), 92
Wilson, Woodrow, 24
Winnicott, D. W., 23
Wittgenstein, Ludwig von, 159–60
  (causal reasoning in aesthetics)